THE
NEW
FOODS
GUIDE

THE
NEW
FOODS
GUIDE

What's Here, What's Coming,
What It Means for Us

John Elkington
& Julia Hailes

VICTOR GOLLANCZ
LONDON

First published in Great Britain in 1999 by
Victor Gollancz
An imprint of Orion Books Ltd
Orion House, 5 Upper St Martin's Lane, London WC2H 9EA

ISBN 0 575 06806 X

Printed in Great Britain by
Clays Ltd, St Ives, plc

Contents

There's a revolution going on in what we eat – and in how it is produced. To get a flavour of where we are headed, it helps to know where we have come from. This chapter fast-forwards the reader through a million years of food history.

We try out the three types of new food now on the menu. In each case, we ask: What are they? How are they made? What are the issues? Why all the excitement? What do the critics say?

3: INGREDIENT WATCH

New foods don't just drop like manna from the heavens. They are often concocted from a growing range of food ingredients. What ingredients are now being used to make which foods? Why are they being used? What are the health implications? What's going on in the GM corner? And what's new?

4: ALONG THE SHELVES
Product by Product 113

What's new under each main category of food and drink? What are the latest GM, Functional and New Organic products? Who is producing them? What are the issues? And what sort of benefits are we being promised?

5: PERSONALISED MENUS

Good for You 215

We run through some of the more important ailments, conditions and diseases – and investigate some of the new food items now on offer as cures or palliatives. In each case, we ask: What's in? What's out? And what's new?

6: **FOOD FIGHTS**
Behind the Scenes

What's on tomorrow's menu? Will there be enough food to go around? Are we paying too much for our food – or too little? What are the deep trends that will shape what we eat in the 21st century?

7: FUTURE FOODS
What's Next on the Menu 267

What can we all learn from the anti-GM backlash – and from the continuing boom in demand for organic foods? What can each of us do to ensure that tomorrow's menus are future-friendly? And which food businesses are already heading in the right direction?

Acknowledgements

The New Foods Guide has been great fun to write, and we are very grateful to all those who have given their time and energy to help us make the book as informative, accurate and entertaining as we could. Among those to whom we owe tremendous gratitude are Sara Menguc (our literary agent) and the publishing team at Gollancz/Orion that included Malcolm Edwards, Sara Holloway, John Mitchinson, Mike Petty and Rebecca Porteous (our copy-editor). Thanks, too, to Alison Groom for the cover design and to Helen Ewing for designing the book.

We would particularly like to thank Julian Melantin and Dr Michael Heasman, co-editors of the *New Nutrition Business* newsletter. Julian was a veritable goldmine of information on functional foods. If you are interested in this area, there is no better source of regular briefing and information than *New Nutrition Business*. And thanks, too, to Sue Dibb of the Food Commission for first putting us in touch with Julian.

People who have made a major contribution to the process of putting the material together are: Francis Blake (Soil Association), Jeroen Bordewijk (Unilever Nutrition Research Centre), Christiaan Brakman (Unilever Nutrition Research Centre), Dr Lyndon Davies (independent food consultant, formerly of the Institute of Food Research), Christèle Delbé (SustainAbility), Lynne Elvins (SustainAbility), Geoff Lye (SustainAbility), Onno Korver (Unilever Nutrition Research Centre), Dorothy McKenzie (Dragon International), Jon Walker (Out of this World), Tricia Walsh (research), Jan Weststraat (Unilever Nutrition Research Centre), Marcus Williamson (Connectotel) and Amanda Wynne (British Nutrition Foundation).

Others who have helped us along the way have included Michael Antoniou (independent consultant), Laura Barrington (Soil Association), Ian Bentley (Rhodia Ltd), Peter Berry-Ottaway (Berry-Ottaway & Associates), Nicola Burger (Yakult), Ian Christie (Demos), George Dent (Christian Ecology Link), Chris Holmes (Procter & Gamble), Dr Vyvyan Howard (University of Liverpool), Lilian Huber

(Sustainability), Dr Vernon Jennings (when with SustainAbility; now at Novo Nordisk), Lindsay Keenan (Genetix Food Alert), Lise Kingo (Novo Nordisk), Sarah Langely (herbalist), Professor Barry Law (independent food consultant), Tim Lobstein (Food Commission), Jeanette Longfield (Sustain), Jørn Mahler (Novo Nordisk), Sue Mayer (GeneWatch), Greg McEwen (McEwen Parkinson), Andrea Muller (Nutritionist), Peter Riley (Friends of the Earth), Nick Rowcliffe (*ENDS Daily*), Robin Soames (pig farmer), Robert Vint (formerly of the Religious Education and Environment Programme), Nilufer von Bismarck (Slaughter & May) and Hugh Warwick (Genetics Forum).

We found the work of Hartmut Meyer, co-ordinator of the Europe-wide network on genetic engineering – Genet News (website: http://www.gene.ch/) – enormously helpful. And we also benefited from a number of transatlantic conversations and e-mail exchanges with Paul Hawken (Natural Step Foundation, USA) on the trends in America.

One of the more ambitious elements of our research was the GM Food Survey, carried out in April 1999. In this, we covered all the UK's major retailers (and many others), most major caterers and over a hundred food manufacturers. The industry and company contact details for the survey came from *The Grocer Food & Drink Directory 99*, published by William Reed Directories in 1998. We began the survey just as the anti-GM snowball really began to roll in the UK. As a result, many of the companies that responded were in some disarray. In many cases, their GM policies were still being formulated or just hot off the press and it was clear that many were using our questionnaires as guides to the issues that might come up in the future. Because of the speed with which things were – and still are – moving, we decided not to convert the replies into statistics. Instead, you will find that we have salted the responses through the book, with particular concentration in chapters 4, 5 and 7.

In addition, we contacted hundreds of companies by telephone and e-mail. We visited several companies, among them Unilever's Nutrition Research Centre outside Rotterdam, and are grateful for the time they devoted to us. We also made extensive use of the Internet.

Among the number of excellent books that we drew on were *The Food Bible*[1], *The Nutrition Bible*[2], *The Optimum Nutrition Bible*[3] and *The Shopper's Guide to Organic Food*[4], all highly recommended. Other useful books were: *Foods That Fight Pain: Revolutionary New Strategies for Maximum Pain Relief*, Neal Barnard, Bantam Books, 1999; *Functional Foods: The Consumer, the Products and the Evidence*, edited by Michèle Sadler and Michael Saltmarsh, The Royal Society of Chemistry, 1998; *GM-Free: A Shopper's Guide to Genetically Modified Food*, Sue Dibb and Dr Tim Lobstein, Virgin Publishing, 1999; *Grocery Revolution: the New Focus on the Consumer*, Barbara Kahn and Leigh McAlister, Addison-Wesley, 1997; *What the Labels Don't Tell You*, Sue Dibb, Thorsons, 1997; and *The Food We Eat*, Joanna Blythman, Michael Joseph, 1996, now published in paperback by Fourth Estate. And useful periodicals included: *The Food Magazine, Healthy Eating, Inside Food & Drink, New Nutrition Business* and *Which? Online*.

Finally, our heartfelt thanks to our families for their extraordinary support during this latest project – and for the time that should have been theirs. At Tintinhull, thank you Ed, Liz (Paice), Minker (Soames), Connor, Rollo and Monty. And in Barnes, thank you Elaine, Gaia and Hania. We hope you will all feel it has been worth it.

FOOD TIME

Introduction

Fancy a taste of the future? That's what you'll find in *The New Foods Guide*. The following pages are jam-packed with information on some of the extraordinary new food products that are beginning to appear on the supermarket shelves, others that are in the pipeline and still more that are just a gleam in food scientists' eyes.

THE NEW FOODS REVOLUTION

The food business today is changing at high speed. By the time *The New Foods Guide* went to press, public concern about GM food had even overtaken concerns about BSE in the UK. Indeed, we had actually set out to write a book called *The GM Foods Guide*, but quickly discovered that there was a lot more to tomorrow's menus than the genetic modification of crops. We also recognised that the GM food controversy is increasingly connected with two other major new food developments: 'New Organic' and what are called 'Functional' foods.

So, in *The New Foods Guide* we focus on these three, which we have identified as the most important elements of the food revolution. Our aim is to give you a balanced overview, so that you can have an informed idea of what you like about each of these food types, and what you don't. For each food type, we look at the processes involved in producing it, why the food industry is so excited about it, what the critics are saying, and who is – or is meant to be – in control in terms of regulations and standards. Throughout, we focus on the extent to which they are likely to be 'future-friendly'. In chapter 2 we explain what is going on in more depth, but here's a brief overview.

■ **GM FOODS:** Nowadays, GM (or genetically modified) foods hardly need an introduction. They are rarely out of the headlines. Less well understood is how far genetic modification is already in use, what foods of the future are on the drawing board, and the extent to

3

which the GM foods industry is likely to go 'functional' in the coming years.

● **FUNCTIONAL FOODS:** At the moment, functional foods are much less familiar to the public than either GM or organic foods, but they will explode into the news in the first decade of the 21st century. They comprise all food products designed to give extra health benefits. Some are simply 'vitamin-enriched' or based on 'low-fat' formulas, but increasingly we will come to see a whole range of novel 'miracle' ingredients being added to our food. These ingredients will promise to do just about anything, from boosting your immune system to making you happy.

◆ **NEW ORGANIC FOODS:** This is a term we have coined for *The New Foods Guide*. Traditional organic food was – and still is – bought at the farm gate or local market, but in most cases has not yet made it to the supermarket. 'New Organic' food, on the other hand, is mass-produced, often imported and widely available in supermarkets. Demand is exploding and, as a result, big food companies like **Mars** and **Unilever** are competing for a share of the cake.

Anyone who has studied food, as a shopper trying to make sense of food labels or as a professional, knows just how complex today's food ingredients have become. In chapter 3, we give the inside story on all the ingredients used in food production, explain the current thinking on how they might affect our health and predict what we are likely to see more of – and less of – in the future.

Among the questions we ask are: What new diet ingredients are being introduced? Should we really be buying products with added vitamins and minerals? What are 'bio-cultures'? Is all cholesterol bad? And how are GM enzymes being used in food?

So far so good, but where do these new ingredients pop up in the foods we buy – and where will they appear in the future? In chapter 4, we take the reader along the shelves, product by product, explaining where each product stands at present in terms of our three categories, and how it might develop.

Among the questions we ask here are: What is the future of milk? Can eggs be made functional? Is fish farming really 'future-friendly? Do sports drinks make a difference? And what *are* some of the new food brands like *Benecol, Columbus Egg, Olestra* and *Yakult?*

For most people 'I'm on a diet' means 'I'm trying to lose weight', but growing numbers of people are beginning to understand the profound influence that our diet can have on our health. For people on special diets, we show in some of the ways that new foods might help in chapter 5. The focus moves from children to pregnant women, slimmers to cancer sufferers, sport players to depressives. In each case we look at the theories about which foods help and which don't.

In chapter 6, we examine the major issues and debates that are helping to shape the future of our food – and of the food industry. And just in case all of this makes it seem that we have no option but to swallow whatever the food industry cares to dish out, in chapter 7 we launch a 10-point New Foods Manifesto, identifying the changes that the Government and food industry must make, as new food products are developed and introduced.

To give credit where credit is due, we conclude by spotlighting a handful of 'New Food Stars': companies that are doing at least some of the right things spectacularly well.

THE NEW FOODS TIME MACHINE

A sense of how our diet has changed in the past might help us to understand just how dramatically it could change in the future. Some foods that we eat without a second thought today would have seemed outlandish to people living only a century or two ago, let alone our really distant ancestors.

What, for example, would our great-grandparents think of growth-promoting hormones and antibiotics? Fish farms and battery-hen houses? Airline meals and takeaway hamburgers? Or microwave-ready meals and 'supercarbonated' canned drinks?

Imagine that we have a time machine that can zoom us back to the world of 1,000,000 years ago, 100,000 years ago, 10,000 years ago, 1,000 years ago, 100 years ago and 10 years ago. All aboard? Then let's set the controls for somewhere around a million years BC[s].

1,000,000 years ago

Our first contact is with someone who would be difficult to introduce to the neighbours. Like everyone else of his time, he is a scavenger. He eats almost anything he can get his hands on, competing with hyenas and other wild animals for scraps. His diet consists of things like berries, nuts, termites and bone marrow. When we mention cooking, he is baffled. Cooking won't be invented for another 600,000 years or so.

100,000 years ago

This time we meet a skilled hunter. He tracks down and kills large animals like hairy mammoths and sabre-toothed tigers, and then he cooks the meat. He doesn't know when his people learned to cook, but the use of fire is already hundreds of thousands of years old.

10,000 years ago

Agriculture has now radically altered human culture and eating habits. A woman in the Near East proudly shows us the cleared plots where people – and they are mainly women – are using sharpened sticks to plant and cultivate wild grass seeds. Goat's milk has been on the menu for over a thousand years already, but bread as we know it is still thousands of years ahead.

1,000 years ago

As the first millennium AD ends, we meet a peasant farmer in England. Over the past thousand years, invaders like the Romans and Normans have introduced new types of food, including oysters and rabbits, to the country. Even so, the farmer tells of recent famines in 975, 976 and 986, when woods and hedgerows had to be scavenged for beechnuts, acorns, nettles and wild grasses. Now, although bread is the real 'staff of life', his family enjoys foods like pit-roasted beef, mutton and pork, game-birds, fish and even poultry, still something of a luxury.

100 years ago

On the threshold of the 20th century, we find that agriculture and food are undergoing a period of profound change. The Industrial Revolution has enabled food to be shipped over large distances (the first really successful shipment of frozen meat from Australia arrived in England in 1880), and to be increasingly processed.

We meet a gentleman farmer. He is quite familiar with a number of names we recognise today, including Mrs Beeton, who published her famous cookery and household management book in 1861; **Sainsbury's** and **H. J. Heinz**, both formed in 1869 (**Heinz** adopted their '57 varieties' slogan in 1892); and *Coca-Cola*, bottled for the first time in 1899.

But, like his neighbours, our gentleman farmer still uses horses and oxen to plough his fields – and his wife cooks almost all their meals from scratch, using very few processed foods. Asked about his dreams for the future, he admits that he is thinking about buying a new-fangled invention called a tractor. It's steam-powered and weighs in at eight and half tonnes!

10 years ago

On our final time trip, we meet a food scientist. She is well aware that genetic engineering is used in the drugs industry, but her only experience of GM technology in the food industry has involved new tests for food contamination. She has recently read about functional foods appearing in Japan, but has not yet tried them.

She tells us that new and deeply felt issues are coming into play in the food world. People are more interested in 'health foods' than ever before, and most consumers have at least a passing understanding of the importance of vitamins and minerals in their diets. By the same token, they are worried about the whole range of additives now found in processed foods, among them colourings, flavourings and preservatives.

The environment has come on to the agenda in a big way, but our scientist reports that although organic products are beginning to be sold in some supermarkets, their availability is patchy, prices are uncomfortably high and the quality is variable.

So much for time travel. Whatever device we use to get a sense of the pace of change, it's extraordinary to think that the modern farming technology we take for granted, from tractors and combine harvesters to synthetic crop-protection chemicals and satellite monitoring systems, has all evolved in the last 100 years.

A very high proportion of food is now grown using chemical fertilisers and pesticides. It is shipped around the globe in vast containers, is highly processed and sold in packaging that gives it a long shelf-life. Processed foods contain ever larger quantities of the cheapest raw materials of all: air, water, wheat, salt and sugar, in that order. And the pace of change is accelerating sharply. Experts say we will probably see more change in the next 10 years than we saw in the last 50. Let's take just one example of the sort of development we're talking about.

As we worked on *The New Foods Guide*, one of the odder stories we came across was about the 'smart spud'. In a laboratory experiment, scientists inserted a gene from a jellyfish into a potato, which makes it glow green – if viewed through a special instrument – when it needs more water.[6] If these GM potatoes are planted, you won't be able to see the green glow in the way that we now see fields of yellow rape and sky-blue linseed lighting up the countryside, but it's one more indication that we stand on the threshold of extraordinary times.

None of this is inevitable, of course. It remains to be seen where society will draw the line. The GM foods controversy in Europe – and increasingly in the USA – has shaken the food industry at its roots. How foods will develop could be very different as a result. So let's turn now to the key issues that are mapping the future for our foods, menus and diets.

2

THE NEW FOODS TRIO

GM, Functional, New Organic

Some people can't wait to get their teeth into new foods. Others find the whole idea unappetising, even disgusting. And some of us flit from one response to another with each new 'miracle' food – or whenever there is a food scare. It's all pretty confusing. So let's start by examining exactly what we mean when we talk about 'new foods'.

The first discovery is that different people mean different things. However, we shall take 'new foods' as a label for the three new food trends that will dominate the future: GM foods, which have been hogging the headlines recently; functional foods, which are only just beginning to surface in the media; and New Organic foods – an emerging sector from which all food producers and retailers could learn new tricks.

Most of the food innovations you will see reported in the media in the next decade will fall into one or more of these groups. For each group, we spotlight the key trends and issues – and explain what makes some people excited and others gloomy.

◼ GM FOODS ◼

What are GM foods?

This is an area full of jargon. We need to hack a way through. GM itself is shorthand for 'genetic modification' or 'genetically modified'. Some people talk instead of 'genetic engineering' (GE). When we talk of a GM organism we mean a genetically modified organism (or GMO). So GM foods are primarily foods that have been genetically modified or, more usually, that might contain GM ingredients.

The ability to identify, modify and move genes is a key part of modern biotechnology, which involves the industrial use of living things. Just as engineers work with inert materials like metals, biotechnologists work with biological systems, such as microbes, plants and animals.

But where do genes fit in? Think of it like this: when building a car, an engineer needs a blueprint showing the overall design and how all the bits should fit together. The blueprint will specify, for example, whether there is one windscreen wiper or two, how fast they will move and so on. In much the same way, genes provide the blueprints for the characteristics of our bodies, and indeed the body of every living thing. Our genes determine whether we are going to be short or tall, heavy or light, blonde or red-haired, blue-eyed or brown. They can also influence subtler characteristics such as the way we think, and even our tendency to be happy or depressed.

By changing the genes in plants or animals, genetic engineers hope to program them to do things that they wouldn't normally do. For example, they have already produced fish that grow faster, fruit that takes longer to ripen and therefore lasts longer, lentils that don't give you wind and cows that produce milk similar to human breast milk. To make these small miracles happen, genetic engineers remove the genes – or parts of genes – responsible for a certain characteristic from the genetic code or blueprint of one organism. Next, they copy the genes in question and insert the copies into new organisms. In one extraordinary case, scientists took the gene responsible for fluorescent colouring from a jellyfish and transferred it into mice. The result: 'fluorescent mice' that glow in the dark.

Extraordinary, yes, but this is not just science for science's sake. With this technique, genetic engineers hope, as we have seen, to produce crop plants that can signal to the farmer when they need more water. And if these signalling crops are still a part of the future, real examples of genetically modified food are already very much in existence. The global area planted with GM crops almost trebled between 1997 and 1998. From zero in 1994, the area covered by GM crops had exploded to nearly the size of the Philippines by 1998. By 1999, 35 per cent of all US corn, almost 55 per cent of all US soy beans and nearly half of all US cotton were GM.[7]

Examples of GM foods?

For a better idea of how genetic modification works in practice, let's look at a few real-world examples:

Herbicide-resistant soya: Most of us have at least heard of this one. Scientists have inserted a gene from a soil bacterium into soya plants. The idea is that the gene, which protects some bacteria against a commonly used herbicide, will do the same for the GM crop plants. As a result, when the crop is sprayed with that particular herbicide it is not harmed. This allows for a heavier dose of herbicide to be sprayed on the crop at the best time for really knocking back the weeds, while ordinary crops, which don't tolerate such a high concentration, require repeated sprays. The scientists behind this innovation claim that the result is a significant reduction in the amount of chemicals sprayed onto the crops. They also say that the chemical used is safer than many of the alternatives. But all these claims are seriously challenged (see below).

Insect-proof corn: Corn is a crop that many insects love to eat in the field. Most farmers use chemical insecticides to control pest damage, but now GM corn plants can fight off the pests themselves. Scientists have taken the 'Bt' gene from a soil microbe (*Bacillus thuringiensis*), and transferred it into the corn plant, where it helps produce a protein that can kill more than 50 species of moth and (most importantly) kill their plant-damaging caterpillars. Unfortunately, scientists in the USA have discovered that such GM crops could hit the already endangered monarch butterfly.

Longer-lasting tomatoes: Nature sees fruit and vegetables as carriers of seed, programming them to ripen and rot. Rotting helps plants spread seed, and speeds germination, but for the food industry it is a nightmare. Sometimes rotting is triggered by ethylene gas, produced by the plants themselves. Genetic engineers therefore wondered whether they could switch off the gene responsible for producing ethylene. It turned out that they could. Avocados, bananas, melons, tomatoes and strawberries have all been experimentally engineered to produce less ethylene and thereby slow the rate at which they rot. Delayed ripening can mean better flavour (fruit can stay longer on the vine), higher yields (less fruit is lost to rotting) and a longer shelf-life in stores. But although fresh GM tomatoes are sold in the USA, no fresh fruit in the UK is yet GM.

Milk boosters: This is another controversial category. Dairy cows produce milk partly thanks to BST (or bovine somatotropin), a hormone that occurs naturally in their bodies. The issues to do with BST are discussed in more detail in the BST milk box in chapter 4. Normally cows produce just enough milk to satisfy their calves. The challenge for modern farmers has been to find a way of boosting this amount. Now genetic engineers have programmed bacteria with the BST gene so that the bacteria can churn out the hormone in fermentation tanks. The BST is then injected into cows where it stimulates their bodies into producing more milk.

Super-growing salmon: Fish can be genetically engineered too. In some cases, as with farmed salmon, the idea is to produce fish that are even more efficient in converting feed into flesh. In the UK, genes from Chinook salmon were inserted into the eggs of 10,000 Atlantic salmon. About half of the Atlantic salmon grew to be four times as large as they would normally have done, with no signs of any abnormalities. The media, inevitably, called them 'Franken-Fish'.[8] The fish were destroyed at the end of the experiment, but the potential had been demonstrated.

Leaner pigs: Although some meat-eaters like the fat from pork, ham or bacon, healthy eating has spurred interest in leaner pigs. GM techniques promise to help breeders produce pigs that put on lean meat faster. Either growth hormones can be injected into the pig or, more fundamentally, appropriate genes can be inserted in the pig's genetic make-up. One proposal was to insert a human gene into pigs, which, not surprisingly, proved highly controversial. It will almost certainly happen – and find commercial applications.

Don't forget, though, that despite all the talk about 'Frankenfoods' and the more sensationalist experiments, the GM ingredients in our food today consist almost exclusively of 'herbicide-resistant' or 'pest-resistant' soya or maize.

Why all the excitement?

 The greatest threat to us all would be a future without the benefits that [GM] technology has the potential to bring to society.

DuPont response to GM Food Survey

Many food companies responding to our GM Food Survey did not communicate any great enthusiasm for GM foods. But a few brave souls – like **Bird's Eye** – chose to stand out from the crowd. They said, 'We support the responsible use of biotechnology, including genetic modification.' But even they having been moving away from GM.

Here are some of the reasons why GM food supporters are enthusiastic about the prospects for their products:

Reduction of chemicals: They may not count as organic but, as we have seen, some GM crops can get by with fewer sprayings of herbicides. The benefits are even clearer with crops designed to be resistant to insect pests. The American company **Monsanto** claims that, thanks to its genetically modified cotton, there has been an 80 per cent reduction in the pesticides needed to protect cotton grown in Alabama. Cotton is a crop that has traditionally required particularly heavy doses of chemical insecticide.

Lower cost: One key objective of GM technology is to boost the productivity of a given acreage of land, crop plant or animal. Among other things, increased productivity can mean lower costs for producers and consumers. However, in most cases so far, as with GM soya, the savings have flowed to farmers and the GM crop companies, not consumers.

Greater efficiency: The idea here is to use GM technology to get a more saleable product from less raw material. So, for example, GM tomatoes can be designed with a higher 'goo' factor, which means you can get more tomato purée from a given number of tomatoes. Because the fruit is more concentrated and contains less water, less energy is needed in the production process, as well.

Powerful tools: With the use of GM tools, a genetic trait can be transferred in as little as a single generation, compared with the several generations required for conventional selective breeding techniques. Also, traditional breeding methods restrict the selection of genes to those of closely related plants or animals. With GM tools, on the other hand, you can cross the species barrier and, for example, put a scorpion gene into a vegetable.

Higher profits: Some of the life-science companies that are introducing GM technologies look set to make vast profits. Some even predict that the power of their technology will explode, in much the same way that computer technology has. In the process, these companies hope that they – and their shareholders – will become fabulously wealthy.

Consumer Opinion

THE CONSUMER IS ALWAYS RIGHT – EVEN WHEN WRONG

Consumer opinion is make-or-break for food giants like **Nestlé** and **Unilever**. So you could hear the frustration in the two companies' announcements that they would drop GM foods in the UK market. 'There were never any concerns about the foods,' said a **Unilever** spokesman. 'But we're market-driven, and if the [British] public no longer likes the foods with GM ingredients, we are obliged to get rid of them.' The companies still see GM as a 'promising technology' – and continue to use it in other countries.

What do the critics say?

If you are worried about GM foods, there are plenty of concerns to focus on:

Allergies: The number of people suffering from allergies is increasing.

Allergies are often caused by proteins, such as those found in nuts, and, if not properly controlled, genetic engineering could result in such proteins popping up in totally unexpected places. So it may be more likely that particular GM foods will trigger allergic reactions in some people. The other side of this allergy coin is that there are GM foods being designed specifically to help people with allergies (pages 131 & 221).

There have even been claims that allergies among the British public to soya increased by 50 per cent in 1998, coinciding with a large increase in imports of GM soya from the USA. One scientist, Dr Mae-Won Ho, warned that herbicide-tolerant soya beans might pose a serious food-allergy problem. She pointed out that the GM beans contain genes from a virus, a soil bacterium and the petunia plant, none of which have been in our diet before. No link has yet been proved between the imports and the allergies.

Antibiotic resistance: Another concern focuses on the use of antibiotics. In experiments, scientists take a gene that is resistant to normally lethal doses of antibiotics. Known as 'marker genes', these are inserted into the plant at the same time as the new gene that is being experimented with, and the plant is then exposed to high levels of antibiotics. If the plant shows antibiotic resistance, the scientists can then be sure that the transfer of all new genes into it has been successful. The worry is that this antibiotic resistance might itself be passed on to other species once the GM crops are grown in the open environment. In theory, at least, this resistance could also be passed on via the intestines of animals fed unprocessed GM maize. It's technically possible to remove the antibiotic resistant marker genes in the GMO once they have done their job. Indeed most scientists believe it is sloppy science to leave them in. Responsible companies have taken note of the dangers, and are exploring safer alternatives for the future.

Biodiversity: Traditional low-tech farming focuses on crops that suit the local environment and culture, helping preserve at least some biodiversity. GM crops, however, may be developed to survive in a wide range of environments, for example grape-vines may be modified to flourish in cold climates. One risk is that such plants might then push out local plant varieties – and help create global monocultures.

Environmental issues: To begin with, the critics of GM technology were most concerned about the risk of GMOs 'escaping' from laboratories. Microbes or seeds, for example, could be accidentally released into the environment, with the risk that they might then proliferate.

Now that GMOs (be they micro-organisms, crop plants or animals) are graduating from the laboratories and being planted in the general environment, the focus of concern is shifting to deliberate release. This raises fears that GM crop might cross-pollinate with other crops, and that widespread GM crop plantings would therefore begin to undermine the organic option altogether (see the Organic Dilemma box, page 42), because of the doubts about whether it's possible to preserve the integrity of organic produce that is farmed anywhere near GM crops.

This is one of the reasons why field trials are being carried out. One group of scientists working on pollen-free flowers and grasses – which they suggest may help hayfever sufferers – have also suggested that their work could help tackle the cross-pollination issue (see also super-weeds, below).[9]

Finally, as we saw with the antibiotic resistance issue, there could be problems for the environment with what some call 'genetic pollution'. This happens when modified genes are transferred from GMOs into wild species – or from GM crops into organic crops (see above). In Norway, escaped farmed fish have already undermined the biodiversity of the wild stock, now believed to be outnumbered by their fat cousins by five to one. Even though these fish are not yet GM, their influence on the wild stock is wholly damaging (page 144).

 We shall soon have an unprecedented and unethical situation in which one farmer's crops will contaminate another's against his will.

Prince Charles in a public statement, summer 1999

Ethics: GM technologies have already sparked a number of extraordinary controversies. Vegetarians would clearly wish to avoid vegetables containing animal genes, but even non-vegetarians might prefer not to become – as some would put it – 'cannibals' if and when human genes are used in our food. No such products are likely to get to market, but as matters stand it would not be illegal. And whatever their religious beliefs, many of the most forceful critics argue that

19

those producing GMOs are assuming powers – and responsibilities – that historically have been left to God (or at least evolution).

Health: One of the biggest fears over the introduction of GM foods is that they may be harmful to human health, particularly the health of children. This concern was whipped up to fever pitch following the revelations of Professor Pusztai. He conducted research on potatoes and concluded that it was at least possible that genetic modification could affect our immune systems. Even he did not say that his evidence was irrefutable, but one thing was clear: no one can yet say with certainty that GM foods are safe to grow or eat. These products have not been thoroughly tested for their long-term effects, and, what is more, no testing has yet been done on humans – except, of course, that many of us are already eating the stuff. When safety assessments are carried out, they are done on a case-by-case basis, without any consideration of the likely overall impact of a series of new developments.

Power: A small number of major agrochemical corporations are buying many of the seed banks around the world. This could eventually mean it would be almost impossible to buy seed that was not produced by one of these corporations.

Monsanto has been active in this area, and **DuPont**, another chemical company that has been diversifying into crop biotechnology and is now the second largest chemical company in the world, recently bought **Pioneer International**, the world's largest seed company. As the *Food Magazine* put it, 'DuPont can now sell you the seed, sell you the chemicals to grow the seed, purchase your harvest and process the harvest for American breakfasts.'[10]

Profits: Some financial analysts have been wondering aloud whether the GM foods industry is going to be profitable in the foreseeable future? They note that growing demands for separation of GM crops and crop products could well result in real financial problems for the industry. In the summer of 1999, for example, Germany's **Deutsche Bank** downgraded the shares of **Pioneer International** from 'Hold' to 'Sell'. Such decisions can cause financial shock-waves

'Substantial equivalence': This is the complicated term used by regulators and the food industry to describe GM foods. But it's interpreted by critics as a serious loophole. Although the DNA or protein of a GM

food product is detectably different from that of its non-GM counterpart, producers argue that many GM food products are not changed significantly enough to merit extra testing and labelling requirements. For example, a GM soya bean that has been genetically engineered to be resistant to herbicides, is, in terms of taste, texture and how it can be processed, identical to an ordinary soya bean. In legal terms it is therefore 'substantially equivalent' to an ordinary soya bean. But even as some manufacturers say their GM products are substantially equivalent, they still assert their right to patent them.

Super-predators: Most genetically engineered animals or organisms would probably die out if they escaped into the wild, because their energy is diverted into activities that are not helpful for their survival. But what if we should produce a super-pest? Those who saw the film *Jurassic Park* should remember, however, that this is less likely to be a new version of T-Rex than an accidentally released super-virulent mosquito.

Super-weeds: Most of the GM crops now being grown are designed to resist commonly used herbicides. The worry is that their herbicide-resistant gene might be transferred to nearby weeds, resulting in new strains of super-weeds, which could not be eradicated by any known treatment.

 It's unacceptable to impose a risk on the entire global population.

Patrick Holden, the Soil Association

Third World impact: The biotechnology industry claims that GM crops will help feed the Third World, because of their potential to increase productivity. However, the industry does not concentrate its time and effort on overcoming world hunger. Nor is lack of food the only significant cause of starvation. More often than not, malnutrition and famine result from problems in distribution, usually caused by politics, corruption and war.

Some critics argue that, far from helping the Third World, GM technology will devastate some of its economies, by enabling substitutes for products such as coffee, sugar or palm oil to be grown in other parts of the globe – or even produced in factories. Development organisations like **Christian Aid** warn that the GM revolution will concentrate power in too few hands, stripping farmers of their independence. If this happens, the risk of famine will *increase*. Others worry about the impact of technologies like the 'Terminator' gene.

Single-cycle seeds

THE TERMINATOR GENE

If a computer company develops a totally new form of hardware or software, it can apply for patent protection. Biotech companies have been patenting GM organisms, including animals like the 'Oncomouse', in the same way. But many GM companies, and their customers, want even more control. They are working on ways to stop GM plants from breeding – or at least breeding true – after the first crop has been produced.

The reason for this interest is obvious: they want to protect their profits against farmers who would otherwise simply replant the seed year after year, as they do with 'normal' seed. Around the world, companies and government agencies are working on technologies that promise to limit GM crop plants to one seed cycle.

When **Monsanto**, the international GM company with the highest public profile, announced its plans to buy the **Delta and Pine Land Company (D&PL)**, a storm broke out. **D&PL** owned the rights to the so-called 'Terminator' gene, one of a whole family of technologies developed to achieve gene control in commercial crops.

Monsanto's critics believe that the new technology will give the company too much control over the food cycle. In particular, they worry that this sort of technology could have a devastating impact on smallholder farmers in countries like India who rely on one year's saved seed to provide growing stock for the next.

Experts stress that such gene-lock technologies will not enter the market until 2005 at the earliest.[11] But the issue spotlights a crucial question: who will own and control tomorrow's food?

Toxicity: Many plants, as our ancestors found to their cost, produce a range of toxic compounds as part of their natural defence. Some of these substances are already present in today's food at levels that are apparently safe, but what would happen if genetic engineering accidentally raised their levels? Or produced a new toxin? Would the regulatory authorities detect the problem before we did?

Unintended effects: Experience shows that unexpected side-effects to new technologies are more or less guaranteed. GM technology is ultra-sophisticated, and it is certainly a long way ahead of where we were a few decades ago, but given the complexity of the systems we're now trying to manipulate, we are still pretty much in the biological Stone Age.

Some of the effects of gene transfer may be unpredictable, others undetectable until it's too late. Putting a human growth gene into mice produces giant mice, but the same gene inserted into pigs can produce animals that are skinny, cross-eyed and suffer from arthritis. The use of BST (page 149) boosts milk production, but requires greater use of antibiotics to control the resulting increase in mastitis. As a result, the antibiotic contamination of milk goes up.

Already, after only two or three years of using GM crops, significant resistance to Bt is being found in the insect pests that GM cotton and maize were designed to control. This could have serious implications for organic farmers, who are allowed to use Bt sprays because they break down within 24–48 hours of spraying. Organic farmers believe that resistance would not have developed if it had not been for the GM crops.

Yields: GM is supposed to increase yields, but industry rumours suggest that some farmers are experiencing a crippling combination of lower yields and no reduction in costs, while being bound to the biotech companies with tough contracts. At this stage, it's difficult to know what is going on; but a study by the US Department of Agriculture of crop yields in 1997 and 1998 has shown that GM crops do not automatically produce better yields or significantly lower pesticide use. 'I would have a lot of trouble attributing any sort of "yield bump" to biotechnology,' said one economist involved in the study.[12]

Your choice: Finally, an overriding concern focuses on the issue of consumer choice. Consumers have not been given a choice of whether or not they want GM crop ingredients in their food, and, as we saw above, the use of GM may actually restrict our choice by genetically polluting organic crops – grown nearby – so that they can no longer be certified and sold as organic. But consumer pressure in both Europe and Japan is having its effect. As *The New Foods Guide* went to press, one of the largest US soya and maize exporters – **Archer Daniels Midland** (**ADM**) – announced that it would move to segregate GM crops. The company, which buys a third of US corn, wheat and soya, was signalling a significant shift in the world's most important food market. If this approach spreads, the cost implications for the GM crop sector could be profound.

In the spotlight

MONSANTO AND ITS COMPETITORS

Monsanto may have been in the news recently, but it is only one part of what looks set to become a major industry of the 21st century. Many of the early GM pioneers were small companies, with names like **Biogen**, **Celltech** and **Genentech**. They attracted a great deal of media attention, partly because of the investment 'goldrush' they triggered and partly because of early fears about possible *accidental* releases of GMOs. Later, many were taken over by big chemical and drug companies.

Some of those same large companies began to develop their own life science (biotechnology) businesses, including chemical giants such as **Dow Chemical**, **DuPont**, **Monsanto** and **Novartis**. **Monsanto** alone has spent nearly $8 billion since 1996 to buy various seed banks and companies.[13] To put it mildly, these activities were not always welcomed by campaigners and the media. Some of the companies, already targeted by campaigners on a range of environmental issues, have triggered new concerns with their growing interest in GM crop plants and the *deliberate* release of GMOs.

One of **Monsanto's** early bio-products, the dairy hormone known as BST, was banned in the EU. Other companies, among them **Eli Lilly**, were also trying to push BST into the market, but **Monsanto's** approach meant that it attracted much of the negative publicity. Much later, **Monsanto** returned to the fray with products based on GM soya, designed to tolerate high concentrations of the company's chemical herbicide *Roundup*. At a time when **Monsanto's** chief executive was calling for a shift to more sustainable (or future-friendly) forms of technology and trying to win the support of leading environmentalists, the company seemed willing to use surprisingly robust political tactics to get its way.

In what follows, **Monsanto** will inevitably be mentioned a number of times. In the longer term, its technologies may well become hugely successful in the GM foods market, but for the moment the company seems to be swimming against the tide of public opinion.

Who's in control?

With medicines, the patient usually benefits alongside the doctor, hospital and drug-maker. With most GM food products to date, the benefits have gone to farmers and the life-science companies, while many of the risks appear to be carried by the consumer. So who is keeping an eye on these new technologies and products?

The short answer is that it's our government's job, both nationally and at the EU level. The government, in turn, is advised by a number of expert bodies. In the UK, the **Advisory Committee on Novel Foods and Processes** (ACNPF), for example, reviews new product applications. **The Ministry of Agriculture, Fisheries and Foods** (MAFF) grants licences for trials of GM crops. The **Nuffield Council on Bioethics** considers ethical issues raised by products like GM foods. And organisations like **English Nature** are responsible for nature conservation issues.

One particularly controversial area involves the labelling of GM foods. The **European Commission** (EC) is responsible for setting the labelling requirements. There are a number of different ways in which GM technology is made use of in the food we eat, and each requires particular labelling criteria. The EC has broken down GM foods into these categories:

- *GM crops*: These are crops that have been genetically engineered, such as soya, maize and tomatoes. Products containing GM soya or maize (but not GM tomatoes or any other crop) must be labelled as such. An exception is made, however, for products that have been so highly processed (see GM crop-derived ingredients, below), that it would not be possible to detect any GM ingredient in the product.

- *GM crop-derived ingredients:* These are ingredients which have been made using GM crops, but which do not normally contain any detectable traces of the GM processes. They include the emulsifier lecithin, corn oil and corn starch. There is no requirement to label such ingredients.

- *GM bug-derived ingredients:* This category covers foods or food ingredients produced by GM micro-organisms, such as enzymes (page 93). Examples here would include the GM rennet used in cheese, brewer's yeast and some vitamins. There is no requirement for these foods to be labelled – and it's unlikely that they will be any time soon.

- *GM-treated animal products*: This category embraces all produce from animals treated with GM products, for example BST milk. In the USA, BST milk is mixed with the general milk supply and there is no labelling requirement. If BST milk is introduced in Europe after it comes up for review in mid-2000, the same approach may be adopted, although in the current climate this seems unlikely.

- *GM animal products*: None of the GM animals that scientists have been experimenting with – such as leaner pigs, disease-resistant chickens or super-fast growing salmon – have been cleared for human consumption, even in the USA. Given the public concern over GM foods, it's almost inconceivable that they would not be labelled, but the further away the suppliers – and the more opaque the supply chain – the greater the chance that someone may try to pull a fast one.

- *GM fed animal products*: This category covers food from animals that have been fed with GM crops or feed additives. In the UK, all non-organic meat, milk and eggs could qualify for such labelling. Although no UK-grown GM crops are used in feed, 20 per cent of animal feed is imported and will almost certainly contain some GM-crop products. There is unlikely to be any requirement to label animals fed with GM crops, but the producers of animal feed may have to label their products – this will make it possible for farmers to avoid GM feed should they so wish. This issue surfaced on the supermarket and food manufacturers' agendas later than others, but many of them are realising that to be genuinely GM-free they will have to avoid products from animals fed with GM crops.

Manufacturers claiming to be totally 'GM-free' may not be clear about whether their products contain 'GM bug-derived ingredients'. In the responses to our GM Food Survey, most companies left this item blank or said it was 'under review'. Some, though, were able to send us evidence that they were buying what are known as 'identity preserved' ingredients.

'Identity preserved' products

TRACEABILITY IN ACTION

The idea is simple – but often infernally difficult to put into practice. When consumers demand GM-free ingredients, a whole chain of processes has to be GM-free: growers have to buy and plant GM-free seed; the resulting crops have to be harvested separately – and kept separate – from GM crops at the farm and when they arrive at the processor's plant; and separate transportation and storage have to be provided right through to the moment when the customer chooses the food from the supermarket shelf.

The process must be audited and documented throughout. If the distribution channels are designed for this from the word go, there is no problem, but when they aren't, the cost of doing everything twice can make the GM-free stream of products more expensive. Nevertheless, growing numbers of food companies and supermarkets have been moving in this direction, including **Linda McCartney's** vegetarian food company, which started using what are known as 'identity-preserved' ingredients when it was discovered that it had unwittingly allowed GM contamination of its products.

It remains to be seen how the new GM food labelling laws will work in the UK. The government plans to broaden the focus of the labelling rules from GM maize and soya ingredients to force the labelling of *all* GM additives and flavourings in foods. The challenge for the catering industry is going to be huge.

◆ FUNCTIONAL FOODS ◆

What are functional foods?

Most people have not yet heard of functional foods. But they will. This type of 'new food', although its impact may be relatively small at present, is set to rocket into public consciousness over the next few years, propelled by the surging interest in healthy eating. In the last five years our understanding of the links between our food and our health has broadened dramatically.

At first sight, the term 'functional foods' is an odd one if we consider that all the foods we eat have a function – to keep us alive by providing calories and a range of vital nutrients. But when the food industry talks of functional foods – or nutraceuticals, a term often used in the USA – it refers to foods especially designed or formulated to improve our health or boost our performance in some specific way.

So far, the health benefits in functional foods have been achieved on the whole by cutting the amount of unhealthy ingredients in the food (like saturated fats); boosting the level of health-promoting ingredients that might already be present (like folic acid); or adding ingredients that would not normally be found in the food (like artifical sweeteners).

Unlike GM or New Organic foods, however, functional foods cannot be easily pigeon-holed, because the definitions are, to put it mildly, fuzzy; and,despite the implications of functional foods on our future eating habits, the term 'functional food' has no legal status as yet. A working definition might run along the following lines: *foods that have been changed – either by the addition or removal of (a) particular ingredient(s) – in order to confer an extra health benefit.*

Food with added nutrients – usually called 'fortified foods' – have been around for a long time. Indeed, it is now compulsory to fortify products such as flour and margarine to compensate for the nutrients lost during processing. But the range of things now being added to our food is expanding way beyond simple fortification.

Food fads and health nuts go back a very long way, but in the late

1960s, there began to be great public interest in the possible links between our diet and health and a dramatic growth in the numbers of health and fortified foods followed. Some offered low fat, low salt or low sugar content, others offered high levels of dietary fibre, thought to improve digestion and prevent various forms of intestinal disease and cancer.

But the revolution of functional food as we shall come to know it in the next twenty years began in Japan in the late 1980s, triggering an avalanche of new products. The first functional food was probably *Fibe Mini*, a fibre-enriched soft drink launched by **Otsuka Pharmaceutical** in 1988.[14] The trend quickly spread to America and Europe, where many big names are now involved, among them **Campbell**, **Kellogg**, **Mars** and **Quaker**.

The number of different terms used in this area continues to explode: 'designer foods', 'foodaceuticals', 'nutraceuticals', 'pharma foods', 'smart foods'. Whatever we call them, functional foods have already begun to trigger major controversies. Let's look at some of the products that are coming to market and at some of the issues they raise.

Examples of functional foods?

As some experts see it, there have been three generations of 'health' foods to hit the market. First came foods with reduced fat, sugar or salt; then came foods free of certain additives which consumers were beginning to see as 'unnatural'; and now come foods designed to have a specific health effect, particularly on the main diseases linked to diet – cancer, cardiovascular disease, diabetes and obesity. The foods produced in all three of these 'generations' could be thought of as functional.

One of the exciting developments in the area of functional foods is the rapidly growing understanding of plant and animal ingredients that it's encouraging in us. Herbalists may have known for years the power of particular plants in healing, but until recently they have not generally had the means to know which particular compound is responsible for the therapeutic effect, and how it might be reproduced. In order to develop functional foods, scientists will continue to turn to nature, using it as a toolbox from which they pick and choose ingredients to add to foods in which they would not normally be found.

 These are not Frankenstein foods. These are not chemical soups. These are naturally occurring substances used in new ways.
Clare Hasler, Functional Foods for Health Program, University of Illinois[15]

Here are some of the purposes of functional foods:

High: Some foods contain health-promoting substances naturally. When the value to human digestion of high-fibre foods was discovered, a flood of products, like breakfast cereals with added bran, came on to the market. Added vitamins have been a feature of processed foods for a long time and are now widely accepted. Some ancient foods, like tea, are also turning out to have interesting chemistry. And many other foods are being investigated in the hope that any natural health-promoting properties may be boosted and new fortified foods created.

Low: Other food ingredients are harmful to health when taken in excess, and correspondingly there has been a stampede to offer products that are low-fat, low-salt, low-sugar, low-whatever. The next stage of this trend can be seen with the advent of products like non-fattening fats (page 70).

Quick: Some new foods are designed to give you a jolt of energy or nutrients needed when you are being highly active. 'Sports drinks' (page 206) fall into this category.

Slow: Alternatively, foods can be designed to ensure that they release their calories and nutrients in a steady, sustained way. Cereals and other starch-based foods have always worked like this, which is why marathon runners tank up on starchy foods, but it's easy to imagine future slow-release foods designed to help people control chronic health problems like migraines or pre-menstrual syndrome (PMS).

There are new foods that are beginning to blur the boundaries between food and medicine, such as cholesterol-lowering spreads and gut-friendly yoghurts. In the future, there might conceivably be spaghetti that keeps arthritis at bay, egg sandwiches that cut the risk of heart disease and cornflakes that help prevent breast cancer.

FRUIT ON PRESCRIPTION

For the moment, food companies are making functional foods primarily by adding new ingredients at the processing stage. In the longer term, however, the hope is that the ingredients can be engineered into the crops that produce the raw materials.

This will eventually allow for the production of foods specifically designed to act as medicines. Food products are not, at present, allowed to make medicinal claims, even though some come very close to it. Medicine foods, however, will be tasty foods like fruits that have been genetically modified to supply the consumer with the drug or vaccination that he or she may need. As with the drugs familiar to us today, some of them will have to be prescribed by a doctor. Instead of fussing with needles, eating an apple, a potato or half a banana could protect against a range of diseases, such as chickenpox, cholera, measles, polio and typhoid.

GM potatoes are being developed as a source of the hepatitis B vaccine. Every year, many millions of people around the world become infected with the virus, which causes extreme fatigue, abdominal pain and nausea. Unfortunately the potatoes have to be eaten raw, because cooking destroys the vaccine, but the basic idea is attractive, given that this approach produces a much cheaper vaccine. Researchers are looking for a more palatable vegetable or fruit to use. Banana chips are high on the list of possible ways of delivering the vaccine in future.

Why all the excitement?

Functional foods have not yet caused tremendous excitement. But they almost certainly will. Here are some of the reasons why:

Health benefits: Some functional foods will be designed to prevent health problems from occuring in the future, while others – including foods that remove cholesterol from your body – might reverse damage that has already been done.

Profits and pricing: Most food markets are commodity markets, with intense competition and enormous pressure on pricing and profit margins, but products that provide significant health benefits, or that consumers believe will do so, can be sold at higher prices.

Treats: Some functional foods, such as those including 'smart' ingredients like non-fat fats, put a new spin on the notion of being able to have your cake and eat it too. You can enjoy something that was once considered to be unhealthy, but get the nutrients you need and avoid the ones you don't.

 Everybody wants to be healthy and live forever – and food companies are there to provide the magic bullets.
> *Professor Debbie Perosio, Cornell University Food Industry Management Program*[16]

What do the critics say?

Functional foods have not yet come under the same level of attack as GM foods, although there have been controversies – about products making excessive health claims, for example – and there will be many more. Among the challenges to date, the following stand out:

Confusion: As the number of functional foods grows and producers try to jump onto the bandwagon, it's likely that we will see increasing confusion about which foods contain what – and how to achieve a healthy, balanced diet. Supermarkets have been offering crisps and corn snacks labelled as 'a source of fibre', despite the fact that such foods are high in fat, salts and additives, and patently not good for your health. And why spend more on fish-oil-enhanced bread when you could just as easily, and more usefully, eat mackerel, sardines or salmon?

False or misleading claims: You would hardly guess it from reading the packets, but scientists have identified relatively few specific substances guaranteed to cut the risks of particular diseases. There is a real likelihood that the 'functional' label will be used as a marketing ploy to differentiate products rather than genuinely to promote public health improvements. A range of drinks in the USA contain a number of ingredients described as 'metabolic enhancers'. These are promoted as 'liquid liposuction', something that will draw off the pounds. Believe it if you must, but don't give up the exercise just yet![17]

Health risks: Surveys have shown that many fortified foods fail to warn of potential health risks. Some products claiming to be a source of added vitamin A, for example, have failed to warn women who are, or might become, pregnant that they should be careful about their vitamin A intake.[18] As a greater range of functional ingredients, including powerful herbal remedies, are added to products, this problem is likely to get worse unless regulators tighten up controls.

Junk food: The UK **Food Commission** is among the bodies that have warned of the risk of 'junk food with added nutrients'. One or two extra functional ingredients do not transform junk food into health food. Adding vitamins to sweet soft drinks, for example, doesn't make them good for your teeth.

Poor regulation and labelling: This is another area where food industry innovation has run ahead of the regulators. A growing body of opinion is expressing the need for functional foods – and the claims made on their behalf – to be better controlled. Critics point out that manufacturers are not required to prove that their new food products are effective before they go onto the market. If these were drugs, clinical trials would be required, but, as things stand, labelling requirements in most countries are weak to non-existent.

Who's in control?

The fact that the term 'functional food' is not yet scientifically or legally accepted results in confusion and raises questions about the integrity of some of the claims. Leading consumer organisations in Japan, the UK and USA have called for a crackdown by government agencies on the marketing of all so-called functional foods.[19] One report asserted that these foods risked becoming 'the snake oil of the next century'.[20]

In Japan, where the functional food trend first took root, manufacturers wanting to make specific health claims must submit their products for extensive testing. Many products have to be certified by the government as a Food for Specified Health Use (FOSHU). But some companies describe their products as 'health foods' to avoid the need to apply for FOSHU certification. The Japanese government has now expanded the FOSHU scheme to embrace all health foods marketed with functional ingredients.

In the USA, the **Food and Drug Administration** (FDA) is a powerful watchdog, but some products have been sold as 'dietary supplements' to avoid the need for some of the more rigorous types of government clearance. The **FDA** has now closed the dietary supplement gap, and requires, among other things, that functional ingredients be proved safe, and that any claims to functional status be based on scientific consensus and approved by the **FDA** before marketing begins. Labels must inform consumers of the quantity of functional ingredients per serving, with warning information where appropriate.

In the UK, there is a voluntary code for the food industry. Recommendations made in 1990 by the **Food Advisory Committee** (**FAC**), which advises the government agriculture ministry **MAFF**, were largely turned aside by the government. There is a set of Food Labelling Regulations, which covers certain claims made about foods, either on labels or in advertisements (among other things, the regulations insist that no food should be labelled as 'capable of preventing, treating or curing human disease' unless it has been cleared under the Medicines Act), but there is no legislation yet specifically relating to functional foods.

The sort of claims that tend to attract particular attention from the regulators are those that suggest that a food does one of the following:

- lowers cholesterol

- strengthens or boosts the immune system

- fights gum disease

- stops cravings for – or 'burns' – fat

- increases metabolic rate

- stimulates or calms the nervous system

- maintains the water balance.

The words that ring alarm bells include 'restores', 'repairs', 'eliminates', 'counteracts', 'combats', 'clears', 'stops', 'heals', 'cures', 'treats', 'avoids', 'protects' or 'prevents'. All of these suggest some form of medicinal effect.

It is clear that the very word 'functional' is virtually meaningless to consumers today, but that position will change. The fact that companies like **McDonald's** are beginning to introduce functional hamburgers, for example, will drive these issues into the headlines. New initiatives will be needed to ensure that industry's claims are properly vetted.

One new initiative in the UK suggests a possible way forward. This is the **Joint Health Claims Initiative**, based on a voluntary code of practice drawn up by the **Food and Drink Federation, LACOTS** (the **Local Authority Coordinating Body on Food and Trading Standards**) and **Sustain**. From early in 2000 manufacturers would be required to submit evidence to support any claims, which will then be assessed by a panel of consumer, trading standards and industry representatives. The idea of this voluntary code of practice is to assist trading standards officers to uphold the law, to encourage the food industry only to make valid claims and to protect the public against misleading labelling and advertising.

However misleading some of the early claims may prove to have been, functional foods are guaranteed a central place on tomorrow's menus. Over time, they will offer increasingly real and attractive health benefits, which will make them irresistible to many consumers. And, eventually, some of these foods will offer functional benefits that can only be achieved via GM means, potentially providing a way of re-introducing GM foods even into markets that currently reject them.

● NEW ORGANIC FOODS ●

These are boom times for the organic farming sector. The industry is being driven by enormous consumer demand, and at present, fuelled partly by fear over residues (see Residues box, page 40), food scares like BSE and the GM issue. Demand is outstripping supply. If current growth trends continue, it is predicted that 10–20 per cent of agricultural land will be farmed organically by 2010. In Denmark, they plan to be 50 per cent organic within ten years.

But organic farming is nothing new. Indeed, it goes back a very long way – over 10,000 years, to the very dawn of agriculture. For most of history, the world's farmers have relied on natural fertilisers and pest control methods (such as manures and natural pest predators). They were organic farmers because they had no alternative. Then, as we saw in chapter 1, world agriculture went through a series of revolutions, each one helping to accelerate the next. As human populations grew in the 20th century, farmers began to use more chemicals and more expensive equipment, and the average size of farms grew rapidly, to the point where many of them now bear a closer resemblance to industrial facilities than they do to the farms of previous centuries.

> What's happened in the past 50 years, and especially in the past 30, is that we have picked apart the fabric and biodiversity of our landscape and degraded it to such an extent that it will take a major reconstruction job, not just a bit of tinkering, to get it back.
>
> *Patrick Holden, Soil Association*

What are 'New Organic' foods?

In recent years, supporters of organic farming have begun to position themselves in direct opposition to high-tech, chemical-intensive farming, and they have also emerged as a powerful voice against the introduction of GM foods. Organic produce is grown with no synthetic chemical pesticides, no synthetic chemical fertilisers and with great attention to the health of soils, animals and ecosystems. Organic farmers aim to build soil fertility by working with natural systems and cycles. They seek always to minimise the input of elements from outside those systems and cycles.

The real difference between the 'organic' farming that our ancestors practised and the emerging New Organic sector is that the latter is driven by the same need to be competitive that all modern food production sectors are subject to. It draws on the latest agricultural science, is constantly seeking to improve its production methods, ships produce over considerable distances (70 per cent of Britain's organic food is imported) and aims to supply supermarkets with large volumes of high quality products.

For most people 'organic' represents 'purity' or an assurance that their food will not be contaminated with pesticides, fertilisers and increasingly, GMOs. If the word 'natural' means anything in the context of today's food, it means organic. And for those with broader concerns, organic food is not only better for health, but for the environment too. At a time when food poisoning incidents have increased 400 per cent in just ten years, the demand for the 'guarantee' of purity is growing at an extraordinary pace. Supermarkets like **Waitrose** and **Sainsbury's** now stock over 400 organic lines, and the size of lettering for the word 'organic' is growing all the time. Organic food is breaking out of the ghetto and is starting to be viewed as the 'gold standard' in some areas of food and drink, for example chocolate.

 Once seen as a quirky fad, organic foods have made a big impact on mainstream retailing – multiple supermarkets account for 60–70 per cent of organic food sales.

New Covent Garden Soup Company

Examples of New Organic foods?

Not so long ago, if you wanted organic produce you generally had to buy it direct from the farm. Nowadays there are many more options for the organic shopper.

Organic box schemes: These either deliver to your home a box containing a selection of organic fruit and vegetables, or let you pick up your box(es) of organic produce from a collection point. Happily for organic consumers, there has been a proliferation of these schemes in the last couple of years. The vegetables are usually fresh, always seasonal and often considerably cheaper than organic produce bought at supermarkets.

Farmers' markets: In a rediscovery of the past, farmers who live and work within a reasonable distance of a town come and sell their produce direct to the public. These markets are not necessarily organic, but a lot of organic suppliers are using this outlet – because it is *local*.

Mail order: Whether you are looking for fresh meat, fruit, vegetables or processed ready meals, organic offerings are also now available from a growing number of mail-order companies.

Small shops: Many farm shops, wholefood shops, health food shops, greengrocers and delicatessens pioneered the organic trend, and although supermarket competition is intense, many are fighting back with an ever-expanding range of organic products.

Alternative supermarkets: A number of alternative supermarkets, such as **Out of This World** and **Planet Organic**, have started up around the country. They generally have the widest range of organic produce and products on offer.

Supermarkets: Most of the mainstream supermarkets have now recognised the demand for organic produce. Some offer own-brand organic products, and although many of them are imported, even the supermarkets are waking up to the benefits of locally grown produce, where feasible.

Why all the excitement?

If organic farming is to fulfil its potential by 2010, it has huge strides to make. At the moment the organic sector is close to the 10 per cent mark in countries like Austria, Denmark, Finland, Germany, Sweden and Switzerland, but it's still at only around 1 per cent in the UK, and the European average is around 2.5 per cent. Organic enthusiasts proclaim a virtual A-to-Z of benefits, including:

Animal welfare: The criteria for organic certification take account of animal welfare.

Biodiversity: Organic growers not only protect the countryside, but are also likely to plant a broader range of plant varieties than conventional growers. Studies have shown that organic farming boosts both the size and the diversity of local wildlife populations, a major advantage now that species loss is very much on the agenda.

Environment: Organic farmers work to protect the quality of soil, water and air, to cut waste to a minimum and to conserve as much as possible of the fabric of the countryside. They are content with smaller fields and more hedgerows, and they actively encourage wildlife, partly as a means of pest control.

GM-free: The recent furore over the introduction of GM foods provided a massive boost for the organic sector, but for at least some organic supporters, it was by no means obvious that the GM option should be rejected for organic criteria.[21] Eliminating pesticides is a key organic principle, and some GM crops are designed to do just that. Some farmers therefore argued that GM crops should be accepted as organic. In the event this was rejected by the leading standards-setting bodies, and organic produce must now, by definition, be 'GM-free' (see Organic Dilemma box). As it has turned out, this has become a key selling point. You can now even buy dog food billed as organic and GM-free. Pet food manufacturer **Pascoe's** says that when it interviewed dog owners, 30 per cent were more concerned about what they fed their dog than about what they fed their partner. But, as *The Observer* put it: 'You may able to take the pesticides out of your pooch, but this is still an animal that regularly licks its own bottom.'

Health: Clearly one of the main advantages of organic produce is that there is less risk of chemical residues (see Toxic Boomerangs box below), although a small amount may be found as a result of pesticide 'drift'. Even better, studies have shown that organic produce generally has lower levels of potentially harmful nitrates, higher levels of vitamin C and more essential nutrients and minerals.

Residues

TOXIC BOOMERANGS

Much of our food contains chemical residues, such as pesticides. The most commonly used pesticides are insecticides (to control insects), fungicides (to control fungi) and herbicides (to control weeds). Any non-organic products may contain detectable residues of these and other agrochemicals.

Agrochemicals may have boosted crop yields, but some surprisingly toxic chemicals are still used. Before they are used, all insecticides and herbicides have to be approved by government agencies, but this does not prevent chemical residues from being left on fruit and vegetables. So-called 'systemic' pesticides are designed to work inside plants and their fruit, which makes it even more likely that they will leave some form of residue.

In a recent **Consumers' Association** survey, it was found that roughly three-fifths of apple and lettuce samples contained residues of agrochemicals. Although none were near the legal limits set by the government, tests of imported foods reveal traces of pesticides that are illegal in the UK. In some cases, these banned chemicals are made in the developed world and then exported to the developing world where laws and controls on their use are less stringent. The treated produce is then sold back to the developed countries – hence the expression 'toxic boomerang'.

Residues can present an acute risk to health, with immediate effects. Potentially more serious, however, are their cumulative, chronic effects – the ones that build up over time. Over a generation ago, in her prophetic book *Silent Spring*[22], Rachel Carson warned that an entire class of chemicals – the organochlorines, including the pesticides DDT, chlordane and heptachlor – were polluting the tissues of virtually every man, woman, child and animal on the planet. Dubbed 'gender benders', these chemicals are thought to affect our reproductive health and in severe cases to render us infertile. The effects have been described in books such as *Our Stolen Future*[23] and *The Feminisation of Nature*[24].

We cannot be sure whether these products are solely to blame because of several factors, including the proliferation of other chemicals to which we are all daily exposed, the extraordinarily small amounts of some hormone disrupters needed to produce undesirable effects, and the subtlety of some of the perceived effects – such as learning difficulties in children.

While we were writing this section, a major UK supermarket was found unwittingly to have sold sweetcorn sprayed with illegal and potentially harmful pesticides. Apparently a farmer had sprayed his aphid-infested sweetcorn crop with *Metaphor* – an organophosphate nerve agent that was not licensed for use.[25] A couple of years later, when *Metaphor* was no longer available, he used three more unapproved pesticides. He allegedly failed to mention the fact because he knew that the supermarket would not buy crops treated in this way. Once it came to light, of course, he lost his contracts to supply the chain.

Nutrients: Organic produce is often eaten fresher, which means it's likely to have retained more nutrients. Because it takes longer to grow, the natural sugars and other foodstuffs that make it up are also more easily digested.

Profits: In the USA, the organic farming sector is now valued at $5 billion a year. It is the fastest-growing and most profitable sector of American agriculture.[26] Profit is by no means guaranteed, however – farmers planning to switch to organic often face difficult transition periods and government grants are generally pitiful.

Sperm counts: Several studies have shown sperm counts have dropped in western males, resulting in rising infertility. There are many views on why this is happening, but one possibility is that there is a link to the use of pesticides. Incidentally, a Danish study revealed that the sperm counts of organic farmers and growers were 50 per cent higher than average. More research needs to be done before these findings can be taken as conclusive evidence of a link.[27]

Taste: For most organic produce it would be difficult to tell the difference in a blind tasting – where the tasters are given no clues to which products are organic and which not. However, organic enthusiasts argue that it's easy to detect the improved flavour in vegetables like carrots, cauliflowers and cabbage.

Transparency: In a time of food scares and rising concern about what is in the foods we eat, a major benefit offered by all organic producers is the way they maintain the transparency of the food chain: in order to be certified organic, food must be traceable back to its origins, wherever it is produced, and guaranteed organic from field to plate. Obviously, this poses a greater challenge when the produce comes from the other side of the world than when it comes from a nearby farm, but the New Organic sector is now taking traceability to such heights that it could teach some mainstream farmers a thing or two. We will examine this trend in more detail later.

How GM-free is GM-free?

THE ORGANIC DILEMMA

Organic criteria require that products and ingredients should be 'GM-free'. But is this really possible? Let's take a look at what it means in practice. There are a number of ways that genetically modified organisms (GMOs) might find their way into organic produce:

1. *Seeds:* Organic producers must use GM-free seed. With more GM crops, it could become harder to guarantee that seeds for organic produce have not come from GM plants.

2. *Cross-pollination:* Pollen from GM crops can be blown on to organic crops. If this happens, organic farmers – or gardeners – could lose their organic status.

3. *Animal feed:* Although organically reared livestock must be given organic feed, farmers are permitted by the standards-setting bodies to feed even organic animals up to 10 per cent non-organic feed for ruminants and 20 per cent for non-ruminants. The **Soil Association** requires non-GM declarations for all non-organic feed components, but standard-setting bodies in other countries may not be so rigorous.

4. *Animal manures:* Organic farmers use a great deal of manure on their land. Unless this manure comes from organically reared animals, there is a possibility that it could contain GMOs. This is a real problem, but one that could ease if supermarkets start to require that livestock should not be given GM feed.

5. *Ingredients:* Labelling rules require that a minimum of 70 per cent of the agricultural ingredients of organic food (i.e. not processing aids such as water and salt) must be organic where the product is labelled 'product made with x % organic ingredients' – and a minimum of 95 per cent where products are labelled as 'organic'. The 30 per cent and the 5 per cent must come from a specific list of ingredients, some of which are not yet available in organic form. A limited number of additives and processing aids are also allowed, although a declaration

must be obtained from suppliers that they are made from non-GM materials.

The net result is that it's rarely possible, even for organic producers, to make a '100 per cent 'GM-free' guarantee. Indeed, the Soil Association cautions against the use of 'GM-free' labelling, preferring instead to push towards GM-free farming systems, which would ensure more or less GM-free products.

Obviously, this will become more difficult as more GM crops are grown, which raises the key question of whether we have a 'right' to organic produce – and, if so, whether this 'right' is being threatened by GM? Whatever the answer to the first question, the evidence suggests that GM agriculture poses a genuine threat to the integrity of organic farming.

What do the critics say?

Here are some of the main criticisms of organic food:

Appearance: Thanks to modern farming and supermarket quality control, many of us have become accustomed to eating uniform and blemish-free produce. Organic produce, on the other hand, comes in all shapes and sizes, might well have some insect damage, and can even be wilted and shrivelled. To date the latter problem may have been caused by low turnover, poor distribution, or infrequent deliveries, but with growing interest in organic, the sector is benefiting from economies of scale. Increasingly there is no real reason why we should accept poor quality organic produce.

Contamination: As the pressures build on GM foods, the inevitable backlash against organic foods has begun – and it will probably build. Concerns have been raised about harmful bacteria like *E. coli* and *Salmonella* being spread in manures used by organic farmers. Whether these concerns are valid or not, it is clear that hygeine concerns will also surface in the organic foods sector.

Cost: Whichever way you cut it, organic food usually costs more. More people are needed to produce it and more land can be required, and, furthermore, organic farmers pay for social and environmental improvements that most conventional farmers don't tackle. There are some who argue that on top of these expected expenses, supermarkets charge a high premium for organic foods. Whether this is true or not – and although there are honourable exceptions among the supermarkets – organic foods are often beyond the reach of the less well-off.

 Safeway supports organic foods by regularly promoting organic products to our customers with price offers.
Safeway response to GM Food Survey

Efficiency: Organic farming generally entails doing things more slowly. For example, an organic carrot might need to be in the ground for up to three weeks longer than a conventional one. The use of growth promoters (including the routine use of antibiotics) is also banned in organically reared livestock, whereas mainstream UK farmers are still allowed to use them, thus producing higher yields.

Practicality: If you ask a non-organic farmer why he/she does not convert to organic, the answer will almost certainly be 'it's impractical' or 'it wouldn't work on my farm'. The reason for this is that converting to an organic system involves a radically different approach to how the farm operates, which goes far beyond just feeding animals organic food or replacing the use of chemical fertilizer with organic. For example, one of the principles of organic agriculture is to be as self-sufficient as possible, which means organic monocultures don't really work. Farmers need to diversify, perhaps even rearing animals as well as growing crops so that the animals can provide manure.

Productivity and Third World issues: These generate the fiercest debates over organic farming. 'World food production has tripled in the past 30 years,' said one **Monsanto** executive. 'If we used the same methods as 30 years ago, we would need another billion acres.' Many people also believe that organic agriculture is a luxury for the rich and would not help feed the Third World. It's true that organic food still tends to be more expensive to produce than conventionally farmed produce, and that crop diseases and pests can spread faster in the tropical conditions often found in many Third World countries. On the other hand, the **Soil Association** claims that 'organic or low impact systems that are well managed have been shown to produce the same level of production as intensive agriculture achieves'.

Organic operations also encourage self-reliance and improved food security, and Third World organic producers are often small scale enterprises that put more back into the local community than the large-scale, global operators. This argument will run and run.

Who's in control?

Organic standards in the UK are set and monitored by **UKROFS**, part of the **Ministry of Agriculture Foods and Fisheries** (**MAFF**), which implements the relevant EU regulation.[28] **UKROFS**, in turn, licenses private bodies to inspect and certify organic farms and food processing. The **Soil Association**, whose staff has exploded from five at the beginning of the 1990s to about 80 today, is the largest of these bodies, with 75 per cent of the market. Its standards tend to be higher than those set by **UKROFS** (see Eggs, for example). For example, products conforming to their criteria will be labelled with their symbol.

At the international level, the EU organic regulation requires that any produce imported into the EU must be produced and certified to equivalent standards. The **International Federation of Organic Agricultural Movements** (**IFOAM**) runs an accreditation scheme to ensure this equivalence at the international level.

As consumer and commercial interest grows, there is a battle under way for the soul of the organic movement, which looks set to intensify. The outcome will decide whether organic farming remains one small sector among many or – as more people now believe is possible – becomes part of the food production mainstream. When one UK farmer was forbidden to use the word 'organic' on his winter beans by the **Soil Association**, because the biotech company **Agrevo** was growing an experimental crop of GM spring oil-seed rape nearby, another certification agency, **Organic Farmers and Growers**, stepped in with its own rating. Organic Farmers and Growers was once the marketing arm of the **Soil Association**, but broke away in 1975. Its chairman is blunt about the organisation's objectives. 'With us,' he says, 'the commercial side was always to the fore, rather than the socialistic, charity side.'

Traditionalists in the organic movement are becoming anxious about some of the methods used in the New Organic sector.

Supermarket chains, for example, were found to be using chemical ways of washing organic salads (page 127), which were not permitted for organic produce.

Such paradoxes could become harder to swallow as the sector tries to match the range of conventional foods on offer and to extend the shelf-life of organic products. For example, some 500 food processing aids are permitted by the EU. Around 50 of these (such as vitamin C) are acceptable to organic specialists, whereas others (among them stabilisers and emulsifiers) are not. As the market expands, the organic movement will increasingly have to balance its aim of being as natural as possible against the realities of which ingredients are available and what the market demands, particularly as more and more processed foods seek organic accreditation. What happens if the boundaries blur and more of these aids are used? 'The danger is,' warns one leading organic expert, 'that one day we will all wake up and find that we have an organic food industry that none of us recognise.'[29]

There seem to be at least three possible futures. The first would see the organic sector fail to live up to the consumer demands now being made upon it and pushed to the sidelines again, returning to its specialised niche market. The second would be marred by dramatic splits in the movement as some chose to stick with the philosophy and principles on which their movement was founded while others attempted to join the mainstream and dilute the criteria to give it greater mass market appeal. And the third would see the standards of the organic sector itself slowly influencing the mainstream of sustainable farming around the world.

Whatever happens, one thing is clear. Much of the popularity of organic foods derives from qualities – among them purity, sustainability and traceability – which mainstream food producers could do well to learn to imitate. Perhaps this will prove to be the organic world's greatest legacy, as a model for safer, saner and more sustainable farming and food production.

We have looked at what we mean by new foods. In the next chapter, we go into close-up to look at new food ingredients. We look at what is currently going into our food, how that is changing and how this might affect our health.

3

INGREDIENT WATCH

Inside Stories

From antioxidants and preservatives to vitamins and flavourings, we are all having to make sense of an ever-expanding array of food ingredients. Some people love the chase, and hunt down information on even the most obscure substances, but most of us are simply baffled.

In this section, we zoom in on some of the novel ingredients now popping up in new foods, and on some of the other major ingredients used in food processing. We look at familiar ingredients, like sugar, salt and fat, and explain how they are being formulated in new ways. We look behind some of the common claims such as 'added fibre', 'low-fat', 'no added sugar' or 'no artificial additives', and at some of the new claims, like 'cholesterol-lowering' and 'encourages friendly bacteria', asking whether these products live up to their promises – and whether they are worth the extra cost.

ADDITIVES AND
PROCESSING AIDS

Additives are not foods in themselves. They are used as preservatives, and to alter the taste, texture or appearance of foods. Each additive approved for use in Europe is given an E number, which must be shown on the label. So many additives and processing agents are used by the food industry today that shoppers feel they need a chemistry degree to understand the labels. Certainly most people are suspicious, worrying that the more strange names there are on a label, the worse the product is likely to be for their health.

Here, we take a look at the range of additives and processing agents, including food colouring, emulsifiers and stabilisers, gums and thickeners, flavourings and flavour enhancers, preservatives, and anti-caking and glazing agents.

The organic movement by and large shuns the use of all but a few additives. And recently, the spotlight has been on the enormous array of GM ingredients and derivatives that – it turns out – are already in our food.

Colours
Rainbow foods

WHAT

Our acceptance of – and appetite for – foods is hugely influenced by the way they look, and colour is a key element in the eye appeal of food. Food colourings can be either natural or synthetic. In 1900 there were around 80 man-made colour additives in use, a number that has since tumbled as public demand for natural ingredients has grown. Unfortunately, natural colours are much less stable when it comes to cooking, so manufacturers greatly prefer the synthetics, derived from coal tar.

WHERE

Food colourings are used to make food look good; to offset colour loss caused by light, air, moisture, temperature changes or storage conditions; to compensate for natural variations in food colour; and to provide a dramatic appearance for 'fun foods'. The rainbow effect can be found just about everywhere. Tinned peas are transformed from murky grey to bright green, chickens are fed with yellow colouring – carotenoids – to make egg yolks brighter orange, fizzy drinks are dosed with a range of colours depending on the flavour they are simulating, and sweets, cakes, biscuits, puddings and squashes also often contain added colour.

HEALTH ISSUES

Colours are often used in foods that are poor in quality or low in nutritional value, to make them look more appetising, and most of us have got so used to these artificial colours that food without them would seem to be less fresh and even less nutritious.

Some colourings, such as cochineal extract, a red colouring extracted from the cochineal beetle, can cause allergies – and clearly would be unappealing to strict vegetarians. But it is not always easy to tell which colours have been used.

Other reservations that people have about colourings have included fears that they may be carcinogens. For example, the Citrus Red 2 additive used can cause cancer in laboratory animals. There are also concerns that they may be a cause of hyperactivity in children. Although these fears have not always been valid, they have resulted in a number of products being banned – and, perhaps more importantly, in a fairly widespread reduction in the use of artificial colourings.

☆ ☆ ☆ ☆ ☆ ☆ **WHAT'S NEW?** ☆ ☆ ☆ ☆ ☆ ☆ ☆

- *An organic no:* Colourings – ironically, even most natural ones – are not permitted in organic foods, with the exception of 'annatto', a natural extract that is permitted in Red Leicester and Double Gloucester cheese to give them their traditional orange colouring.

> ### GM Spotlight
> # WHAT COLOUR IS GM?
>
> Food colours that could be made from GM maize or other crops include caramel colouring (E150: used in beers and some spirits); carbon black (E153); cryptoxanthin (E161c: a yellow food colour); and lycopene (E160d: a red dye made from tomatoes and used in biscuits, cakes, snacks and drinks).

additives & processing

☆ ☆

Emulsifiers and stabilisers
Good mixers

WHAT

Emulsifiers help mix together ingredients that would normally separate; stabilisers are used to stop them separating again. Examples of stabilisers include agar (extracted from seaweed), guar gum (extracted from cluster beans) and pectin (which occurs naturally in plants and fruit). Synthetic emulsifiers are often used to combine something fatty, like butter, with something acidic, like lemon. They are made from animal and vegetable fats. Lecithin is the most widely used emulsifier and it is almost always made from soya.

As well as holding emulsions together, emulsifiers also slow the staling of bread, make non-dairy creamers dissolve on contact with hot coffee, stabilise whipped toppings, prevent starches from crystallising, and ensure the creaminess of ice-creams.

WHERE

These products are typically found in processed foods such as baby milk, bakery products, bread, chocolate, cream (UHT and reduced calorie), desserts (e.g. mousses and flans), ice-cream, margarine, mayonnaise, milk drinks, pasta (fresh), slimming drinks and spreads.

HEALTH ISSUES

There are no significant health issues relating to emulsifiers.

☆ ☆ ☆ ☆ ☆ ☆ ☆ **WHAT'S NEW?** ☆ ☆ ☆ ☆ ☆ ☆ ☆

GM Spotlight

WHERE CAN I FIND GM-FREE LECITHIN?

- The food industry says that there is no commercially viable alternative to using soya flour (which is likely to be GM) to make lecithin. Alternatives such as sunflower and rapeseed lecithin have several drawbacks, including poor flavour, reduced functionality and limited availability.
- For those wanting to go GM-free, the **Soil Association** offers a list of recommended organic suppliers of lecithin.

☆ ☆ ☆ ☆ ☆ ☆ ☆ ☆ ☆ ☆ ☆ ☆ ☆ ☆ ☆ ☆ ☆ ☆ ☆

GM crop-derived ingredients

WHERE ARE THEY?

Before food manufacturers and supermarkets introduced 'GM-free' policies, it was estimated that something like 70 per cent of UK processed foods could contain GM ingredients. Surprisingly, all these ingredients stem from only two crops: soya and maize. Let's look at both crops.

MAIZE

Corn means different things to different people. To English farmers, it has meant 'wheat', to Scottish farmers 'oats' and to American farmers 'maize': here we use the American definition. Today, corn varieties range from tiny popcorn to plants producing enormous cobs – there are over 60 varieties of sweetcorn alone.

Why GM?: The main reason for corn being genetically modified is to enhance insect resistance. For example, Bt-corn, as it's known, is designed to resist pests like the European corn borer.

Where: GM corn is now widespread in the USA and is not segregated from non-GM corn. Early in 1999, it was the only GM crop being commercially grown in Europe – in France and Spain. Although only 0.7 per cent of the 1998 European harvest of maize was GM, this was not kept apart either. As a result, even manufacturers sourcing

additives & processing

their maize from Europe found that they could not guarantee that they had totally GM-free maize.

Corn is used in an extraordinarily wide range of food-processing ingredients, including ascorbic acid, anti-caking agents, caramel colouring, carbon black colouring, corn flour or starch, corn oil, corn syrup, cryptoxanthin colouring, dextrose, emulsifiers, fats, flavourings, fructose, glucose, maltodextrin, maltose, modified starch, monosodium glutamate, sucrose, vitamin C and xanthan gum. Many of these ingredients, even where they appear in European foods, are actually produced in the USA.

•••

Safeway's approach to eliminating GM soya and maize from their products was representative. They said, '**Safeway**'s position on GM soya and maize is that they fail to offer any tangible benefits to our customers. For this reason, **Safeway** has undertaken a systematic programme of work to eliminate such ingredients from our own-brand products.'

•••

SOYA

What: There are now over a thousand varieties of soya beans, which are variously black, brown, green, red or yellow. Soya is sometimes described as the richest natural vegetable food known to man. When soya beans are processed, they yield 80 per cent flour (high in protein and low in carbohydrate) and 20 per cent oil (high in polyunsaturated fats, making it highly nutritious).

Why GM? Among other things, soyabeans are being modified for herbicide-resistance, particularly for **Monsanto's** *Roundup* herbicide.

Where: Soya was introduced into the USA from China, and today the USA is the biggest producer. Virtually all soya imported into Britain comes from the USA, and the first GM soya reached Europe in 1996. By 1998, 30 per cent of soya in the USA was genetically modified, and in 1999 the figure was expected to be around 50 per cent. Other major soya-producing countries include Argentina and Brazil. Although GM soya is being grown in Brazil, there is support in the region for the development of large GM-free zones and the country could yet become the biggest supplier of GM-free crops.

About two-thirds of all manufactured food products have contained derivatives or ingredients made from soya. It can be used to make soya flour, soya oil, soy sauce, soy milk, miso, *tamari* and tofu. It is used in food processing ingredients such as anti-caking agents, colourings, emulsifiers, flavourings and vitamins. Soya oil, which is the basis of many margarines, is also used in cooking oils.

Soya beans are extremely important to vegetarians, because the protein they contain is the natural substitute nearest to meat protein. Vegetarians and vegans often replace cow's milk with soya milk, which, when enriched with various additives, can be used for baby milk. They also eat it as soya-protein isolate, which comes in granule form and is added to processed foods, as well as so-called 'textured vegetable protein' (TVP, discussed on page 111), a substitute for meats like chicken, steak, ham and bacon. **Provamel** runs an information service called *Soy Source*, which consumers can call or write to for more health information on soya products.

Gums and thickeners
In the thick of it

WHAT

Invisible they may be, but a wide range of gums and thickeners are used in processed foods. Starches and other thickeners are used to bulk up foods, to give them a standard consistency and to enhance the 'mouth feel' of foods like soft drinks and yoghurts. They are used to thicken foods, to prevent sugar crystals from forming in sweets, to stabilise beer foam, form a gel in puddings, encapsulate flavour oils in powdered drink mixes and to keep oil and water mixed together in salad dressings. Look out for them – used to replace fat – in low-fat ice-cream and baked goods. Food manufacturers have found gums of various descriptions to be a useful ingredient because they swell up and don't break down easily.

Starches are also found in baby foods, gravies, sauces, pie fillings, puddings and a vast spectrum of 'instant' products and mixes. A fair number are modified with chemicals, such as aluminium sulphate (a key ingredient in baking powder), to make them easier to use.

HEALTH ISSUES

Interestingly, the health-promoting effects of gums already used in our food, such as gum arabic, are now being discovered – or rediscovered. They are an important source of dietary fibre, and they can help us digest our food more efficiently. But thickeners also tend to be cheap, and sometimes replace more expensive ingredients. Starch-thickened baby foods, for example, have been found to contain as little as 25 per cent of the fruit ingredients found in full-fruit baby foods.

 **WHAT'S NEW?**

GM Spotlight
GM GUM

Xanthan gum can be made with GM maize. Corn starch is also a common thickener – and may be made with GM maize. If it hadn't been for the GM backlash, manufacturers producing organic processed foods might have found it difficult to find GM-free gums and thickeners.

Flavourings and flavour enhancers
Questions of taste

WHAT

Flavourings and flavour enhancers add new flavours, replace lost ones and make flavour consistent. In the days when spices were imported from the East, the main idea of flavourings was that they should cover up the taste of strongly preserved, or even rotting, foods. Today, when food is preserved more easily, our palates are more demanding, and food designers can now draw upon an enormous range of flavourings and flavour enhancers to achieve the particular effects they are after.

Flavourings have been used in foods since ancient times. To begin with they were herbs, spices, gums and some animal products, and over the centuries, people learnt how to extract distinct flavours. Then in the 19th century it was found that the characteristic flavours of some natural products could be reproduced synthetically, although others are much more difficult to mimic. To create the aroma of orange oil artificially would take at least 100 different substances, coffee would take over 1,000, and the smell of roasted meat 2,000–3,000! For those who find it hard to give up meat, 'vegetarian beef' flavours have been created.

The main types of flavouring include *natural flavourings*, such as herbs and seeds (or their oils); *nature identical flavourings*, which are chemically the same as natural flavourings, but have been made artificially; and *artificial flavourings*, which do not try to copy nature except in their taste and are favoured by food manufacturers because they are usually stronger, cheaper and more stable.

Flavour enhancers don't taste particularly good in themselves, indeed they may even be completely flavourless, but they do intensify or accentuate other flavours in food. Salt is a long-established flavour enhancer, while perhaps the best-known modern flavour enhancer is monosodium glutamate (MSG: E622). Another is citric acid, also used as a preservative, and as a flavour enhancer in soft drinks. Phosphoric acid, a form of the mineral phosphorus, is used in cola drinks to boost the characteristic cola flavour as well as to make it fizzy.

WHERE

Most processed foods contain some form of added flavouring. They are particularly common in savoury foods, snacks, sauces and meat products, and ready-made meals are a particular growth sector. Monosodium glutamate (MSG) is a favourite ingredient in Asian cooking.

HEALTH ISSUES

Something like 3,000 additives are now routinely mixed into our food, and around 2,000 of them are flavourings and flavour enhancers. Not all of these have yet been tested for safety, partly because they are used in such minute quantities. An EU-approved list of flavourings will not be introduced until 2004, which is why they do not yet have E numbers.

Among flavour-enhancers, salt, of course, has been linked to high blood pressure, and monosodium glutamate is thought to cause headaches and other symptoms by over-exciting brain cells in a few people. In some countries, it is required that all food containing

MSG should be labelled accordingly. Baby-food manufacturers have been forced to stop adding it to their products altogether, because of its potential dangers – and, if the truth be known, they were adding it mainly to make food taste better for parents!

☆ ☆ ☆ ☆ ☆ ☆ ☆ **WHAT'S NEW?** ☆ ☆ ☆ ☆ ☆ ☆ ☆

Exotic flavours: Our growing taste for exotic cuisine, partly because of all the travelling we now do, has meant that the food industry has been using much more exotic flavours. Indian, Chinese and Mexican foods have all become part of many people's daily diets, whether we're looking for curries, spring rolls or tortillas, as have tropical fruits.

Tailor-made: Over time, it will presumably be possible to use GM technology to produce foods with more intense flavours, which may well begin to make flavour enhancers redundant.

GM Spotlight

THE FLAVOUR OF GM

- Soya and maize, which may well be GM, are widely used as 'carriers' for flavours.
- The flavouring maltodextrin is made from corn, which could be GM.
- Monosodium glutamate is industrially produced, some with GM bacteria. In the fermentation process, the bacteria are fed on nutrients made from glucose preparations, which may also be based on GM maize.
- Citric acid is industrially produced, by fermentation, but no-one in the western world yet seems to be using GM technology for this. However, again, some manufacturers may be using GM crops to make glucose, which is needed to produce citric acid. On top of that, about 10-15 per cent of the citric acid used in Europe is imported from China, where they are thought to be using GM technology for fermentation. Companies who are aware of this issue may specify guaranteed 'GM-free' sources, which are available. But it seems that some companies have not realised there is a GM issue here.

Preservatives and preservation

Shelf lives

WHAT

Food poisoning caused by bacteria is one of the main reasons for using preservatives. Most foods also go off fairly rapidly, particularly in hot weather, unless they are preserved in some way. Traditional methods include drying, smoking, fermentation and cooking, as well as adding ingredients like salt, vinegar, sugar and spices.

Most preservatives fall into one of two main categories. They are either antimicrobials, used to control the growth of bacteria and mould, or antioxidants, which stop food from going brown or rancid. Interestingly, many of the spices long used to preserve foods turn out to contain substances that kill bacteria, and are also full of antioxidants. For example, hot curries and chilli dishes, which evolved in hot countries where food spoilage is a particular problem, tend to be particularly high in natural preservatives. Cinnamon has been found to be effective in controlling *E. coli* bacteria, and research in the USA has shown that food bacteria can be killed not only by cinnamon, but also by cloves and garlic.[30]

Bacteria

BUGGED FOODS

This may seem an odd inclusion in a chapter on ingredients, but there is growing concern about the hidden bacteria in our food. This is mainly due to the fact that food poisoning outbreaks have increased sharply in recent years. Possible reasons why unwelcome bacteria are getting into our food include more antibiotics being used in farming; more animals being transported over longer distances to abattoirs, causing them to collect bacteria on the way; faster production lines in abattoirs; waste from abattoirs being spread on grazing fields; poorly trained meat handlers; more people eating out; and more fast food, such as hamburgers, on our menus.

Here are some of the villains, their roles and their likely haunts:

Campylobacter jejuni: Causes upset stomach that can last a week or more, abdominal pains and profuse diarrhoea. It is now the biggest cause of bacterial food poisoning world wide. Found in raw (or poorly

---

cooked) poultry and meat, in unpasteurised milk and contaminated water.

Clostridium botulinum: This bug produces a deadly toxin which causes botulism. It may be found in canned foods such as hams, luncheon meats, shellfish, sausage, soups and vegetables (such as beans, corn and peas). If cans are not sterilised properly, they can get contaminated, but because the bacteria produce gases, the cans will often bulge.

Clostridium perfringens: Nicknamed the 'cafeteria bug', this is responsible for a significant number of food poisoning incidents in countries like the USA. It's generally found in foods like meat or poultry which have been left for some time at room temperatures.

Escherichia coli: Better known as *E. coli*, this was once a relatively harmless intestinal bug. Even now, most cases cause mild diarrhoea, but now a deadly strain – *E. coli* 0157:h7 – has surfaced. In the 1980s, there was a wave of food poisonings in Canada and the USA, caused by rare hamburgers at fast-food restaurants, and in 1997 there were serious *E. coli* outbreaks in Scotland, resulting in several deaths, and an outbreak in Devon in the summer of 1999 killed one child and infected 12 others. Cross contamination of raw and cooked foods can be the problem, as well as poor hygiene.

Listeria monocytogenes: This type of food poisoning affects people whose immune systems are weakened, such as the elderly or AIDS and cancer patients, but it is particularly serious for pregnant women, which is why they are recommended to steer away from soft cheeses (particularly unpasteurised ones) and patés, where the listeria may lurk. Interestingly, GM scientists have worked out how to introduce listeria-killing genes into cheese, but they have not yet developed such products for market.

Salmonella: This is not a single bacterium, but a cast of thousands. The symptoms are like those caused by intestinal flu. It has surfaced all over the place in recent years, causing major problems for manufacturers of products including meat, poultry, mayonnaise, ice-cream and even meringue toppings (the last three of which may be made with raw eggs).

Staphylococcus aureus: This bug lives on the skin and in the respiratory tract, so it can be spread when a cook or waiter sneezes. The problem is caused not by the bug itself, but by the toxins it makes. Once these toxins get into food, no amount of cooking can destroy them.

Found in meats, poultry, eggs and egg products, cream-filled cakes and pastries, gelatins, creamy salads and other foods allowed to stand too long at room temperatures. This bug loves to breed in warm, moist foods. This virulent bacteria causes pneumonia, abscesses and potentially life-threatening bloodstream infections, with symptoms such as impetigo, a rash with a slightly golden crust on the surface around the face and mouth. It is a particular problem for the elderly and anyone with a weakened immune system. A number of people died in Japanese hospitals because of staphylococcus strains that were resistant to antibiotics.

Acidulants make food acid (and therefore taste sour), and are commonly used as preservatives. Many of them come from natural sources, such as citric acid from citrus fruits, malic acid from apples and lactic acid from dairy products. Acid foods are better able to resist microbial contamination.

Anti-caking agents are used to keep products such as dried milk and salts free-flowing, and glazing agents are used to produce a protective coating or sheen on meat and fruit pies.

Packaging and refrigeration are alternative approaches to preserving food. As frozen food is convenient and of high quality, there seems little doubt that it will continue to be an important aspect of the 'new foods' menu.

WHERE

Preservatives are found in most processed foods. In many countries, foods now have to be labelled to show which preservatives they contain and what they are meant to do. In the UK, all food ingredients have to be listed on the label, including preservatives, although it's not required that it should say what they do. Regulations for labelling of alcoholic drinks are different – not all the ingredients have to be listed.

HEALTH ISSUES

Ironically, the vast array of preservatives now put into foods to prolong their shelf-life and make them safer causes many people deep concern. Lack of information is partly to blame, and things are not helped by claims that when we die our bodies last several days longer than they did a century ago because of preservatives. This may be simply an urban myth, but like all good myths, it rings true!

Clearly, there is a balance to be struck here. Preservatives help protect us from food poisoning and even potentially fatal diseases, but some have themselves been suspected of causing health problems. Sulphiting agents – for example, sulphur dioxide (E220) –, which are used to stop discolouration in foods like dried fruit, 'fresh' shrimp and chipped potatoes, as well as to control bacterial growth in wines, can also destroy vitamin B1 and cause severe reactions in asthmatics. There has also been concern that the nitrates and nitrites (E249–252) used to cure meat might be carcinogenic.

Packaging

LEARNING FROM BANANAS

New foods often require new forms of packaging. Recent innovations include ring-pull openers on tins – which may mean we can say goodbye to can-openers for good – and reclosable plastic pour devices on milk and juice cartons.[31] Even pet food is now available in single-serve, squeezable pouches.

Used in the right way, packaging helps preserve food, ensures product security and provides vital consumer information. Whatever future we move towards, the packaging industry will have a key role to play. Among other things, it will help with information on how the product has been produced and where ingredients have come from.

But packaging itself has raised some health and environmental concerns along the way:

Health: Recently, there has been controversy over the effects of phthalates, once widely used as plasticisers in PVC packaging, including cling film. Bisphenol-A is another suspect chemical, thought to have an adverse effect on fertility – and still used in the lacquer coatings found on the inside of many cans.

There have even been concerns about recycled paper packaging, with warnings that if the recycled paper or cardboard contains old carbonless copying paper – that used by most office photocopiers – any food in direct contact with the materials can be contaminated by so-called DIPNs (or diisopropylnapthalenes). Of 34 branded and own-label products tested, 30 were found to have traces of the toxin.[32] There is no evidence of any harm to health, but this is one more illustration of the need for packaging materials to be managed properly.

Over-packaging: In recent years there has also been much criticism of the 'over-packaging' of many products, and of the large number of materials used. Too often, products are packed in multiple layers of multiple materials, making them difficult to recycle. Packaging designers are now being briefed to come up with less wasteful solutions that protect the products and still look attractive.

Quick-chill, global warming: Even in a climate of heightened awareness of both environmental and health issues relating to pack-aging, one horror innovation got through. Some readers may remem-ber the quick-chill can for soft drinks that used powerful greenhouse gas – 1,300 more powerful than carbon dioxide. The resulting media storm meant that the product was redesigned. But it's astonishing that contemporary designers could have brought such a product to market.

Ideally, future food packaging would be as intelligent as a banana skin. A banana's packaging is highly attractive, you can tell at a glance what state the product is in by looking at the colour and texture of the skin, and the material is highly biodegradable once its useful life is over.

☆ ☆ ☆ ☆ ☆ ☆ ☆ **WHAT'S NEW?** ☆ ☆ ☆ ☆ ☆ ☆ ☆

Whatever the validity of consumer concerns about chemical preser-vatives, it seems likely that we will see less of them used, in favour of physical methods to keep food fresh, such as freezing. Some other approaches are being tried.

High-pressure foods: In an attempt to stem the tide of food poisoning, researchers are now exposing foods to pressures as great as 9,000 times normal atmospheric level. The idea is that many of the bugs responsible for food poisoning outbreaks will be killed in this way, while the foods (instead of collapsing into a mush, as you might expect) are only minimally affected. The process, which has been tested on meats, poultry, fruit and vegetables but is only being used for liquid or semi-solid foods at the moment, is good for keeping nutritional value, taste and colour.

Pasteurisation of eggs: Publicised outbreaks of salmonella poisoning (page 59) have made people more wary of eggs. Now an American company, **Pasteurised Eggs**, has worked out how to pasteurise them. This is quite an achievement if one thinks that normally to raise an egg's temperature to 72°C over an hour would leave it lightly cooked. With this new process, the salmonella bacteria are destroyed, yet the egg is virtually unchanged. The head of the company is bullish: 'It won't be long, maybe a couple of years,' he says, 'before it will be impossible to buy an unpasteurised egg.'[33] Watch this space.

Irradiation
....

PROS AND CONS

Irradiated foods may not be 'new foods' but they do represent a radically different way of preserving foods, new or old. Foods are exposed to high doses of irradiation, although if done properly this does not make the food radioactive. Irradiation has many possible benefits. It can kill insects and pests that infest foods; reduce levels of dangerous bacteria, such as salmonella, listeria and campylobacter; delay ripening and decay, so foods can be kept longer; and completely sterilise food, making it fit for hospital patients with damaged immune systems.

But it does have disadvantages.[34] It is difficult for meats and not suitable for dairy foods. It can substantially reduce levels of key nutrients – including minerals, phytonutrients and vitamins – in the same way that heat processing does, and yet it may leave some active bacteria, which can then reproduce rapidly if not controlled, and it is ineffective against viruses. It's also likely to kill off 'good' bacteria alongside the 'bad'. It could enable dishonest traders to disguise food that is unfit for human consumption, and may reduce flavour in some foods because the fat oxidises. Finally, it is relatively expensive.

Consumer resistance in Europe has slowed down the introduction of irradiation. When it does appear, treated foods should be labelled as 'irradiated' or 'treated with ionising radiation'. But be warned: this labelling requirement does not apply to ingredients that make up less than 25 per cent of a labelled product. In the wake of several *E. coli* outbreaks in the USA, there have been clamorous appeals for wider use of irradiation, including for some meat products. One possible reason: the attempted introduction of irradiation in Europe coincided with the Chernobyl nuclear disaster, Americans were further away from Chernobyl and therefore less worried by its implications.

Organic shelf-lives: Some preservatives, such as citric acid and ascorbic acid, are permitted in organic foods, but not many. And sulphur dioxide is allowed in wines, but only at half the normal level.

FATS AND SUGARS

Fats and oils
Good, bad and ugly

WHAT

Fats are an important group of naturally occurring substances that are essential for our health. Some (such as oleic, palmic and stearic acids) are solid at room temperatures, while others (oils) are semi-solid or liquid. Fats play a number of roles in our bodies. They help to regulate cholesterol, transport vitamins around the body, process certain vital chemicals, insulate the body, give energy, cushion vital organs and maintain healthy skin.

In the environment in which we evolved, fatty foods were often hard to come by. Most fruit and vegetables contain very little oil, and their fibre content helps limit fat intake. Even when early humans were able to scavenge or kill game, the animals were usually pretty lean, unlike modern farm-fattened stock. Today, however, fats are much more readily available. Coupled with our increasingly sedentary lifestyle, our growing consumption of fats can cause real health problems. To show how dramatic the change has been, it's thought that our ancestors' diet probably included around 6 per cent fat, in contrast with modern intake levels – which can exceed 35 per cent. The unwelcome results include expanding waistlines, heart disease, diabetes, arthritis and breast cancer.

Fats can come from a number of sources and in various forms. In this section, we begin by looking at the different types of fats and at the health issues involved, and then we turn to one of the biggest areas of new food development: the revolution in low-fat and non-fat foods, and, somewhat bizarrely, at what we might describe as non-fat fats.

HEALTH ISSUES

Fish oils: Not so long ago, people used to be forced (it tastes revolting) to swallow a spoonful of cod liver oil as a healthy start to the day.

Nowadays, fish oils are recommended for a large number of conditions, including arthritis, brain development in infancy, pregnancy, breast cancer, depression, male infertility, migraines, blood clots, bone mass problems, and pre-menstrual syndrome.

Omega-3 is a fish oil, and one of the new ingredients attracting attention. It comes in two main forms: eicosapentaenoic acid (EPA) and docosahexaenoic acid (DHA).

It has been claimed that DHA will 'vitalise the brain', 'improve memory and learning ability' and 'make you smart'. Although there is little evidence to suggest that DHA provides these benefits for adults, whose brain and eye tissues are already developed, there is evidence that for unborn and infant children it is very important.[35] A foetus will even draw DHA from its mother's body and brain during the last three months of pregnancy, when the child's own brain is developing. It's thought that if women are not taking in enough DHA at this time, the lack of it may be partly responsible for the absent-mindedness that pregnant women and new mothers often complain about.

Studies carried out in Australia showed that breast-fed babies whose mothers have enough DHA in their diet may have a 10-point IQ advantage in later childhood. DHA in the breast milk of Japanese mothers is three times higher than in the UK, because they have such a high fish diet,[36] which is thought to be a key factor in the lower rates of coronary heart disease found in Japan.

Helpful oily or fatty fish, in descending order of benefit, include herring (not kippered or pickled), mackerel, tuna, salmon, and sardines, as well as anchovies, cod, halibut and many shellfish.

Those using fish oil supplements need to be aware, however, that overdosing can cause bleeding, anaemia and even strokes.

Saturated fats: Saturated fats are the least healthy fats. They raise 'bad' cholesterol levels (as well as 'good' cholesterol levels) and are thought to be a key factor in cancer, heart attacks, strokes and obesity, among other things. High quantities are found in many fast and junk foods, as well as in meat fat (such as lard) and dairy products (such as butter, cream and cheese). They are also found in some plant-derived fats, including coconut and palm oils.

fats & sugars

Cholesterols

GOOD AND BAD

These days, we all know we don't like cholesterol – but what is it? The answer is a form of waxy fat. More accurately, there are two different types: the 'good' form is called high density lipoprotein (HDL), the 'bad' low-density lipoprotein.

The 'good' HDL cholesterol is used to make oestrogen, testosterone, vitamin D, bile, skin oils and nerve- and brain-cell sheaths. But too much LDL cholesterol, a problem for about 70 million adults in the EU alone, can kill us. It furs up our blood vessels, leading to heart disease and strokes.

The reason HDLs are thought of as 'good' is that they can remove cholesterol from the cells and take it to the liver, which uses it for vital bodily functions. LDLs, on the other hand, are thought of as bad because when they 'carry' the cholesterol in the blood, they tend to drop bits along the way. These bits then stick to the artery walls, hardening over time and leading to blockages.[37]

Unsaturated fats: These come in 'poly' and 'mono' forms. *Polyunsaturated fats*, for example those found in sunflower and corn oils, are usually liquid at room temperature. A certain amount of these fats is needed in our diets, because they contain *essential fatty acids*, as well as vitamin E, which our bodies need. They also lower 'bad' LDL cholesterol. However, caution is recommended even here – because cooking with polyunsaturated fats may produce free radicals (page 80). *Monounsaturated fats*, of which high levels are found in olive oil and rapeseed oil, as well as in many nuts and avocados, are also usually liquid at room temperature. They are the healthiest fats, because they are thought not only to lower levels of 'bad' LDL cholesterol, but possibly also to boost levels of 'good' HDL cholesterol. They are thought to be one of the active principles in the healthy 'Mediterranean' diet, which is linked to increased longevity, reduced cancers and a lower incidence of heart disease and obesity. Oleic acid, for example, is found in canola, corn and, most of all, olive oil.

Trans fats: These are also known as hydrogenated fats, because they are made using hydrogen, in a process introduced in 1900.

Margarines and other spreads were created with a similar consistency to butter, by turning polyunsaturated fats into saturated fats. Unfortunately, it was later discovered that these fats could have the same negative impacts as traditional saturated fats.

Evidence is emerging to suggest that *trans fats* may be even worse for your health than saturated fats because, in addition to raising 'bad' LDL cholesterol, they may lower 'good' HDL cholesterol. Hence the continuing debate over the health merits of margarine versus butter. Some big-name margarine brands, such as *Flora*, have been reformulated to contain very little trans fatty acids.

☆ ☆ ☆ ☆ ☆ ☆ ☆ **WHAT'S NEW?** ☆ ☆ ☆ ☆ ☆ ☆ ☆

fats & sugars

GM Spotlight

GM IN OILS

• Vegetables oils are blended, and may well contain oils from GM crops such as maize, soya or cotton seed. Fried foods, such as crisps or chips, may be fried in these oils.

EXTRA OMEGA

Hi-Q boosts Oz diet: Australians have discovered that people in the lowest income brackets tend to have the lowest DHA levels, because they cannot afford to eat lots of fish. A white bread, called *Hi-Q*, has therefore been developed, which is targeted at these people. Critics might point out that it's wrong to encourage the idea that eating white bread is a healthy option, but the pragmatists' counter-argument is that if people will go on eating white bread it makes a great deal of sense to make it healthier.

Eggs and Omega: Columbus Eggs (page 160) have been developed by a Belgian company and are available in the UK. Flax seed oil, one of the richest plant sources of Omega-3, is injected into the chicken feed. In the USA, *Omega Tech* eggs are produced by chickens fed on oil from cultivated natural algae, also a good source of Omega-3. The levels of DHA in these eggs are said to be equivalent to those found in eggs 50 years ago, when chickens were fed on a more diverse diet.

Milk fat: In Italy and Spain, meanwhile, they have introduced milk with added Omega-3. Removing the unhealthy saturated fats, as they do with skimmed milks, the manufacturers have replaced them with Omega-3; and in Australia, DHA is being added to baby formula milk. None of this is yet happening in the UK.

CHOLESTEROL-LOWERING

Something like 70 million Europeans, as we have seen, have elevated LDL cholesterol levels, which can signal heart disease. Not surprisingly, there has been an explosion of interest in cholesterol-lowering products, with a growing number already on the market. We look at some of the main ones below.

Cholesterol-lowering

HEARTY SPREADS

Food scientists had long suspected that plant sterols, natural components of all plants, would lower 'bad' cholesterol, but no-one was able to work out how to get them into foods. Then, in the early 1990s, a Finn working at Helsinki University discovered the trick. He made plant sterols from pine trees into a family of taste-free, odourless, fat-soluble food ingredients (known as 'plant stenol esters'), which were then added to edible fats.

Interestingly, these plant sterols had always been a by-product of the paper industry, and a small amount of them were used for pharmaceutical and cosmetic uses – the rest were thrown away. Now they are the 'magic ingredient' in one of the leading functional foods.

The *Benecol* brand of margarine that resulted from this work hit the Finnish market in 1994. Extensive clinical trials had shown that, when eaten by people enjoying a normal healthy diet, *Benecol* cut their cholesterol levels by 12–14 per cent. The new ingredient passed through the body without being absorbed.

Benecol now offers 'full-fat' and 'low-fat' versions of its margarine spread, as well as cream cheese – available in the UK, Netherlands, Belgium and the USA. Approval in Europe was automatic, because the product had been approved in Finland before the country joined the EU. Competitors have not always been so lucky. Although **Unilever** launched their own cholesterol-lowering spread, called *Take Control*, in the USA, it has yet to win approval for its European version, *Flora Proactiv*. While *Benecol* uses plant sterols from pine trees, **Unilever's** spreads take them from soya (non-GM).

Critics of these cholesterol-lowering products worry that although plant sterols have been passed as safe, they could be consumed in far bigger quantities than would occur naturally in our diet. There is also scepticism about the efficacy of these products for people eating a particularly high- or low-fat diet. Trials were carried out on people eating a balanced diet.

Even trickier for the European regulators is the fact that cholesterol-lowering pharmaceuticals have to go through rigorous and expensive safety tests, when food products with much the same effects do not.

Other companies expected to launch plant-sterol-based, cholesterol-lowering products in the near future include **Monsanto** and **Novartis**. (Although both of these companies are active in GM technology, they do many other things too.)

Oats: Thirty years of research have confirmed that oats have cholesterol-lowering properties, thanks to their soluble fibre, which comes in the form of beta-glucans. In the USA, companies are allowed to make this claim on their products, and **Quaker Oats** have done so on their porridge, but apparently it has not made a great difference to sales. *Psyllium* is a grain product which is rich in soluble fibre and thought to have cholesterol-lowering properties. Naturally occurring in wheat-bran, psyllium is being used by **Kellogg** in a new product range, *Ensemble*, which they are testing for sale in the USA. They are permitted to make cholesterol-lowering claims on packs in America, as long as they use this convoluted statement: 'Soluble fibre from foods such as oat bran, as part of a diet low in saturated fat and cholesterol, may reduce the risk of heart disease.' Even this type of wording is not permitted in Europe.

Yoghurts: Some yoghurts have been touted as cholesterol-lowering. A Dutch yoghurt called *Fysiq* had its claim challenged in 1994, but the manufacturer won the case. In the UK, a similar challenge by the **Food Commission** against *Gaio*, launched in 1995, was successful, and the product, manufactured by **MD Foods**, was later withdrawn. The **Advertising Standards Authority** concluded that the health claims were unsupported by scientific evidence, and that the graphics exaggerated any effects.[39] Paradoxically, *Gaio* is now a leading brand of bio-yoghurt in Denmark.

FAT-LESS

Low-fat: This is a boom area, with innumerable foods, from biscuits and crisps to yoghurts and ice-creams, being produced and sold as low-fat. (In America, it sometimes seems as though there is nothing that is full-fat any more.) Foods traditionally high in fat, such as spreads and ice-creams, have the fat removed. Many low-fat spreads tend to replace the fat with water. The 'low-fat' label is used to tantalise health-conscious consumers, but ironically many low-fat products can be high in sugar and are not necessarily low in calories. These foods appeal to dieters because of the general awareness that, gram by gram, fat is the highest-calorie food there is.

Calories

WATCHING OUR WEIGHT

Calories are units used to measure energy. Specifically, one calorie is the amount of energy needed to heat 1 gram of water by 1°C. Food energy is also measured in calories, with different foods providing different amounts of energy. The higher the calorie content, the greater the available energy content.

Almost all foods provide some energy. To give an idea of the range: 1 gram of fat accounts for 9 calories, 1 gram of alcohol for 7 calories, and 1 gram of protein and 1 gram of carbohydrates for 4 calories each.

The number of calories we need daily varies according to our height, weight, age and activity. It also depends on whether we're trying to put on weight, take it off or stay the same. So, for example, a young, fit male runner will need more calories than a pensioner who walks the dog once a day.

Some reduced-fat foods, such as **McVities'** *Go Ahead* biscuits, have been hugely successful, with fewer calories and less fat than equivalents. More controversial, however, have been products like **Walker's** *Lite Crisps* produced by **Frito-Lay**, a company owned by

PepsiCo. At the time of its launch the brand had reduced fat content from the normal 35 per cent to 28 per cent. But critics pointed out that other crisps – not promoted as 'low-fat' – were available with a lower fat content, including **Walker's** own *Dorito* brand of tortilla chips. It was also pointed out that since whole-fat milk only has a fat content of 4 per cent, it seemed bold to make 'low-fat' claims for a product with seven times more fat.

Fat-free: While 'low-fat' products contain between 0.5 per cent and 2 per cent fat, 'virtually fat-free' or 'fat-free' normally means that a product contains less than 0.5 per cent fat. Fat-free products include skimmed milk and an amazing array of products like chocolate and puddings.

Fake fats: Conventional low-fat or fat-free foods can be dry and unappetising. Manufacturers are aware of the in-built human love of fatty foods and are therefore rushing to produce substances which behave and taste exactly like fat but have none of the calories – fake fats.

Benefat: This is a fat substitute that has been developed by **Nabisco**, the American company which makes products including *Ritz Crackers*. Based on a substance called *Salatrim*, it has the physical properties of regular fat, but the maker says it provides only about 55 per cent of the calories, because the stearic acid in the product is poorly absorbed. Critics, however, claim that the calorie reduction is not as great as claimed and that too little testing has been done to determine its effects on humans. Small amounts are not thought to be harmful, but eating 30 grams a day, it's alleged, may increase the risk of side effects such as stomach cramps. At the time of writing, there was no evidence of products containing *Benefat* being on the UK market.

Olibra: Made from oat oil and palm oil, *Olibra* is an appetite suppressant designed to keep you feeling full for longer. Used in Swedish products like **Skåne Dairy's** *Måväl* yoghurts, *Olibra* is not yet strongly promoted for slimming, possibly because its benefits have not been sufficiently proven.

fats & sugars

fats & sugars

Olestra

THE NO-FAT FAT

The *Olestra* story shows just how hard it can be to get a new food ingredient to market. Made by **Procter & Gamble**, and licensed for use in the USA, *Olestra* is a synthetic fat that is not absorbed by the body. It looks like a fat, cooks like a fat and tastes like a fat, but passes through the body unchanged – which for the diet-conscious means no calories. The idea is that using *Olestra* for frying chips and other foods will allow people to eat fatty foods without putting on weight or risking heart disease.

On the plus side, *Olestra* supplies no calories, and it blocks the absorption of dietary cholesterol, reducing blood cholesterol too. There is real concern, though, that *Olestra* encourages people to eat food that may have other unhealthy ingredients, such as salty crisps.

Fierce debate also rages about the possible side-effects of *Olestra*. It has been alleged to cause diarrhoea, loose stools, abdominal cramps and flatulence. The regulatory authorities and the manufacturer are adamant that this is not the case – and have published large-scale clinical trials to support their position. But products containing *Olestra* still have to be labelled with warnings ('may cause abdominal cramping and loose stools'). It is also thought to reduce the body's ability to absorb essential vitamins from fruit and vegetables, so vitamins A, D, E and K are added to compensate.

Procter & Gamble first asked the US **FDA** to approve *Olestra* in 1987, as a general-purpose fat substitute. At the time, one industry analyst predicted that the product would be 'the single most important development in the history of the food industry', but the subsequent problems encountered in getting *Olestra* on to the market have spotlighted the potential hurdles facing all new food producers.

Final approval for the first use of *Olestra* in a food product came in 1996, when the **FDA** cleared it for use in savoury snacks such as crisps, crackers and tortilla chips. Early products to market in the USA have included **Frito-Lay's** *Wow! Chips* and **Procter & Gamble's** own *Fat Free Pringles*.

No products containing *Olestra* have been launched in Europe to date and no applications are currently in progress. For the GM-conscious, it's worth noting that the key raw materials used to produce *Olestra* are soya and cotton, both likely to be GM crops if sourced from the USA.

Spuds: Some potatoes have been genetically modified to have a higher starch content, so that they absorb less when fried. These GM potatoes are not yet permitted in the UK, but are used in the USA, particularly for pre-prepared chips supplied to catering companies.

The outlook: With the growing awareness of the role of certain fats in causing such health problems as heart disease, and despite the difficulties the industry has experienced in bringing no-fat fat products to market, this is an area in which there will be continuing huge investment as companies compete to develop novel functional foods. If consumer concerns about GM foods are eventually overcome, the chances are that we will see many of these products not only based on GM raw materials but also themselves being genetically engineered to achieve particular nutritional or health effects.

fats & sugars

Sweeteners
Sugar & Co.

In the past, the main way we satisfied our craving for sweet foods was by eating ripe fruit and vegetables, which are easy to digest and offer a good balance of vitamins, minerals and other nutrients. Today, however, we are surrounded by sweet processed foods like chocolate, sweets, biscuits, cakes and soft drinks. Even medicines and dietary supplements like vitamins are often sweetened, to 'sugar the pill', and sugar is added in large quantities to foods that are ostensibly savoury, such as tomato sauce, baked beans, mustard, sandwich spreads and soups.

Britons are regarded as having particularly sweet teeth. Perhaps this can be tracked back to the days of Empire and cheap, slave-grown cane sugar. Whatever the reason, some food manufacturers apparently increase the sweetness of products specifically for the UK market!

This is another area which has been affected by health awareness, and in which new foods are booming. We'll look at what's new in sugar, and then look at the complicated area of artificial sweeteners.

WHAT

There are a huge number of commercial sweeteners. They include natural products like honey, and natural sugars such as dextrose; fructose, a fruit sugar made through fermentation; glucose, found in starchy foods like pasta and potatoes and carried around in the blood to fuel the body; lactose, also known as milk sugar; maltose; sucrose, which is the same as table sugar; and sweeteners like corn syrup.

Super-sweet, low-calorie sugar substitutes have been created in response to the health issues surrounding sugar, especially in the drive for lower calories and healthier teeth. These substances act on the tongue's receptors in such a way that they taste hundreds of times sweeter than ordinary sugar. Some are now widely used, although they still appear to leave a sour taste in some mouths. And they also bring their own health problems with them. Getting these products to market – and keeping them there – has therefore turned out to be something of a challenge.

HEALTH ISSUES

When we eat lots of sugar our bodies have to use up stored nutrients in order to process it. High sugar consumption is linked with health problems such as tooth decay, obesity, heart disease and diabetes. And although many people have managed to reduce their intakes of fats, sugar intake has increased massively. Some studies seem to indicate that if your body is getting lots of calories from sugar, which are not being burnt off, then the sugar also turns to body fat. But it should be said that this is not yet proven.

The quest for new super-sweeteners has yet to come up with the Grail itself, but there are plenty of would-be candidates:

Acesulfame-K: Sold in the USA as *Sweet One* and *Sunett*, and in the UK used in **Wrigley's** *Icewhite* chewing gum, this sweetener is 200 times sweeter than sugar – and yet it's calorie-free. It is still under scientific scrutiny, however, because its chemical structure is close to that of saccharin (see below), long suspected of being a mild cancer-causing agent. Despite this concern, consumption is increasing. In 1998, for example, the USA allowed it to be used in soft drinks – as well as in the baked goods, chewing gum and desserts in which it is already used.

Aspartame: Made from amino acids (page 109), aspartame is around 200 times sweeter than sugar. Critics in the USA have mounted an intense campaign to have the product banned, claiming that it may cause serious health problems. However, the manufacturers have strongly rebutted all allegations and the campaigners have not been backed up by the regulatory authorities.

A three-year study was launched by British scientists in 1999 to look at possible links between aspartame and brain cancer.[40] The focus will be on one ingredient of the sweetener, methanol, which it is suggested might enter tissue and change DNA. Manufacturers of the best known brand, *NutraSweet*, have responded by pointing to the current scientific consensus that there is no such problem.

We do know for certain that aspartame is unsafe for those suffering from phenylketonuria (PKU), an inherited condition that makes it impossible for the body to break down phenylalanine. One in 10,000 people have this defect and babies are routinely tested (the Guthrie test) soon after birth, when a blood sample is taken by pricking their foot. So you should already know if your child is affected.

Cyclamate: This sweetener was banned in 1969, because it was found to cause bladder tumours in rats.

Saccharin: The scientist who discovered saccharin in 1879 stumbled across it by accident. He found that it passed safely through the body, and was therefore good for diabetics and people trying to take off weight. Food manufacturers enthusiastically embraced saccharin and its use soared when cyclamate (see above) was banned.

However, animal research seemed to show that the sweetener, which is 500–700 times sweeter than sugar, caused bladder tumours in rats. It is now banned in the UK, except as a sugar substitute in crisps and snacks, and available in France only by prescription. By contrast, it is permitted in the USA, after strong lobbying by manufacturers, so long as it carries detailed health warnings. Saccharin is thought to be particularly risky for young children,

fats & sugars

pregnant women, white men who are heavy smokers and non-white women.

Sorbitol: This sweetener has been around for a long time, in many different applications. Only half as sweet as sugar, sorbitol is used in commercially prepared diabetic foods such as canned fruit and juices, jams and preserves, chocolates and chewing gum, and it also helps keep shredded coconut and marshmallows moist. However, some people find that even small amounts can cause gas and diarrhoea.

Sucralose: This is a new artificial sweetener, approved for use in the USA in 1991 and now used in 27 countries around the world. Invented by **Tate & Lyle**, sucralose is the only low-calorie sweetener created from sugar, so it tastes like sugar. It is 600 times sweeter than sugar, and contains zero calories. Called *Splenda* by its manufacturer, **Johnson & Johnson**, it is more stable than aspartame, which means that its flavour does not fade over time, nor is it affected by cooking. It is found in bakery mixes, cereal, chewing gum, confectionery, fruit drinks, iced tea, jams, sauces, soft drinks, table-top sweeteners and yoghurts. The product underwent the most extensive safety and environmental trials ever carried out on a food additive, and is now cleared for more food types than any other low-calories sweetener.

☆ ☆ ☆ ☆ ☆ ☆ ☆ **WHAT'S NEW?** ☆ ☆ ☆ ☆ ☆ ☆ ☆

Sweeter sugar: It is still at the research stage, but the Dutch are working on a genetically modified sugar beet with enhanced sweetness. This would be an alternative to artificial sweeteners.

Low-cal sugar: Genetic engineers, also in Holland, say they have created a non-fattening sugar. Made from sugar beet, it is based on fructans (which the body finds hard to absorb), tastes as sweet as normal sugar, but only contains about half the calories.

Organics: Organic honey and sugar are now widely available.

fats & sugars

GM Spotlight

SWEETENERS

- GM maize is often used to make corn syrup – and dextrose, fructose, glucose, maltose and sucrose can all be made from corn syrup.
- High fructose corn syrup (HFCS) has largely replaced ordinary sugar used in soft drinks and many other foods, largely because it is cheaper. Corn syrup is a sweet, thick liquid made by treating cornstarch (which could be made with GM corn) with acids or enzymes. Those enzymes are likely to have been produced by GM microbes.
- Aspartame (widely used in low-calorie foods and drinks) is produced using GM technology in the USA. But, apparently, the same product supplied to UK food producers is not.

fats & sugars

VITAMINS AND MINERALS

In this section, we look at antioxidants, those superstars of the new food universe, and at other vitamins and minerals which were once superstars in their own right. These ingredients play a key role in new foods – in functional foods especially. Vitamin- and mineral-enriched foods, such as milk and cereals, were among the earliest functional foods. We all got used to seeing the percentage of our recommended daily allowance (RDA) of particular minerals and vitamins on our cereal boxes.

Now, with the increasing interest in health, these ingredients are added to an extraordinary range of products – and in increasingly extravagant quantities. Often a food can contain hundreds of times the RDA of a particular vitamin. However, the health effects are still not fully understood, and for some vitamins an excess can be detrimental. That said, it seems inevitable that we will see both more health claims being made for antioxidants and more foods containing them in the future.

Antioxidants
Life extensions

WHAT

All antioxidants are vitamins, but not all vitamins are antioxidants. Simply stated, antioxidants are chemicals that keep other substances from being oxidised – that is, turning brown (like apples) or going rancid (like butter). But they also seen to have huge potential for disease prevention and control. In Europe, they are given E numbers, which run from E300 to E321.

WHERE

Natural antioxidants include vitamin E, found in vegetable oils, vitamin C, found in citrus fruit, among other things, and beta-carotene, found in a range of orange coloured fruit and vegetables, including carrots, mangos, melons and pumpkins. Prunes have the highest levels of antioxidants, and raisins, blueberries and cherries also have high levels.

Some of the main types of antioxidant derived from plant sources are listed in the box below. Among the artificial antioxidants used in food processing are butylated hydroxyanisole (BHA) and butylated hydroxytoluene (BHT), which do not have the star status of their natural counterparts, but do not cause any health problems either.

PLANT-BASED SOURCES OF ANTIOXIDANTS

Antioxidant	Sources
Carotenes	apricots, cantaloupes, carrots, chicory, greens, herbs, kale, mangos, pumpkins, red peppers, spinach, squashes, sweet potatoes, herbs
Copper	avocados, asparagus, bananas, blackberries, blackcurrants, gourds, grapes, guavas, kiwi fruit, lychees, mangos, mushrooms, olives, plums, potatoes, pulses, raspberries
Flavonoids	apples, broad beans, citrus fruits, grapes, greens, onions, peanuts, strawberries, tea
Isoflavones	pulses (especially soya and linseed)
Lutein and zeaxanthin	celery, greens, herbs, kale, leeks, onions (shallots or spring onions), spinach
Lycopene	guavas, pink grapefruits, tomatoes
Manganese	bananas, beetroot, blackberries, greens, pineapples, pulses, raspberries, spinach
Organo-sulphur compounds	chives, garlic, leeks, onions (all allium vegetables)
Polyphenols	apples, black tea, cocoa (and dark chocolate), kidney beans, raisins and red wine
Ubiquinol	beans, garlic, spinach
Vitamin C (ascorbic acid)	blackcurrants, green peppers, guavas, gourds, greens, strawberries, kiwi fruits, citrus fruits, paw-paws, Brussels sprouts, new potatoes
Vitamin E	asparagus, blueberries, broccoli, herbs, kale, spinach, sweet potatoes, tomatoes

Sources include: *Functional Foods: The Consumer, the Products and the Evidence*[41]

vitamins & minerals

HEALTH ISSUES

Our understanding of the benefits of antioxidants is growing rapidly, with some scientists arguing that they may help slow down the ageing process, boost the immune system, limit the damage done by cholesterol LDLs, and even reduce the likelihood of cancers, strokes and cataracts.

American studies have shown that people who eat lots of tomatoes have a substantially decreased risk of numerous cancers, particularly cancers of the prostate, lung and stomach. Processed tomatoes often have a higher lycopene content than fresh ones, but there is concern that these benefits may be offset by the increased fat and sugar contents they may contain.

It seems that some antioxidants destroy so-called free radicals (described in the box below), which are pollutants made when energy is produced in our cells as part of the process of fuelling our bodies.[42]

Polyphenols are the antioxidants largely responsible for the popular medical recommendation to drink a regular glass of red wine as an effective way to reduce the risk of heart disease and some cancers. And isoflavones are thought to be one of the reasons that soya is considered to be particularly healthy.

Free radicals

THE ENEMY WITHIN

To convert food to energy our bodies need oxygen,[43] which is converted to water in our body cells. But this process does not always work properly, and in about 2 per cent of cases 'oxygen free radicals' are created. Free radicals are also formed by smoking, air pollution and exposure to sunlight. And they may be made by our immune cells, as a weapon against invading bacteria.

Free radicals in our body can damage healthy proteins and fats, as well as our DNA, perhaps even causing it to produce cancerous cells. They may also help trigger heart disease and, because our body may become less elastic, can spur into action other ageing problems, such as cataracts and cancers.

Our body is naturally equipped with an effective system to protect it from free radical damage, but antioxidants give extra protection. Although some are naturally present in our body, others must be obtained from our diet.

vitamins & minerals

☆ ☆ ☆ ☆ ☆ ☆ ☆ **WHAT'S NEW?** ☆ ☆ ☆ ☆ ☆ ☆ ☆

Overall, the future for antioxidants looks pretty bright. According to Lester Packer, in his book *The Antioxidant Miracle*, 'There is now over-whelming scientific evidence that those of us who eat a diet rich in antioxidants and take antioxidant supplements will live longer, healthier lives.'[44]

Juicy antioxidants: One manufacturer who added extra antioxidants to their fruit juice claimed that they slowed down the ageing process (of the drinker, not just the drink!). In the UK, no brands (as far as we're aware) have actually stated that they contain antioxidants, but many – such as **Immergut's** *Sport Yo Yo* drinking yoghurt, **Petty Wood's** *Epicure V-Fruity* and **Gusto's** *Gusto Goddess* – contain vita-mins A, C and E – all antioxidants.

☆ ☆ ☆ ☆ ☆ ☆ ☆ ☆ ☆ ☆ ☆ ☆ ☆ ☆ ☆ ☆ ☆ ☆ ☆

Minerals
Salts of the earth

WHAT

Minerals are substances not formed from plant or animal matter, but which turn to ash when burned. Many of them are essential for our health, so let's look at some of the most useful ones found in food.

Calcium: Good sources of calcium include all dairy products, except butter; dried peas and beans; most dark leafy greens; the soft bones of canned fish; fruits, nuts and seeds; and tofu.

Fully 99 per cent of the calcium we absorb goes into our bones and teeth, from where it is moved around our body and used for other processes, such as blood clotting, nerve signalling and absorb-ing vitamin B12. It seems to play a much wider role in ensuring human health than was originally imagined, helping to ease the symptoms of pre-menstrual syndrome and cutting the risks of heart disease, strokes and colon cancer.

Interestingly, the **New Zealand Dairy Advisory Service** takes the health benefits of calcium so seriously that it doesn't just promote dairy products, but also lists a range of other good sources, including salmon, muesli, almonds and tofu.

vitamins & minerals

Fluoride: Naturally present in tea and fish, fluoride is sometimes added to water and toothpastes, because it helps to prevent tooth decay in children. The medical evidence suggests that fluoridation of drinking water is both safe and effective at protecting our teeth against decay, but critics argue that too much fluoride can damage health. True, but the consensus among doctors appears to be that there is no problem.

Iodine: Found naturally in milk and seafood, iodine is also added to some types of table salt. A lack of this mineral can cause goitre, where the thyroid gland swells in an attempt to find and process enough iodine. The result can be a large unsightly swelling of the neck, as well as mental retardation in severe cases.

Iron: The main source of iron in our diet is red meat and offal, although it is also found in vegetables, pulses and nuts. It helps to create red blood cells, and so increases resistance to infection and helps the healing process. A deficiency can result in anaemia. Food such as cereal already has added iron, and other iron-fortified foods may well become more common in future as the industry targets women, because they typically need twice as much iron as men. This is partly because of their periods but also because they are more likely to be vegetarians.

Magnesium: This mineral is found in many foods, but particularly in wholegrain cereals, nuts, garlic and peas. It helps cells and muscles work efficiently and a lack of magnesium can therefore cause irritability, fits, tiredness and – in extreme cases – heart attacks.

Phosphorus: Found in dairy foods, meat, fish and eggs, phosphorus is a key element of the cells in our bodies and is also present in bones and teeth. There are no recorded cases of phosphorus deficiency.

Potassium: All foods contain potassium, except sugars, fats and oils. Bananas have a particularly high content and processed foods tend to have less than 'natural' foods. It helps the body process fluids, and a lack of it can cause fatigue, weakness, mental confusion and, again in extreme cases, heart failure.

Selenium: Found in cereals, meat, offal, fish, cheese, eggs and in very high quantities in Brazil nuts, selenium is an antioxidant (see above). It's thought to help prevent heart disease, premature ageing, some cancers and even AIDS. It works with vitamin E to aid normal

vitamins & minerals

growth, fertility, and thyroid action, and to maintain healthy skin and hair. The selenium content of food depends on the soil it is grown in, and American and Canadian soil has higher levels than elsewhere, so wheat grown there will have a higher selenium content. Research is under way in the UK to see whether the wheat grown here is selenium-deficient.

Selenium deficiency is rare in the developed world, but it can result in heart disease, arthritis and perhaps cancer. High doses (normally from the over-use of supplements) are potentially extremely toxic, resulting in hair and nail loss, nerve damage, irritability, fatigue and stomach upsets.

Sodium: It's the sodium in salt that is linked with stomach cancer, heart disease and high blood pressure. Doctors routinely tell us to cut down our salt consumption, but there are two schools of thought: one says you don't need to unless you are vulnerable to high blood pressure, which many people are; the other that controlling salt intake is necessary to prevent high blood pressure from developing in the first place.

Salts

TAKING THE SEA WITH US

Salts may have got a bad press recently, because sodium salts in particular can raise the blood pressure, but they are essential ingredients in our diet. Long ago, when our early ancestors moved away from the sea, it was vital that they developed a taste for salt, to ensure they ate enough of it.

Salt is now added to so many processed foods as a flavour enhancer or preservative that we can end up eating extraordinary quantities without even being aware of it. As a result, our taste for salt is continuously stimulated.

But not all salts are the same. For the different types of salt on the market, see chapter 4, Along the Shelves. Most of our salt intake is from manufactured foods, although we can make some impact by cutting down on that used in cooking or at the table. Some manufacturers have been gradually cutting down salt levels in products over a period of time, so that consumers adapt, but we will also see alternative means of flavour enhancement used.

vitamins & minerals

Zinc: This mineral is found in high-protein foods like oysters, meat, nuts, wholegrains, seeds and *Quorn* (page 110). It is essential for growth, fertility and a whole range of bodily functions, including the strengthening of the immune system. Deficiency is rare, but an excess – which may be brought about by taking zinc supplements – can interfere with the body's use of copper and, it is thought, may contribute to the development of Alzheimer's disease.[45]

☆ ☆ ☆ ☆ ☆ ☆ ☆ **WHAT'S NEW?** ☆ ☆ ☆ ☆ ☆ ☆ ☆

Calcium-enriched: There are already a number of calcium-enriched products available, including cereals, desserts and drinks. They include *Campina Yazoo* (milk and chocolate drinks), **Haldane Foods'** *Granose* soya shakes, **Kellogg's** *Nutrigrain* bars (which contain 25 per cent of the recommended daily amount), most **Kellogg's** breakfast cereals, **Linda McCartney's** *DairyLike* range, *Provamel* soya milk, *Rivella Rivella* (fizzy drink with calcium and herbs) *Tropicana Plus* (calcium-enriched orange juice) and *Warburton's* sliced bread (with extra fibre and calcium). As long as the populations of many industrialised countries go on ageing, calcium-enriched foods are going to go on growing.

Fortified: Most cereals are fortified with minerals, including iron, calcium etc.

GM mineral boosters: In the future, plants may be genetically modified to increase their uptake of particular minerals, perhaps even to make up for the lack of minerals caused by intensive agriculture.

In organic: Research suggests that non-organic vegetables now have a lower mineral content than in the 1940s, when use of artificial fertilisers and pesticides was less common.[46] Iron levels in non-organic basic vegetables have decreased by over a third in the last 60 years and magnesium levels have halved. Eating organic produce is therefore a good way of ensuring a reasonable balance of minerals.

New salts: Iodised salt was an early functional food when first introduced. *Lo-Salt*, produced by **Klinge**, is low in sodium, getting its salty taste from potassium, and is recommended for people with high blood pressure.

Selenium solutions: High selenium yeasts have been trialled in the

vitamins & minerals

USA and found to be effective, but there are not yet any foods using these yeasts – only supplements – and no selenium fortified foods on the market. Watch this space.

Supplements: It can be difficult to get the minerals you need from supplements, either because they are not in a form that your body can absorb or because you are not eating the right combination of foods to allow them to do their best. It's far better to try to eat a balanced diet naturally containing a good complement of minerals.

☆ ☆

Vitamins
From A to K

The vitamin industry is now huge, but the word *vitamin* only entered our vocabulary in 1912, when the first one – thiamin, or B1 – was isolated. We now know that some of the most devastating diseases of the past were caused by vitamin deficiencies, among them scurvy, rickets and beriberi.

Scientists are convinced that there are more vitamins to be found – and that new roles will also be found for existing vitamins.[47] Many new foods are fortified with extra vitamins and have become, in effect, little more than a glorified way of taking supplements. Critics argue that eating vitamins direct from their natural sources is more nutritious.

Let's review some of the vitamins so far discovered. We will look at vitamins A, B, C, D, E and K, at some of the foods in which they are present, at some of the benefits they provide and at what happens if we are deficient in them.

VITAMIN A

Vitamin A is found in cheese, egg yolks, fatty fish, milk and fruit and vegetables, particularly orange-coloured ones such as carrots, squashes, mangos, papaya and apricots. The orange colour is provided by beta-carotene, needed to make vitamin A – and also used in some processed foods as a colouring.

vitamins & minerals

Although beta-carotene has been promoted as reducing the risk of certain cancers, one Californian study concluded that it may actually increase the risk of lung cancer in smokers – and heavy drinkers should be aware that alcohol can make beta-carotene toxic to the liver. Overdosing can increase the risk of birth defects, and it can also lead to blurred vision, slow growth, increased skull pressure and hair loss.[48]

However, the benefits of vitamin A are overwhelming. It's essential for healthy skin, eyes, bones and teeth and a normal daily dose is not dangerous for anyone.

VITAMIN B COMPLEX

Vitamin B1 (thiamin): Thiamin is found in pork, liver, other meats, whole grains, legumes and nuts. It helps break down carbohydrates and make our appetites and nerves work. Deficiency can cause nerve problems and a tropical disease called beriberi.

Vitamin B2 (riboflavin): Found in dairy products, meat (particularly liver), whole and enriched grains and vegetables, riboflavin helps with digestion, vision and healthy skin. A deficiency can result in dry, scaly, facial skin and a swollen mouth. Vegetarians are often a bit low on this vitamin, and may need to take supplements.

Niacin: The richest sources of niacin include meat, liver, poultry, whole and enriched grains, vegetables and peanuts. Niacin helps in digesting food, particularly in breaking down carbohydrates, as well as in maintaining the health of the skin and nerves. The lack of husks in highly refined flour and grains led to niacin deficiencies. When refined rice products were introduced to Indonesia by Europeans, their lack of niacin caused outbreaks of pellagra, an unpleasant disease causing severely cracked skin and, at worst, insanity and death.

Vitamin B6 (pyridoxine): Found in poultry, fish, meat, potatoes, avocados and bananas, pyridoxine helps break down carbohydrates, fats and protein. A deficiency can lead to nerve damage.

Vitamin B12 (cobalamin): Rich sources of cobalamin include meats (especially offal), poultry, eggs, fish and milk. It helps create red blood cells, which carry oxygen and nutrients around the body, as well as keeping nerve tissue healthy. Pernicious anaemia is caused by a lack of B12.

vitamins & minerals

Folic acid (folacin): Folic acid is plentiful in liver, leafy green veg-etables, beans, whole grains, nuts and oranges. It helps make healthy red blood cells. Pregnant women (and those who may conceive) are advised to take folic acid supplements to prevent birth defects, and it's also recommended for the prevention of some forms of cancer and heart disease.

Pantothenic acid: Found in meats (particularly offal), fish, egg yolks, whole grains and beans, pantothenic acid helps break down carbohydrates, fats and proteins as well as encouraging the growth and maintenance of body tissues.

Biotin: Found in meats, eggs, milk, whole grains, beans and nuts, this vitamin helps break down carbohydrates, fats and proteins, but eating very large amounts of raw egg whites can stop the biotin being absorbed.

VITAMIN C

Also known as ascorbic acid (E300), vitamin C is found in fruit, par-ticularly citrus fruit and soft fruit, and in vegetables like peppers, brassicas, potatoes and tomatoes (although it can be lost in cooking water).

It's vital in our diet because it strengthens blood vessels, helps the absorption of iron, speeds up healing and boosts the immune sys-tem. It is by far the most popular supplement, and some people take 'megadoses', hoping to ward off colds. However, while some increase in vitamin C may help – although this is far from certain – too much can result in dependency, and if doses are later reduced, symptoms of vitamin C deficiency may appear.

VITAMIN D

Although vitamin D is found in egg yolks and fish oils, the main source for humans is from sunlight. Vitamin D increases the absorp-tion of calcium and phosphorus, which helps harden bones and teeth. Old people are often particularly vulnerable to vitamin D defi-ciency if they are not able to get outside much. Overdoses can be toxic, causing stunted growth and weight loss.

vitamins & minerals

VITAMIN E

Vitamin E is found in liver, leafy greens, vegetable oils, margarines, butter, eggs, nuts, whole grains and wheat germ. It works as a natural antioxidant, and prevents the destruction of vitamins A and C, as well as of fatty acids. Recent studies suggest that large doses may reduce the risk of heart disease and cancer, but this is not absolutely guaranteed.

VITAMIN K

This is found in egg yolks, milk, leafy green vegetables and soya bean oil, but we make most of the vitamin K our bodies need. A natural antioxidant, vitamin K helps blood clotting, and recent studies suggest that large doses may reduce the risk of heart disease and cancer. New-born babies are often given extra vitamin K because they are not yet able to make it and may not get enough from breast milk.

☆ ☆ ☆ ☆ ☆ ☆ ☆ **WHAT'S NEW?** ☆ ☆ ☆ ☆ ☆ ☆ ☆

Added beta-carotene: Some soft drinks that contain extra beta-carotene have been promoted as health drinks.

Folate: In the USA it is now a requirement for flour to be fortified with folate (folic acid). In the UK the added folate is optional, but is added to some flour, bread, cereals and even frozen vegetables. Typical labels will say 'with extra folic acid' or 'contains folic acid'. Folic acid deficiency – apparently the world's leading deficiency – can lead to babies being born with nervous system problems or spina bifida. Several studies have also linked boosted folate levels with a reduced risk of cancer in adults. In the USA, for example, it was found that women with high folate levels were 75 per cent less likely to get cancer.

Vitamin-C-enriched: There's nothing new about vitamin C-boosted products. They are everywhere: sweets, chewing gum, soft drinks, squashes, even cough sweets. Expect more.

Multi-vitamins: Some products try to pack in everything they can think of. The cheese spread *Primula Ultra Plus*, made by German manufacturer **Kavli** and launched in 1997, was not only 95 per cent

fat-free, but was fortified with vitamins A, C, D, E, B6, folic acid and calcium!

GM Spotlight
RICH IN GM VITAMINS

- Food manufacturers generally buy vitamins from bulk suppliers, which makes it difficult to establish whether GM technology has been used in their production or not. But, given that many vitamins are made with fermentation technolog, it is increasingly likely that they will be produced by GM means (although the final product should not contain any altered DNA).
- Vitamin B2 (riboflavin) can be made with GM technology, but it's not known how widely this version is used.
- Vitamin B12 (cobalamin) is made through fermentation. Although the GM version has not yet been approved for the UK, it is widely used elsewhere and may well be included in products consumed here.
- Vitamin C is often made from maize, which could be GM. Indeed, very little vitamin C can be guaranteed GM-free.
- Vitamin E can be made from soya, which could be GM.
- Emulsifiers, such as lecithin, are sometimes used in vitamin supplements and could be made with GM ingredients.

☆ ☆ ☆ ☆ ☆ ☆ ☆ ☆ ☆ ☆ ☆ ☆ ☆ ☆ ☆ ☆ ☆ ☆ ☆ ☆

vitamins & minerals

BIO-INGREDIENTS

Our food contains – or is processed using – a growing range of bio-logical ingredients. Some of these are organisms in their own right, others are extracted from organisms – and growing numbers are now synthesised in the laboratory. In this section, we focus on bio-cultures, enzymes, herbs, phytochemicals, and on proteins and amino acids.

Biocultures
It's alive

There is growing awareness that our stomachs and intestines need all the help they can get. At any one time, they contain about 2 lbs (1 kg) of bacteria (that's around 100,000,000,000,000 individual bacte-ria), most of them busily working to break down the food we eat. During an average lifetime the gut will handle something like 65 tonnes of food – roughly equivalent to the weight of a dozen full-grown elephants! Many modern habits, such as eating on the hoof, drinking too much and taking antibiotics, can add to the strain on our systems, and there is a growing interest in foods that will help with these digestive processes.

WHAT

Bio-cultures are essentially live, active bacteria, also known as *pro-biotics*. These bacteria are vital in digesting our food, and also actively fight off the 'bad' bacteria which can produce toxins in the body. There are thousands of different probiotics, but only a few of them have been thoroughly researched and been proven to be beneficial food ingredients. The two best-known bacteria used as probiotics are *Lactobacillus acidophilus* and *bifidus*.

There are others – like *L. casei* in *Yakult* (see *Yakult* box below), and *L. la1* in **Nestlé's** *LC1* Go. Over time, it's likely that other lactic acid bacteria will come in to play as probiotics. One likely candidate is

L. reuteri, which occurs naturally in the breast-milk of healthy women.

Prebiotics are foods (usually soluble dietary fibre) which probiotics feed on, ensuring they are more likely to proliferate. Synbiotic foods are those that contain both probiotics and prebiotics.

WHERE

Bio-cultures (i.e. probiotics) are found in some yoghurts and fermented dairy drinks. So, for example, 'bio-yoghurts' and 'bio-drinks' have extra bacteria added.

HEALTH ISSUES

As George Bernard Shaw is reputed to have said, 'a good set of bowels is worth more to a man than any quantity of brains.' Probiotic and prebiotic foods are geared to maintaining a healthy colon and regular bowel movements. They are also thought to help with constipation, diseases linked to antibiotics, gut infections, irritable bowel syndrome, liver damage and the production of excess gas and of cancer-causing agents in the gut.

But some scientists are sceptical about the benefits of probiotics because, they say, to be effective the bacteria need to reach the colon, and the acidity of the stomach is a serious barrier to this.

Bacteria help create the right sort of acid conditions in the colon. In the process, they strengthen the immune system, lower blood cholesterol, reduce the risk of cancer and help the digestion of food. There is at least anecdotal evidence to show that that bio-yoghurts can also help reduce infections of the vaginal fungus Candida that causes thrush (page 227).

 ☆ ☆ ☆ ☆ ☆ ☆ ☆ **WHAT'S NEW?** ☆ ☆ ☆ ☆ ☆ ☆ ☆

Bio-foods: We are now seeing a growing range of self-declared 'bio-yoghurts', featuring added probiotic bacteria. *LC1* yoghurt, made by **Nestlé**, claims to boost your body's immune system. **Yoplait**, in France, produce a 'prebiotic' yoghurt called *Oligo*, and 'synbiotic' yoghurts with pre- and probiotics include **Müller's** *ProCult 3* in Germany and *Synbalance* in Switzerland. There is also a fruit juice on the market, called *ProViva*, which uses a probiotic bacterium first identified by a Swedish professor. The hospital he worked at fed it

bio-ingredients

through tubes to patients who were recovering from operations, and found that it accelerated their recovery because it fights harmful bacteria aggressively. Extensive tests seem to confirm that it benefits intestinal health.

The first *Lactobacillus* probiotic on the American market was *Culturelle*, made by **ConAgra**, then the world's seventh largest food group. Launched in 1998, this came in the form of capsules containing the lactic acid bacterium *Lactobacillus CG* and designed to promote 'intestinal health'. The company was careful to pace itself, introducing products with proven health benefits before extending the *Culturelle* brand into other foods. 'Americans think that all bacteria should be shot on sight,' explained a leading executive.[49]

Yakult

MEET 6.5 BILLION FRIENDS

Yakult Honsha, the company behind this product, says that one bottle (the recommended daily intake) of *Yakult* contains over 6.5 billion live bacteria. This may be a somewhat surprising addition to the contents of our fridge, but millions of people around the world now religiously consume their daily portion.

The company stresses that *Yakult* is a food, not a medicine. It is a 'probiotic' containing the bacterium *Lactobacillus casei Shirota*. This is billed as able to withstand our gastric juices and bile, so it can reach the intestine intact. Once there, we are told, it helps friendly bacteria proliferate in your gut and discourages their unfriendly competitors. This means that your body can break down and process the food you eat more efficiently.

The manufacturers claim that *Yakult* will help if you are run down, stressed, taking antibiotics, have a poor diet or are recovering from an illness. Positive customer feedback to the company includes claims that *Yakult* has helped overcome complaints such as irritable bowel syndrome, indigestion and poor skin. A normal healthy person with a balanced diet will almost certainly not notice any difference, however, except perhaps more regular bowel movements.

Critics say that *Yakult* is too sweet. It is 10.7 per cent sugar (sucrose), similar to most flavoured yoghurts; but a low calorie version is available in Japan.

bio-ingredients

Probiotic drinks: As well as yoghurts and dairy products, probiotics are starting to be added to other types of foods. *ProViva* blackcurrant drink was launched in the UK, in 1999. The probiotic bacterium used in this product was originally developed in Sweden and given to newly operated-on patients to build up their immune system.

Gum arabic: Acacia gum, or gum arabic, is a non-dairy prebiotic. It feeds the healthy bacteria in the gut, helping maintain a good balance in the intestine and colon. It is the unexpectedly healthy ingredient in some sweets (which can contain more than 40 per cent acacia gum), helping with digestion and problems like constipation.

Enzymes
Miracle workers

WHAT

Enzymes are about the closest you can get to 'miracle' ingredients. They are proteins that speed up biological reactions such as fermentation. They are natural – and pretty much ubiquitous. Every cell in our bodies contains thousands of different enzymes. They make life possible. Each type of enzyme – no one knows how many there are–does only one thing, and does it very fast. Take the enzymes found in 'biological' washing powder. One type dissolves only fat, another only starch, others only egg or chocolate.

There is a long history of traditional enzyme use, but the pioneers had little idea of what made their processes work. People may have used nettle leaves to curdle milk for cheese, for instance, when it was actually an enzyme found in the nettles that did the real work. When enzymes were discovered, manufacturers sought the microorganism, plant or animal, that naturally produced the enzyme they wanted to use – and made a liquid extract. Often these early extracts contained other active enzymes, so the effect could be rather muddled.

Over time scientists became more expert at hooking out the particular enzymes they wanted. But it was the introduction of GM

bio-ingredients

techniques that really transformed the industry, opening the doors to mass-produced, custom-tailored enzymes.

Nowadays most enzymes are produced by the fermentation of different types of micro-organism. The micro-organisms are grown in large closed tanks where they produce the desired enzymes. The trick is to get hold of a micro-organism that can produce the enzyme in large quantities. This can be achieved by using gene technology to transfer the gene responsible for producing a certain enzyme into a safe and effective micro-organism. Here, the enzyme itself is not genetically modified, but the micro-organism producing it is. Such a micro-organism is often called a GMO, a genetically modified organism.

More recently, scientists have worked out how to modify genes so that they can produce enzymes with new properties. The enzymes might be made less sensitive to the heat or chemicals used in food processing, allowing them to work faster and for longer.

One significant benefit from enzymes produced by GMOs is that fewer resources are needed to produce them. As a result, less energy and water is needed to make any given amount of enzyme. To take a specific example, when the enzyme alpha-galactosidase is produced by GMOs the process cuts the amount of yeast used from 236 tonnes to just 10. There are also further substantial savings in other areas.

Yeasts

GETTING A RISE

Yeasts are microscopic organisms that feed on starch and sugar and release carbon dioxide (like the bubbles in fizzy drinks) in the process. The active ingredients in this process are enzymes, produced by the yeasts. The bubbles make the bread rise and add the fizz or sparkle to alcoholic drinks such as beer and champagne.

Yeast is actually quite nutritious. It supplies the body with high quality protein, as well as thiamin, riboflavin, iron and phosphorus. Some yeasts have been trained to absorb high levels of selenium from the nutrient broth in which they are grown. In the process, they can convert selenium into selenomethionine, which is much easier for the human body to absorb. A number of GM yeasts are now cleared for use, for example in the brewing industry.

GM yeasts: Yeasts can be seen as delivery systems for useful enzymes, which they produce when fed on the right raw materials. As a result, it seems highly likely that the 21st century will see growing numbers of GM yeasts being developed and proposed for use in making food and drink products.

In 1990, the UK was the first country to permit the use of a live GM organism in food. The relevant yeast was genetically modified to produce more useful enzymes and, thereby, make bread dough rise faster.[50] Another yeast has been developed which may have the effect of reducing the 'beer belly', even in heavy drinkers. This GM yeast can produce a full strength beer which is low in carbohydrates, and was approved several years ago for use in beer production in the UK – although it's not clear whether or not it has been used commercially to date. GM yeasts are almost certainly now being used in the USA, however.

WHERE

Enzymes are now found in many food production processes, from baking and brewing to producing fruit juices and cheese. It's clear that they can bring major benefits to the food industry and, potentially, to the environment, by making production processes more efficient. Enzymes produced by GMOs are currently exactly the same as those produced by traditional methods, but in the future the enzymes themselves may well be genetically modified, to give them new properties. Below, we look at some of the enzymes used in food production, and at the important issue of their GM status.

Beer: Traditionally, malted barley was the source of the enzymes used in brewing. Key enzymes used in brewing include *alpha-amylase*, which breaks down starch, *papain* to remove protein and *beta-glucanase* to prevent 'chill-haze' (when the beer becomes cloudy upon cooling). Low carbohydrate beers may use *amyloglucosidase* as a sweetener and to remove starch. So far, however, most brewing enzymes are produced using traditional methods, not GMOs.

The use of enzymes is particularly important for making light – or 'lite' – beers. These are low carbohydrate beers and the enzyme most often used for this purpose is *amyloglucosidase*, which breaks down unfermented, unwanted carbohydrates in the finished beer. Industry

bio-ingredients

sources say that enzymes produced by GMOs are very rarely used for this purpose.

One area where enzymes produced by GMOs may be used, however, is in the removal of a bitter-tasting substance known as diacetyl. The enzyme used here is *alpha-acetolactate decarboxylase.*

Biscuits: Among the key enzymes used in biscuits and crackers are *proteases*, used to reduce the level of proteins in flours, because low-protein flour makes it easier for the biscuits to keep their shape. Biscuits and crackers require a low level of protein/gluten in the flour. This reduces the leavening effect of the dough and ensures the flat appearance of the final products. It's unlikely that enzymes from GMOs are currently used for this application.

Bread: Bread quality can be improved by using enzymes at several stages in the process. *Alpha-amylases hydrolyse* are used by yeast to produce gas which makes the bread rise. *Hemicellulases* (including *xylanases*) make the dough softer and easier to handle. And *glucoseoxidase* strengthens the dough, and makes it less sticky and easier to handle.

A special amylase (a so-called *'maltogenic' amylase*) is also used to prevent staling by breaking down some of the starch in the dough. White bread goes stale when the starch granules change from a soluble to an insoluble form, making the bread hard and brittle.

Most of the enzymes used in the bread-baking industry are produced by GMOs. Most of these enzymes are *hemicellulases/xylanases* and are used for making dough softer and easier to handle. Several have been subjected to extensive food safety tests.

Cheese and other dairy products: For the making of cheese, *chymosin* is indispensable. This used to be obtained from the stomachs of slaughtered young animals (typically calves or lambs). Nowadays, using GM techniques, it's possible to produce the enzyme by fermentation. Among other uses in cheese-making, enzymes are used to break down lactose (milk sugars) to make some dairy products more digestible for people with lactose intolerance. GM enzymes cleared in the UK for cheese-making include an *E. coli* K12 bacterium, an *A. niger* fungus and a *K. lactis* yeast.

Fruit juices: In nature, the ripening of fruit such as apples is promoted by enzymes, namely *pectinases*, which gradually make the fruit softer and softer. In the process, the *pectinases* turn pectins into more soluble forms. This knowledge is used in the production of fruit juices. By accelerating the changes initiated during natural ripening, almost all the juice can be extracted from the fruit. Removal of pectins also helps to clarify pressed juices and remove haze. The enzymes commercially available in this area are made using both classical methods and by GMOs, but the majority is non-GM.

Margarine: Lipases are used as a clean and more versatile alternative to chemically catalysed processes used to soften margarines and to increase the proportion of polyunsaturated fatty acids they contain. To date, most lipases are of microbial origin, but are very unlikely to come from GMOs. In the longer term, however, GM technology will enable industry to reengineer enzymes to make them last longer in food processing.

Meat: Traditionally, in tropical countries, meat was tenderised by wrapping it in papaya leaves, or dipping it in papaya or pineapple juice. This worked mainly because of the enzymes that are present in the leaves or juice. These days, the most frequently used enzyme is *papain*, which – as its name suggests – is extracted from papaya. But meat tenderisation is not allowed by the EC, so this is an insignificant area of enzyme use.

Soft drinks: Key enzymes used to make the high fructose corn syrups used in almost all fizzy drinks are *amyloglucosidase* and *glucose isomerase*.

Sweeteners: During times of sugar shortages in Europe, it was discovered that glucose could be made by boiling starch with acid. This technique was far from perfect, however, and the discovery that with enzymes it was possible to convert the starchy material into glucose and then turn some of this to fructose was considered a great improvement.

The enzymes a*myloglucosidase* and *glucose isomerase*, most of which is made using GMOs, are widely used to help turn starch into glucose and glucose into fructose. This takes three enzymatic steps. First, an *alpha-amylase* breaks the starch down into smaller molecules called maltodextrins. Then an *amyloglucosidase* converts these maltodextrins to glucose. In the process, other sugars – such as maltose – are also formed, their quantity varying according to the

bio-ingredients

presence of other enzymes. Finally, an immobilised glucose *isomerase* is used to convert a proportion of the glucose into fructose. In this way, low-value corn starch can be used to make high-value fructose. Fructose is the naturally occurring sweetener in honey and fruits. It is about twice as sweet as sugar, but has about the same number of calories. It is widely used as a sweetener in foods and soft drinks as an alternative to sugar.

Wine: The processes and enzymes used in wine production are in many ways similar to those used in the juice industry (see above). *Pectinases*, b*eta-glucanases* and *urease* are permitted within the EU – and American wine producers also use these enzymes. They are still produced mainly with classically bred micro-organisms.

HEALTH ISSUES

There are no major health issues that arise from enzymes.

☆ ☆ ☆ ☆ ☆ ☆ ☆ **WHAT'S NEW?** ☆ ☆ ☆ ☆ ☆ ☆ ☆

Enzyme technology is developing so fast that all of it could be considered new.

GM Spotlight

WHY GM ENZYMES?

There are two main benefits of GM enzymes for producers and users of enzymes:

- First, enzyme production is more economical and less polluting (see introduction to this enzyme section, above).
- Second, the GM enzyme products tend to be purer, with fewer so-called 'side activities'.

The benefits for consumers depend very much on the enzyme in question and what it is acting upon. With the fruit juices, for example, the main benefits focus on a better use of raw materials, which should translate into lower prices. In the baking industry, products should remain fresher for longer. And with the sweeteners, GM enzymes mean that fewer chemicals, like acids, need to be used in the production process.

It's worth noting that GM enzymes, however they are produced,

---

bio-ingredients

do *not* end up in the finished product. The GM enzymes are processing agents, rather than ingredients, and the foods produced through their means are indistinguishable from foods produced by enzymes made in traditional ways.

Food manufacturers therefore argue that labelling of foods whose processing involves such enzymes would not make sense – and there is no requirement to label in the EU. GM opponents counter-argue that the use of GM techniques at any point in the food production process should be labelled, to ensure consumer choice, and this would include the use of enzymes produced with GMOs.

Whatever your position, there are good reasons to use enzymes in food processing, but information about their use needs to be readily accessible. Our GM Food Survey showed that most food manufacturers and retailers who responded had reviewed the GM status of their products and suppliers, but had not even thought of checking for the use of GM technology in the production of enzymes.

The **Co-op** were the only company that labelled the use of GM enzymes – in their cheese. But even they have not felt it necessary to label any other products containing GM enzymes. With public concern over GM food, it is not surprising that this issue is beginning to attract more attention.

Tate & Lyle was one of the very few companies responding to our survey to talk openly about the use of GM enzymes. It pointed out that one variety of *Tops* yoghurt (strawberry) contains glucose syrup, which, although derived from wheat, needed GM enzymes to produce it. But neither the enzyme nor any GM material is detectable in the finished product, the company said.

Fibre
Roughage works

WHAT

Better known as roughage, dietary fibre is a carbohydrate containing no vitamins, minerals or calories. There are two types, soluble fibre, which dissolves in water, and insoluble fibre, which doesn't.

bio-ingredients

WHERE

Soluble fibres, including pectins, gums and mucilages, are variously found in citrus fruits, apples, potatoes, dried peas and beans, oatmeal and bran. Insoluble fibres include cellulose, found in wheat bran, whole wheat, whole-grain breakfast cereals, broccoli and carrots, and lignin, found in asparagus, wheat bran and pears. Animal products, such as meat, eggs, milk and cheese, do not contain any fibre.

HEALTH ISSUES

Over the course of this century, western diets became increasingly thin on fibre intake; the result was constipation and a correspondingly high demand for laxatives. In the 1980s, people became more aware – partly because of books like the *F-Plan Diet* – that fibre was an important part of diet. Like most good things, this can be taken too far, but it is now generally recognised that eating reasonable quantities of fibre is important. The average Briton eats only about 12 g a day – 6 g less than the recommended 18 g a day. But beware of making a young child's diet too bulky, since they may well then feel full before they have eaten enough food to satisfy their need for essential vitamins, minerals and energy.

Soluble fibre is thought to lower cholesterol levels in the blood and therefore cut the risk of heart disease. It also stabilises blood sugar levels, which is potentially good news for diabetics. Insoluble fibre bulks up your stools, which means that they move through your intestinal system faster, potentially helping cut the risk of colon cancer.

☆ ☆ ☆ ☆ ☆ ☆ ☆ **WHAT'S NEW?** ☆ ☆ ☆ ☆ ☆ ☆ ☆

Added fibre: Psyllium is a natural laxative, full of soluble fibre that comes from dried seeds, as well as occurring naturally in wheat. It's already an ingredient in cereals like *Weetabix* and *Shredded Wheat*. In the USA, **Kellogg** has launched its *Ensemble* range of cereals, biscuits, pastas and breads – all of which contain psyllium, also used for its cholesterol-lowering properties (page 66).

Among the fibre-enhanced foods available in Japan are *Fibemini*, a cheese enriched with fibre; *Fibi*, a fibre-rich soft drink, and *Meiji Seika*, a cereal with added fibre[51]. In the UK, *Ribena Juice & Fibre* contained added psyllium, but it was withdrawn in 1996. There had been

bio-ingredients

complaints that the product's likely benefits had been exaggerated.

Biting into bark: For a couple of weeks each spring, when the sap is rising in Finnish pine forests, people are out collecting the nutrient-rich under-layer of bark for food. The Vikings used to eat this so-called 'phloem' in times of famine, and the North American Indians used it for medicinal purposes. Now it is being formulated into health food products under brand names like *Vitibark*, which has also been used instead of phosphates to bind sausages.[52] These bark products are seen as an excellent source of vitamins, minerals, fibre and antioxidant bioflavonoids.

Food for bugs: Fibre can be useful in our diet as a source of nutrients for healthy bacteria in our stomach and intestine (see prebiotics, pxx). It's therefore added to yoghurts and other fermented products.

Skins: It is the fibre content of potato and other vegetable or fruit skins that makes them particularly good for you. But government advice is to peel fruit and vegetables to avoid pesticide or other chemical residues, so organic produce has an advantage here.

Herbs
Green remedies

WHAT

Herbs have been used since time immemorial to flavour our foods, protect against food poisoning and treat a wide range of ills. Our growing taste for Mediterranean and Asian cooking has meant that all sorts of new herbs and spices have been introduced into western diets, and cooks now use a much broader repertoire of herbs than they did a generation ago. Herbal remedies are also widely available in health food stores and chemists. Herbs range from traditional ones such as sage, thyme, parsley, chamomile, peppermint and basil to more exotic varieties from the east such as ginseng. What's new is that herbs are increasingly popping up in new products, and becoming an important part of the new foods repertoire.

bio-ingredients

HEALTH ISSUES

Before the advent of the modern pharmaceutical industry, they were used as preservatives and medicines. Herbalists learned how to administer them by trial and error over generations, and much of their accumulated, hard-won wisdom turns out to have been remarkably accurate. Part of the secret of herbs' effectiveness is a natural pharmacy of phytochemicals, which can help against an array of health complaints (see chapter 5 for more details).

But be careful not to overdo it. There are numerous naturally occurring compounds in plants we eat that have been shown to cause cancer in experimental animals. And even some plant-based supplements have come under suspicion in recent years.

Here are some of the herbs and herbal products that have been attracting particular attention, and their health benefits:

- *Chamomile:* The dried flowers of chamomile are widely used in teas that are sold as natural digestives, tranquillisers and sleep-promoters. It's caffeine-free, has a long history of successful use and is considered to be extremely safe by herbalists, who even prescribe it to babies with colic or sleep trouble. Chamomile is also a staple ingredient in herbalist's remedies for childhood asthma and eczema.

- *Echinacea*: An old herbal remedy extracted from the purple cornflower, this was once prescribed for everything from 'tired blood' to snake-bite. It's back in the spotlight today as a claimed treatment for colds, flu, chronic fatigue syndrome and weak immune systems. Apparently regular dosing does not make any sense because it exhausts the immune system.

- *Gingko biloba:* Gingko biloba extracts are said to help with problems of the elderly such as depression, headache, ringing in the ears and memory loss. Taken from the ornamental tree whose fruit and nuts have long been prized for their assumed medicinal properties, they are also being used to treat such conditions as asthma and eczema, with promising results.

  Research in Germany suggests that the extracts act as 'vasodilators', increasing blood flow – particularly to the brain. There is also evidence to suggest that they may help mop up free radicals (page 80), which circulate through the blood and can damage cells and lower immunity. But, as with other herbal products, take care to buy from reputable companies. The German tests were carried out on products made and marketed by **Willmar Schwabe**. Some drinks companies are looking at the idea of adding Gingko biloba to their products.

- *Ginseng:* Extracts from this parsnip-shaped root have been used for many thousands of years by Chinese herbalists as a sort of 'fountain of youth'. Talk to some herbalists and you will hear ginseng praised as a treatment for impotence (Louis XIV used it to pump up both his energy and virility), high blood pressure, diabetes, chest-colds and congestion. It's also recommended to ease the pain associated with cocaine withdrawal, to boost the immune system and even to protect against irradiation. Scientists accept that ginseng has stimulant properties, but challenge its reputation as a miracle-worker.

- *Kava kava:* This herb, made from crushed roots, can be used to make an intoxicating drink. **The American Herb Products Association** caution that 'kava', added to juice drinks in the USA and available in capsule form, may affect your ability to drive or operate machinery, but there is no information on products to warn of this effect. This highlights the concern that there are not yet enough controls in place for herbal supplements and additives. A herbalist friend who has tried it says, 'I can guarantee that it does relieve anxiety and stress, but it also renders linear thought impossible!'

- *Spirulina:* Blue-green algae, or *Spirulina*, have become superstars in the field of 'smart foods'. Used as medicines by ancient Chinese herbalists, and harvested by the Aztecs and the Incas, they are packed with nutrients, and easy to absorb.[53] *Spirulina* enthusiasts say that it contains more vegetable protein than any other food on earth, in addition to the antioxidant beta carotene, iron, vitamin B12 and gamma-linoleic acid (GLA). And they may be on to something. When it comes to vitamin B12, for example, *Spirulina* is 2–6 times richer than its nearest rival, raw beef liver.

   Spirulina-based products are seen to be helpful for those who have problems absorbing their food, such as those suffering

bio-ingredients

from chronic fatigue syndrome or severe digestive problems. The **US Cancer Research Institute** has found that chemicals derived from blue-green algae help slow the growth of the AIDS virus – and **NASA** is even testing it as a food for astronauts. Because of their high level of amino acids (page 109), blue-green algae are also being developed as potential brain foods.

There has been recent controversy over one brand of blue-green algae from the USA, because the **UK Consumers' Association** found traces of neurotoxins in some samples.[54] The algae are collected from the wild in Klamath Lake, Oregon, which has been the subject of pollution warnings. Run-off from farming can cause other, toxic algae to grow and – potentially – contaminate the algae used for food.

- *St John's wort:* Made from *Hypericum perforatum*, St John's wort extracts have a long history of medicinal use. Tests show that they are effective as a mild anti-depressant, with few if any side-effects. But mothers should be careful of using such extracts as part of the weaning process if they are also taking anti-depressants, as they seems to amplify the effects and side-effects of anti-depressants. Food manufacturers have seen the potential, and indeed St John's wort has recently been described as 'the most hyped herb'.

- *Valerian:* One plant extract found in many foods comes from valerian. Although the extract used is also found naturally in apples, cocoa, coffee, peaches and strawberries, most of the food-grade material is taken from valerian. It is used in baked foods, candies, ice creams and soft drinks, to help achieve such flavours as butter, butterscotch or rum. Herbalists and health food stores have long promoted valerian roots as a cure for such ailments as insomnia, nervous tension, hysteria and even epileptic fits. Scientists say valerian is a tranquilliser and it's generally thought to be safe for healthy people.

☆ ☆ ☆ ☆ ☆ ☆ ☆ **WHAT'S NEW?** ☆ ☆ ☆ ☆ ☆ ☆ ☆

Herbal ingredients are surfacing in the energy and sports drink sector, and herbs with claims to semi-miraculous properties are also cropping up in a wider range of foods. In the USA, for example, the

bio-ingredients

Hain Food Company offers its *Prescription Kitchen* range of canned soups fortified with herbs such as Echinacea and St John's wort.

Herbal yoghurts: The sort of products we may soon see in the UK are illustrated by the herbal yoghurts launched in New Zealand in 1998. These are 'synbiotics', and come in three different types: one with Echinacea, one with Gingko biloba and one with ginseng. The makers say that the products deliver their benefits when eaten daily over 3–4 weeks.

Spirulina: In countries like New Zealand and the USA, *Spirulina*-enriched drink products are fairly common. In the UK, some drinks bars, such as the one at the Notting Hill organic supermarket **Planet Organic**, serve it and you can buy the *Spirolight Bar*, made by **Life Stream Research**, in health food stores.

St John's wort: Products with added St John's wort include crisps, biscuits, yoghurts and soft drinks. To date, most such products have been launched in the USA, but at least one German yoghurt manufacturer, **Müller,** claims that one of its products containing St John's wort is 'calming and balancing'. Meanwhile, there are plans to introduce to the UK tortilla chips sprayed with St John's wort, which are likely to be advertised as *Happy Crisps*. St John's wort tea, produced by **Heath & Heather**, is already available from UK health food stores, and, as with most herbal remedies, St John's wort supplements are available from chemists.

☆ ☆ ☆ ☆ ☆ ☆ ☆ ☆ ☆ ☆ ☆ ☆ ☆ ☆ ☆ ☆ ☆ ☆ ☆ ☆

Phytochemicals
Natural wonders

WHAT

Any chemical found in a plant is a phytochemical. All the active ingredients in herbs are phytochemicals, but increasingly this term is being used to describe key substances added to functional foods. Scientists are beginning to understand not just the health benefits of different phytochemicals (some of which have been recognised for years), but how they actually work. Because of this, they are likely to

bio-ingredients

be increasingly important ingredients in functional foods, which we will want to understand.

HEALTH ISSUES

Below we look at the most interesting phytochemicals, where they are found and the health effects attributed to them.[55]

Allicin: Found primarily in garlic, onions and chives. It's hoped that allicin may destroy cancer-causing chemicals – particularly those relating to stomach and digestive-tract cancers. Allicin is also thought to lower cholesterol, disinfect the lungs and clean the blood, while boosting immunity.

Caffeine: The best-known phytochemical to date and one that appears in a number of foods. A key ingredient in coffee, tea, chocolate, soft drinks and now even chewing gum, caffeine is a mild stimulant and can boost alertness when energy flags. It is toxic in high doses, causing high blood pressure, heart palpitations, vomiting and even convulsions. It can also sap the body's supply of calcium.

Capsaicin: Found in chillis and peppers, capsaicin is thought to neutralise the cancer-causing agent benzopyrene, created by chargrilling or barbecuing meat.

Catechins: Found in raspberries and strawberries as well as both green and black tea, catechins are thought to reduce cholesterol, boost the immune system and reduce the risk of gastrointestinal cancers. Tea has long been considered a good source, but a recent study has shown that chocolate contains more than three times as much.[56] There is no recommended amount of catechin for protecting against disease, but Japanese research found that animals benefited from drinking the equivalent of ten large cups of tea day.

Chlorogenic acid and P-coumaric acid: These are found in green peppers, pineapple, strawberries and tomatoes. If we consume water or produce containing high levels of nitrates and nitrites, potentially cancer-causing nitrosamines can build up in the gut. Chlorogenic acid stops this from happening. Another way to tackle the problem may be to eat organic produce, where nitrogen fertilisers are not permitted.

Ellagic acid: Found in berries and other fruit, nuts, seeds and vegetables, this is another anti-cancer compound thought to target aflatoxin (a fungal contaminant of nuts) and benzopyrene, caused by char-grilling meat.

Flavonoids and bioflavonoids: Found in beer, coffee, fruits, tea, vegetables and wine, these compounds are thought to reduce the likelihood of breast cancer.

Indoles (including indole-3-carbinol): These compounds are found in broccoli, brussel-sprouts, cabbage, cauliflower, kale and turnips. They protect against cancers of the breast, colon, lung, oesophogus and prostate.

Isoflavones (e.g. genisteen): These are found in soya beans and might reduce the risk of breast cancer (particularly in pre-menopausal women) and prostate cancer, because they are thought to lower blood cholesterol and keep bones strong. In Japan and China, where they eat lots of soya, there is a much lower rate of many diet-related diseases; however, the link with soya consumption is not conclusive, in part because there is also less fat and more fibre in Chinese and Japanese food.

Limonoids: Found particularly in the rinds of citrus fruits, these are thought to boost immunity. They may also reduce the risk of mouth cancer and, as a result, could be added to toothpaste and mouthwashes in the future.

Monoterpenes: These are found in aubergines, broccoli, cabbage, citrus fruits, cucumbers, parsley, peppers, squash and tomatoes. They are antioxidants and boost our immune systems.

Phenethyl isothiocyanate (PEITC): Found in broccoli, brussels sprouts, cabbage, cauliflower and turnips. Tests on animals suggest these may help suppress some types of lung cancer.

Phthalides: Carrots, celery, coriander, dill and parsley all contain these. They are thought to be another effective tool in reducing the body's vulnerability to some cancers.

Phytosterols: Present in soya beans, these are thought to slow down the absorption of cholesterol and may also protect against cancer.

bio-ingredients

Sulphoraphane: Broccoli, brussels sprouts, kale and turnips are good sources of sulphoraphane, which has been discovered to help neutralise some cancer-causing compounds.

Triterpenoids: Found in citrus fruits and soy products, including tofu, these are thought to help reduce the risk of breast cancer.

☆ ☆ ☆ ☆ ☆ ☆ ☆ **WHAT'S NEW?** ☆ ☆ ☆ ☆ ☆ ☆ ☆

Decafs and supercafs: The spectrum of caffeine levels in coffees, teas and other products is opening out all the time. Some of us prefer complete decaffeination and others super-caffeination.

Three different chemicals may be used to decaffeinate coffee: methylene chloride, ethyl acetate and a combination of water with either carbon dioxide or coffee oils. Methylene chloride, historically the preferred method, has been under suspicion for some time as a possible carcinogen. Although very small traces are left in the final coffee, many producers are now shifting to alternatives.

Meanwhile, research is being done to produce non-caffeinated GM coffee beans. One of the problems manufacturers have at the moment is that when you remove the caffeine, you also remove some of the flavour, and the aim is obviously to produce coffee with both good taste and low caffeine. Scientists at the University of Hawaii chased the gene for seven years. When they found it, they also discovered the enzyme responsible for making caffeine – and promptly found a way to neutralise it. It will be some years before GM non-caffeinated coffee is in our supermarkets, however.

GM techniques could also, presumably, produce super-caffeinated food and drink products. Among current products super-caffeinated by conventional methods are some soft drinks and chewing gums.

Benecol: As we have seen, the active ingredients in this and other cholesterol-lowering products are phytochemicals, more specifically plant stenol esters (page 68).

Miracle soya: As with other phytochemicals, the quality of isoflavones depends on the way in which they have been processed. Poor processing of soya beans can destroy isoflavines. The best source is the whole soya bean, with soya milk and flour coming second. Capsules of soya isoflavones appear to be the least effective.[57]

bio-ingredients

There are a number of branded products which promote the benefits of soya. They include *Provamel* organic soya milk and *Provamel* yoghurt (a blend of fermented soya beans); *Burgen Bread*, made by **Allied Foods**, introduced 1997 and also containing linseed; **Tofutti's** soy *Khero*; and the *Preva Bar*, which has been launched with a claim to increase cancer-fighting substances in the blood and reduce the risk of breast, ovary and prostate cancer. The makers of the *Preva Bar* also claim that it can help with osteoporosis and the menopause – and reduce cholesterol levels.[58] It will be amazing if they deliver on all these promises.

GM Spotlight

IS GM SOYA LESS HEALTHY?

- GM soya may be less effective in fighting disease and promoting health. Recent research suggests that GM soya contains between 12 per cent and 14 per cent less phytoestrogens than non-GM soya.[59]

Proteins and amino acids
Building blocks

WHAT

We humans are largely made of protein. Our hair, nails, skin, blood, hormones and enzymes are all protein. Indeed, our bodies contain an estimated 10,000–50,000 different types of protein. All of them, in turn, are made up of amino acids – which our body needs for growth and repair, as well as for the production of antibodies, enzymes and hormones.

WHERE

Good sources of complete protein are meat and dairy products, poultry and eggs, and fish. Good sources of incomplete proteins include beans (including soya), peas, peanuts, grains and potatoes.

bio-ingredients

HEALTH ISSUES:

For a healthy diet, we need two different types of protein: 'complete' proteins (which contain all the amino acids we need) and 'incomplete' proteins (which lack one or more of the essential amino acids).

There is no evidence of protein deficiency in the UK. In fact there is concern that excessive protein consumption is associated with weakening bones (through calcium loss), and a worsening of kidney disease in patients with the condition.[60]

Those on vegetarian diets, however, need to be careful to achieve the right mix of proteins. They need the right combination of incomplete proteins to get all the essential amino acids necessary for health. This may be done by eating dried beans and rice, for example, or pea soup with bread.

☆ ☆ ☆ ☆ ☆ ☆ ☆ **WHAT'S NEW?** ☆ ☆ ☆ ☆ ☆ ☆ ☆

Meaty muscles: Growing numbers of sportsmen and women are taking the amino acid creatine, to help build up their muscles. Lean beef, pork and fish such as tuna, salmon and cod, contain up to 3 g of creatine per pound, but some athletes are taking massive doses – equivalent to eating 25-30 steaks a day. Available as a powder, as tablets or even as chewing gum, creatine works by giving muscles extra food when they are nearing exhaustion.

Quorn: High in protein and fibre, low in fat, and vegetarian, this new food is based on a fungus that was originally found in a field near food giant **Rank Hovis McDougall's** High Wycombe laboratories, after a world-wide search for a micro-organism able to turn starch-based raw materials into a meat substitute. Fed on glucose syrup made from wheat and potatoes, together with a range of other nutrients, the fungus produces cells which can then be coloured, textured and 'woven' into passable imitations of fish, chicken and meat. Commonly used as a meat-free alternative for vegetarians, it's now made into a growing range of products, including 'burgers', 'sausages' and ready-made meals. It ranks alongside grilled beef in its level of nutritional value – and is low in the sort of fats that cause health problems.

Marlow Foods, one of the companies behind *Quorn*, told us that the product 'is not a product of genetic manipulation'. They also noted that 'all the other ingredients used are purchased by us to a specification which requires that they are not genetically modified.' However, ready meals containing *Quorn* may still contain other GM ingredients.

The basic *Quorn* line was dropped by **Out of This World** ethical supermarket because eggs used in the product were not free-range.

GM Spotlight

GM-FREE PROTEIN?

- Amino acid supplements added to many foods are being made using GM techniques.
- Hydrolysed vegetable protein (HVP), also called Texturised Vegetable Protein (TVP), and tofu, used as protein sources by vegetarians, are made with soya (which could be GM). But work is going on both to make an 'all natural' HVP and to make it GM-free.

Tofu: The Japanese word for soya-bean curd. This ancient Asian food was introduced in the USA in the 1960s, when it became a leading vegetarian 'hippy' food. It's widely available, versatile and recommended as an excellent source of protein, iron, phosphorus and potassium. At the same time, it is low in calories and saturated fat, and contains a minimal quantity of sodium and no cholesterol.

Tryptophan: Tryptophan is an essential amino acid found in meat, eggs, fresh and dried fruit, hot milk, bananas, low-fat cheese, bread and peanut butter. Foods rich in tryptophan can help boost our serotonin levels, which can lift depression. It's probably no coincidence that many people crave sweet foods when they are feeling 'down', because these foods release tryptophan as they are digested.

In the form of L-tryptophan, it is taken as a 'natural sleeping pill' and supplement to combat depression and pre-menstrual syndrome, but this has been the subject of a major health scare in the USA (see box overleaf). The strange relationship between L-tyrosine and L-tryptophan in the brain is explained on page 112.

bio-ingredients

EMS

THE ODD CASE OF L-TRYPTOPHAN

One case often mentioned by opponents of GM foods is that of L-tryptophan as a dietary supplement. In 1989 an epidemic of a painful and debilitating new disease hit users of L-tryptophan in the USA. The disease, eosinophilia myalgia syndrome (EMS), made 1,500 people ill and resulted in 31 deaths. The **FDA** then withdrew the product from the American market.[61]

The batch of tryptophan implicated in the EMS outbreak was traced back to a leading Japanese company, **Showa Denko**, which had recently introduced GM bacteria into its production process. This raised the obvious question of whether the genetic engineering step itself might not be to blame.

It transpired that the **FDA** had initially failed to disclose that genetic engineering had been used, for fear of a public backlash against biotechnology in general. Even when media pressure eventually forced disclosure, there was a surprising lack of co-operation from **Showa Denko** itself. The company refused to supply **FDA** investigators with a sample batch of the GM organism for further analysis, and when the investigators asked to visit the production facility, they were told it had been closed down. The result is that real uncertainties remain: no link has been proved between L-tryptophan and EMS, but then again the link has not been disproved. Such lack of transparency at the company level can backfire on the industry as a whole.

In this chapter, we have covered most of the hidden and complex ingredients found in the foods we eat. Some of them are vital to good health, some detrimental. All of these ingredients will be affected by (and used in) new foods. Some, like insecticide residues, will become less common, particularly if organic foods become increasingly popular. Some will become more common, like the vitamins used in many functional foods. Knowing what is in our food is a key first step in deciding what to buy as we walk along the supermarket shelves, which is where we are headed next.

bio-ingredients

4

ALONG THE SHELVES

Product by Product

Supermarket shopping has had such a profound impact on the way that most of us think about food that it's often easiest to focus on the issues by walking along the shelves. In this chapter we investigate all the major types of food, including fruit and vegetables, meat and fish, dairy products, oils and spreads, processed foods and drinks. As we do so, we highlight what is happening today and what might happen tomorrow for the new foods trio. We also cross-link products to our coverage of ingredients in chapter 3 (Ingredient Watch) and diets in chapter 5 (Personalised Menus), and spotlight brands, companies and other organisations that are leaders or laggards.

FRUIT AND VEGETABLES

There is often more in our fruit and vegetables than meets the eye as we browse the shelves. No fresh fruit or vegetable currently on the market in the UK will have been genetically modified, at least as we now understand the phrase. However, GM fresh tomatoes are already available in the USA, and other fruit and vegetables are likely to follow (see individual fruit and vegetable entries). On the other hand, for fresh fruit and vegetables on sale in the UK there is the growing concern that some may have been cross-pollinated by GM crops..

However you look at them, fruit and vegetables are dietary superstars. Indeed, almost all the personalised menus in chapter 5 recommend them for one reason or another. And increasingly, functional foods are using different plant compounds as their star ingredients. We look at some of the fruit and vegetables that might be used for this purpose and what substances the functional food manufacturers might be looking for.

There is no substitute for eating a diet packed with fruit and vegetables. Only a small proportion of the vitamins and minerals they contain are available in pill form, and, more importantly, the nutritional benefits of some ingredients are boosted when eaten alongside others. For a fuller discussion of vitamins, see chapter 3.

One big worry about fruit and vegetables focuses on the huge quantities of pesticides used in growing them. In chapter 2 we looked at the issue of pesticide residues; later in this section we look at organophosphates, a particularly worrying class of pesticide sometimes still permitted for use on fruit and vegetables.

Finally, it's worth noting that the more picky we are about the size and shape of the produce we buy as consumers, and the further our fruit and vegetables have to travel, the more waste there will be. Ponder this: up to 40 per cent of soft fruit and vegetables are thrown away because of damage done during harvesting and transport. In chapter 6 we debate the food miles issue.

FRUIT

Apples and pears

Locally grown apples are still hard to find in UK supermarkets. One supermarket that is pioneering in this field is **Sainsbury's**: in stores local to the area, they sell apples from the **National Fruit Collection** at Brogdale, home to some 2,300 different varieties of apple tree – and well worth a visit. And **Common Ground's** annual *Apple Day* also encourages us to celebrate the country's traditional apple orchards and apple varieties.

■ **GM**: Yes, it's on its way to your fruit bowl. Among the GM traits being developed for apples and pears are disease resistance (using the Bt gene, page 14), slower ripening and reduced browning when the fruit is cut.

◆ **FUNCTIONAL**: An apple a day keeps the doctor away, they used to say. Given the apple's healthy reputation, it seems inevitable that food scientists will try to exploit these properties.

The food industry is meanwhile trying other tricks: take the way that some fruit goes brown shortly after you bite or cut into it, which is pretty unappetising. One approach to this problem, pioneered in Australia, is the so-called *Snack Apple*, which is a ready-peeled apple covered with a coating that stops it from turning brown.

● **ORGANIC**: It's an astounding fact that up to 50 different chemical pesticides are used on apples alone. In the growing season, non-organic apples and pears are sprayed up to three times a week. Even the government officially advises us to peel apples to avoid the resulting residues. Unfortunately, the highest levels of vitamins are found just under the skin.

Bananas

These days, entire economies risk slipping on banana skins. Indeed, this delicious fruit has recently been at the centre of a hard-fought trade war between the USA and Europe. Some critics of the GM food industry suspect that the USA has fought this issue with such intensity because a defeat would make the introduction of tomorrow's GM food products even more difficult.

■ **GM**: GM techniques promise to slow the banana ripening and rotting processes, easing shipping pressures and – possibly – enhancing flavour. As with other fruit, work is also under way to develop GM bananas, which are able to resist some of the fungal diseases that can have such a devastating impact on the commercial plantations where most of them are grown.

◆ **FUNCTIONAL**: Bananas are being developed that would give us the painless equivalent of an injection. One company is also developing a GM banana that contains a vaccine for hepatitis B.[62]

● **ORGANIC**: Conventional banana plantations are allowed to use considerable quantities of pesticides, including organophosphates. Ironically, some of these chemicals are banned for use on other crops in the western countries that are the main consumers of the bananas.

Banana plantations account for the fact that Costa Rica is the world's largest user (per head of population) of agrochemicals, and there have been innumerable cases where low-paid plantation workers have been poisoned by the toxic chemicals they apply to the plants. Plastic bags wrapped around the undeveloped fruit to protect it as it grows, end up infused with pesticides. Even the banana's thick skin is not protection enough against residues

Happily, organic bananas are becoming much more widely available. The UK-based organisation **Banana Link** campaigns on all banana-related issues, such as fair trade, the misuse of pesticides and worker safety.

In an extraordinary recent development, **Sainsbury's** has announced a long-term partnership with the Windward Islands, to encourage them to provide what **Sainsbury's** customers want – top quality organic exotic fruit. Part of this project is to investigate the possibility of converting an entire island to organic production for the supermarket with a dedicated area on each of the other three islands for the same purpose.

Blueberries

◆ **FUNCTIONAL:** Blueberries were recently named 'Fruit of the Year' in one American magazine, because of their rich content of antioxidants (page 78). One group of antioxidant substances are the anthocyanins, the word coming from the Greek for 'plant' and 'blue', which are responsible for the intense blue and red colours found in wild blueberries.[63] Apparently one cup of blueberries has enough antioxidants to improve balance, coordination and short-term memory.[64]

Citrus Fruits

■ **GM:** Among the early targets for scientists working on GM oranges is fruit that would be pest- and disease-resistant, pipless and/or easier to peel. Biologists developing the pipless fruit, in Australia and Japan, have identified a particular gene that causes plants to destroy the seeds in their own fruit. Among the difficulties they face in getting citrus fruits to go pipless is that if the gene switches into action too soon the fruit might not even form – or it might fall off the tree before fully ripened.[65]

● **ORGANIC:** It's a sad fact that even the most succulently natural-looking citrus fruits may have been treated with problem chemicals. For example, artificial colouring may have been used on the skin of some Florida oranges, even though studies have shown that the Citrus Red 2 additive used can cause cancer in laboratory animals.

By contrast, organic citrus fruits are not treated with fungicides, nor do they use edible waxes, such as shellac – an insect secretion – or beeswax. Organic lemons should be kept in the fridge and used within 2–3 weeks. Organic grapefruit usually last longer.[66]

Dried fruit (currants, raisins, sultanas etc.)

■ **GM:** Did you know that vegetable oils are used to coat all non-organic dried fruit, to stop it sticking together? This oil, made by an American company, typically contains soya oil or cotton seed oil, either of which may come from GM sources. In the light of current concerns about GM foods, it seems likely that a guaranteed non-GM oil will be developed that can be used for coating dried fruits. Ask your favourite supermarket what they are doing in this area.

◆ **FUNCTIONAL:** Among the best sources of antioxidants are prunes and raisins. So, for example, a raisin snack of around 100 grams (two-thirds of a cup) provides more than half the daily intake of antioxidants needed for a significant preventative effect.[67]

● **ORGANIC:** Organic dried fruit is either not coated (which makes it more likely to be sticky and clump together) or is coated with sunflower oil – which apparently has a detectable flavour that some people don't like. These products are also likely to be slightly darker than normal dried fruits, because they have not been processed with sulphur dioxide (E220), a preservative that can trigger allergies in some people. Organic dried fruit brands include *Allos* and *Tropical Wholefoods*.

Exotic fruit

■ **GM:** We are very likely to see a growing range of exotic fruits being modified. Papayas, for example, are now being modified for virus resistance in the USA, and GM techniques are being developed for the slow ripening of such fruit as mangos, nectarines, peaches and pineapples, which will enhance their flavour and increase their shelf-life.

● **ORGANIC:** Organic exotic fruits, such as the kiwi fruit, are now quite widely available, but most of them will have been imported – raising the 'food miles' issue (page 258). Surprisingly, organic kiwi fruit is sometimes even cheaper than non-organic. **Sainsbury's** partnership with the Windward Isles (see Bananas) is in part to expand the range of organic exotic fruit on offer.

Melons

■ **GM:** The smell and taste of sun-ripened melons can be quite extraordinary, but these wonderful fruit also go off very quickly. Although they are not on sale in the UK as yet, GM cantaloupe and chantelais

fruit & vegetables

melons have already been produced with a view to slowing the ripening process. And on the GM menu of the future, apparently, are mini-melons without seeds.[68]

Soft fruits

■ **GM**: Like most of the fruits already discussed, soft fruits like raspberries and strawberries are likely to be genetically modified to slow their ripening – and to protect them against fungal diseases and other pests.

The genes responsible for the sweetness, tartness and smell of strawberries have already been discovered. The scientists involved want to develop berries that taste sweeter and richer, and smell more appetising.[69] This makes sense as long as people continue to want such fruits out of season, when they generally are pretty tasteless. Interestingly, however – and in the wake of the GM food controversy – scientists are planning ways of using their knowledge about which gene does what to get the qualities they want through traditional plant breeding methods rather than by GM.

● **ORGANIC**: However hard you look, organically grown raspberries and strawberries are difficult to find. This is of particular concern given that methyl bromide, a highly toxic fungicide and also a 'class 1' ozone-depleter, is still permitted to be used on those fruits in the UK, although in some countries it's no longer allowed. Methyl bromide should not leave harmful residues on the fruit, but its wider impact on the environment is a real problem.

When you are buying and storing organic soft fruit, remember that it will probably not keep as long as the ordinary version, because it will not have been treated with fungicides.

Tomatoes

Although strictly a fruit, see Vegetables.

VEGETABLES AND HERBS

Yes, we know they are good for us. Indeed, there have been increasingly frantic attempts to get children to eat up their vegetables. Not long ago, for example, **Iceland Frozen Foods** and the **Cancer Research Campaign** launched a range of flavoured vegetables. The *Wacky Veg* range (not GM) included baked-bean-flavoured peas, cheese-and-onion-flavoured cauliflower florets, pizza-flavoured sweetcorn and chocolate-flavoured carrots. A brave attempt, but in the event it did not revolutionise our children's eating habits and the range was withdrawn.

In the USA, meanwhile, they are developing super-nutritious vegetables using a range of selective breeding and GM techniques. Scientists have come up with a maroon carrot at **Texas A&M's Vegetable Improvement Center**, for example, which is called *Betasweet* – and contains twice as much beta-carotene as normal carrots.[70]

They have also developed an onion loaded with quercetin (which can help prevent stomach cancer) and peppers with added beta-carotene, vitamin C and quercetin. Other 'superveggies' in the pipeline include beet with boosted folic acid and varieties of corn and broccoli brimming over with vitamins A and E.

The companies involved in such research – among them **Gerber Products** (owned by Swiss-based **Novartis**), **Kraft Foods** and **Monsanto** – are convinced that the nutritional content of vegetables will be a key issue in the next decade. The question is whether people will like the idea of GM functional vegetables, with boosted nutritional contents, or whether they will prefer organic offerings which, it's claimed, naturally contain more nutrients than the non-organic alternatives.

Beans

◆ FUNCTIONAL: The humble broad bean may, it turns out, help prevent bowel cancer, the second deadliest form of cancer in the western world.[71] A protein called lectin seems to be the active principle, stopping pre-cancerous cells in the body from multiplying. (This 'lectin effect' may be one of the reasons why diets rich in fruit and vegetables help protect against cancer.) Expect future functional versions of the broad bean genetically engineered to offer higher lectin levels, while lectin itself may begin to turn up in other foods.

Brassica

■ **GM:** There now is real interest in the GM world in modifying a range of brassica varieties. While pest-resistant varieties are, of course, being developed, varieties of broccoli with boosted anti-cancer properties are also being researched. If this proves successful, the plan is to apply the same techniques to other vegetables, such as Chinese cabbage, turnips and salad rocket.

GM brussels sprouts containing a snowdrop gene to repel pest caterpillars and aphids are being field tested in Holland, and have been targeted by anti-GM protesters.

It turns out that the brassica family are a pretty promiscuous bunch. In theory it's quite possible for them to cross-pollinate with GM oil seed rape, which is part of the same family. In practice, however, this is unlikely to happen because rape seed crops are normally harvested well before most other brassicas flower, which is when cross-pollination could occur.

◆ **FUNCTIONAL:** President George Bush may not have been alone in disliking broccoli, but it turns out that it is a natural functional food, rich in healthy ingredients. For example, eating broccoli is thought to cause at least some pre-cancerous cells in the body to 'self-destruct'. If the GM work outlined above succeeds, it seems likely that the broccoli of the future could be given an even wider spectrum of preventative or curative properties.

● **ORGANIC:** Non-organic brassicas may be sprayed several times with pesticides during growing. In particular, organophosphates (page 126) are commonly used on broccoli and cabbages.

Frozen fruit and vegetables

Many of us assume that fresh produce is always more nutritious than frozen. Surprisingly much of the 'fresh' fruit and vegetables we buy will contain fewer nutrients, such as vitamin C, than frozen food. By the time food has been picked, transported, sold and then cooked, it will have deteriorated far more than food that was frozen soon after it was picked.

■ **GM:** Future crop plants are likely to be genetically modified to ensure that they freeze and unfreeze well.

◆ **FUNCTIONAL:** Among the functional ingredients likely to be added to frozen vegetables is folic acid.

● **ORGANIC:** Frozen food producers tend to like their vegetables to be as near perfect as possible, so the chances are that they will have used a fair amount of crop protection chemicals in the process. If you are looking for organic alternatives, the *Whole Earth* brand range includes frozen organic broccoli, carrots, peas and sweetcorn, and other organic brands are now available at some mainstream supermarkets, including *ODC Organic* made by **Oerlemans Foods UK Ltd**, which is sold through **Tesco**.

Herbs

■ **GM:** As far as we can discover, no GM technology is used to produce either fresh or dried herbs, but it seems only a matter of time before things go in this direction, either to protect vulnerable plants like parsley against pests and diseases, or to boost a particular herb's functional properties.

◆ **FUNCTIONAL:** Herbs have long been recognised as a healthy element of any diet (see the Bio-Ingredients section of chapter 3). Once again, you could see them as nature's functional foods, partly because of the extraordinary number of phytochemicals (page 105) they contain. Many of these substances are antioxidants, which help prevent cancer, but you will find in herbals that these plants are also used to prevent or cure an astonishing range of illnesses.

● **ORGANIC:** Herbs may be healthy, but don't assume that they are all organic. Remember, too, that some dried herbs were an early target for irradiation (page 63). If you are looking for organic herbs, **Kitchen Garden** produce a wide range of fresh and dried herbs, and **Hambledon Herbs** offer an extensive range through mail order.

Mushrooms

■ **GM:** The compost used to grow non-organic mushrooms is usually based on manures from animals fed on a proportion of GM crop-based feed – not something to get unduly worried about.

● **ORGANIC:** Part of the attraction of organic produce is obviously what the producers don't use. In addition to GM compost, producers of non-organic mushrooms might use chemical pesticides, chlorinated water for disease-control and formaldehyde for sterilisation. They may also employ methyl bromide (see Soft Fruits above) as a fungicide, and treat composts with fungicides once the harvest is complete. *Chesswood Produce* is the main UK brand of organic mushrooms and these are widely available.

Onions and garlic

Onions and garlic have long been known to be good for you, but the evidence just keeps building.

■ **GM:** It may be happening, but we haven't heard of GM garlic, leeks or onions. They are obvious candidates for future GM functional products.

◆ **FUNCTIONAL:** Eating garlic has a real – positive – impact on your health. Among other things, it can act as an antibiotic, tackle hypertension and lower cholesterol. Research has also now shown that eating 18 grams (less than an ounce) of garlic a week can help protect against cancer. A clove weighs approximately 3 grams, so to eat a clove (not a bulb!) of garlic each day, cooked or raw, should be enough. People who eat this amount of garlic are proved to be 30 per cent less likely to develop colon cancer and 50 per cent less likely to develop stomach cancer, according to research in China, Italy and the USA.[72]

● **ORGANIC:** One problem with organic onions is that, because they are untreated, they may sprout faster. If you can, keep them dry and ventilated – advice that applies to all stored onions.

Potatoes

■ **GM:** GM potatoes designed to provide a higher starch content are already on sale in the USA. Developed by companies like **DuPont** and **Monsanto**, these potatoes are used primarily for chip frying – and the higher starch content means that they absorb less fat. It is not yet legal to import GM potatoes into Europe, although in April 1999 suspicions were raised that GM potatoes for chips or crisps might have been illegally imported because of a European potato shortage.

In addition to the direct GM issues, mashed potato products may contain GM emulsifiers and riboflavin. Chipped potatoes may also be coated with corn starch and monosodium glutamate, and fried in GM vegetable oils.

In one extraordinary development, signalling possible future trends, German genetic engineers accidentally created the world's largest potato, weighing in at 3.2kg (just over 7 lbs). They managed this feat by putting a yeast gene into the potato plants.[73]

GM potatoes are also being developed as a source of the hepatitis B vaccine.[74]

● **ORGANIC:** Non-organic potatoes are sprayed with chemicals while they are growing and – to make them last longer – once they have been harvested. Unfortunately, residues are often found in the potato skin, which is where much of the goodness is. Organic potatoes have also been found to contain a quarter more zinc than chemically grown varieties.[75] If you are interested in digging deeper into the world of organic potatoes, the **National Centre for Organic Gardening** (also known as the **Henry Doubleday Research Association, HDRA**) has an annual *Potato Day*, when they display a fascinating range of potato varieties.

Root vegetables

■ **GM:** To date, we're not aware of GM root crops being sold in the UK, but many root crops, particularly sugar beet, have been engineered in laboratories, and in July 1999 field trials of sugar beet in the UK were targeted by protestors who tore them up.

◆ **FUNCTIONAL:** Existing root vegetables have at least some functional ingredients, for example the beta-carotene found in orange vegetables like carrots and swedes.

Most of us have been taught that raw carrots are better for us than cooked ones, because cooking – and particularly boiling – vegetables can remove the vitamins. However, new research suggests that cooking releases disease-fighting chemicals and makes vegetables easier to digest. Recent research also suggests that the antioxidants found in carrots are better absorbed when they have been softened by cooking.

● **ORGANIC:** Non-organic carrots are commonly treated with organophosphates and carrots are not infrequently found to exceed maximum residue levels (MRLs) in tests.

Organophosphates

NERVOUS SYSTEMS

Among the most controversial pesticides are organophosphates, often referred to as OPs. Some of their effects include damage to the nervous system, with headaches, excessive sweating, breathing difficulty, vomiting, blurred vision, slurred speech, slow thinking and loss of memory listed among the early symptoms. Later come convulsions, coma and even – in extreme cases – death.[76]

Nor are these theoretical risks. OPs are under suspicion because of the number of cases of farm or plantation workers being poisoned every year. They are commonly used on a variety of fruit and vegetables, including apples, bananas, carrots, cabbages, broccoli, mushrooms, soft fruits and potatoes. Indeed 400 tonnes of OPs were used on British crops in 1996[77], accounting for about 60 per cent of the arable insecticide market. They are even used in common or garden slug pellets. OP residues are also regularly detected in our food.

The **Pesticides Trust** has drawn up a list of branded products containing OPs, which they plan to update. They are not alone in arguing that OPs should be banned. The **Organophosphate (OP) Information Network**, set up in 1992, is a small, independent organisation campaigning to raise awareness about ill-health related to OP exposure and support victims of exposure.

Salad vegetables

■ **GM:** Chicory is one salad crop plant that has already been modified. Some varieties have been engineered for increased herbicide resistance, and chicory that does not seed has also been produced.

The traditional English round lettuce, first grown some 6,000 years ago by the Egyptians, is also going GM. Researchers have found ways to make these lettuces faster growing, curlier, crunchier and less likely to wilt.[78]

Other vegetables that could be improved in the same way include cabbages and spinach. It's only a matter of time before GM techniques will be used to boost pest resistance and to slow the ripening of most salad and other green vegetables, at least in the laboratory.

● **ORGANIC:** Chemical residues are found in almost all non-organic celery, and multiple residues are common in other salad vegetables. There are seasonal variations in the level of residues. Winter lettuces, for example, are more likely to test positive for residues than summer ones.

A recent controversy has focused on the fact that supermarkets have been washing their organic salad vegetables – as well as conventional produce – with sodium hypochlorite, a chlorine-based chemical. It's only fair to say that it is also used to sterilise babies' bottles, and is considered harmless; but there are alternatives, and it's not permitted for organic foods. Supermarkets were given until the end of 1999 to switch to alternatives. One reason for the use of this disinfectant is the packaging of many salad vegetables in plastic, which may encourage bacteria to breed.[79]

Squash, marrows, courgettes

◆ **FUNCTIONAL:** Orange-coloured squashes such as pumpkins are a rich source of beta-carotene.

● **ORGANIC:** Non-organic squashes tend to be treated far less than other vegetables, and residues are not generally detected.[80]

Sweetcorn

■ **GM**: Given the extent of GM work on maize (page 52), it seems inevitable that we will see GM sweetcorn on sale here early in the 21st century. Maize is used in a vast number of food ingredients, which is why it has been in the GM spotlight. To date, most of the genetic modification of maize has been designed to boost insect resistance, and a key issue is therefore whether commercially grown GM maize could cross-pollinate with organic farm (or garden-grown) sweetcorn.

● **ORGANIC**: If current trends continue, it may eventually be hard to find non-GM corn, but organic sweetcorn is available from **Whole Earth Foods**.

Tinned vegetables

■ **GM**: Some tinned vegetables have added colouring, which may be GM.

● **ORGANIC**: Tinned vegetables are unlikely to be first choice for health-focused consumers, because beneficial nutrients are lost in the tinning process. But the range of organic options is opening out even here, and includes *Biona* (beans), *Bionova*, *Campo*, *Danival*, *Just Wholefoods*, *Kitchen Garden*, *La Bio-Idea*, *Organico*, *Organic Valley* (good quality and inexpensive beans) and *Suma*.

Tomatoes

■ **GM**: Fresh GM tomatoes with a longer shelf life are already available in the USA, but in the UK they have only been sold only as tomato purée. Government approval for GM peeled and canned tomatoes – which sell in the same huge quantities in the UK as baked beans – has been sought.

Tomatoes with Bt-based pest resistance are being tested, and, perhaps most controversially, frost-resistant tomatoes have been genetically engineered using genes from a fish, the flounder. It's widely accepted, however, that the public is unlikely to welcome the transfer of animal genes to plants.

Possible longer-term risks are that GM tomatoes – at least in theory – could cross-pollinate with potatoes, which belong to the same plant family. More likely, perhaps, GM tomatoes developed in laboratories may spread their seed through human excreta. Scientists at one laboratory were photographed eating their GM produce and then chastised because the tomato seeds could 'escape' via the sewage system. However, it turned out that they were actually eating ordinary tomatoes. The anti-GM lobby has taken this as further proof of the attempts by scientists to dupe the public into believing GM produce is safe.

Who knows where all this will lead? One recent report from Xinhua celebrated the fact that Chinese scientists have developed a tomato plant reminiscent of Jack & the Bean Stalk. It grows to 10 metres – and fruits as early as February! Meanwhile, in Wuhan, also in China, they have produced tomatoes smaller than ping-pong balls that can be kept on the shelf ten times longer than ordinary tomatoes.

◆ **FUNCTIONAL**: Lycopene in tomatoes is what gives them their attractive red colour. As we've seen, scientists now also believe that lycopene can help protect against cancer, particularly prostate cancer in men. Some future functional foods may achieve their effects via certain substances added in processing, but there is growing interest in developing GM tomatoes with increased levels of lycopene, as well as in introducing it into other plants.

Studies funded by **Heinz Canada** showed that eating processed tomatoes – in ketchup, tomato sauce or tomato juice, for example – may be an even more effective way of raising your blood levels of lycopene than eating fresh tomatoes.[81]

● **ORGANIC**: Commercially grown non-organic tomatoes are frequently produced hydroponically in greenhouses with their roots in *Rockwool* (the same material used as insulation in many of our house walls). All the fertiliser, nutrients and water the plant needs to grow and fruit are then streamed through the *Rockwool*. It may be a cunning idea, but organic criteria do not permit tomatoes to be grown in this way.

Tomatoes grown in soil have a higher mineral content, and may therefore also taste better. Organic tomatoes have been found in tests to contain 25 per cent more vitamin A than chemically grown varieties and five times as much calcium.

NUTS AND PULSES

Organic commodity products like beans, nuts and pulses are widely available as company own-label brands.

Beans

■ **GM:** To date, GM beans are not on the market here, but GM research is under way to see if the nitrogen-fixing properties of beans and peas can be transferred to other plants. This makes the soil more fertile, and would benefit farmers by reducing the need for chemical fertilisers.

● **ORGANIC:** Organic beans have long been a succulent feature of European summers. Happily, fresh organic beans are available throughout the summer in the UK. **Kitchen Garden** produce organic soya beans, and organic brands of tinned baked beans include *Biona, Bionova, De Rit, Organic Valley* and *Whole Earth*. **Suma** produce organic tinned chick peas, haricot beans and red kidney beans.

Nuts

■ **GM:** GM technology may not yet be used on uncoated and unflavoured nuts, but coated nuts may contain lycopene, used as a food colouring. Some varieties of walnuts have been experimentally engineered for pest resistance. The importance of nuts in our diet and their relatively high commercial value make it almost inevitable that more varieties will be modified in the coming years.

As we have seen, one major worry about using GM techniques on nuts focuses on the fact that some nuts can trigger intense allergic reactions in certain people. It's feared that there is a real risk of creating new allergens, or of spreading known allergens into foods where consumers would not normally expect to find them.

In one case, a GM soya bean was created using a gene from a Brazil nut to boost its protein content. Unfortunately, it turned out that people who were allergic to the albumin of the Brazil nut were also allergic to the GM soya bean. In this case, the bean was not intended for direct human consumption, but there was at least a risk that the allergen could have ended up in the human food chain. This risk is real and the health consequences potentially fatal.

◆ **FUNCTIONAL:** The food industry is certain to try to enhance the existing health benefits of nuts. Already, for example, we are hearing of nuts with boosted calcium levels.[82]

Almonds, like many other nuts, are a complex mix of plant-based protein, monunsaturated fats, fibre, and a variety of micro-nutrients and phytochemicals, which has led some doctors to believe they may play a key role in preventing colon cancer, and laboratory tests seem to have confirmed the hunch. They are also particularly rich in calcium.[83]

Unexpectedly, too, eating peanuts and mixed nuts may help us control cholesterol and shed the pounds, according to new research.[84] The key may be that higher fat diets containing more monounsaturated fats may be as effective in slowing or reversing weight gain as low-fat diets. And nuts are pretty good at satisfying hunger.

Rice

Rice cultivation is the world's single largest market for agrochemicals. As the world's population grows, the demand for rice grows with it, but the land available for rice production is likely to shrink – because of the spread of cities and industrialisation. This was the main reason for the 'Green Revolution' in Third World countries – an intensive effort over decades to boost the productivity of rice crops, which are a staple food for millions of the world's poor.

■ **GM:** At present no GM rice, as such, is permitted in the UK. But it is high on the list of crops being trialed for widespread genetic modification.

Among the research projects underway, one is concentrating on developing a new super-high-protein rice that contains genes from peas. In Japan, too, several companies are working on rice modified so as not to trigger allergies in sensitive people, and there is also Japanese work on rice strains that would actively help lower cholesterol levels in the blood.[85] In China, scientists say they have developed strains that enable them to grow high-yield rice 'on the boundless stretches of the Gobi desert'.[86]

One variety of rice has been genetically modified with a gene taken from daffodils so that it produces higher level of beta-carotene.[87] The hope here is that the fortified GM rice could save millions of children in the Third World from blindness and other potentially life-threatening diseases, among them measles and chronic diarrhoea. In China and India alone it's estimated that some 250 million pre-school children suffer from vitamin A deficiency.

The critical dependence of many developing countries on rice makes this an area where the food politics could be explosive. One American company has already been in conflict with both Indian and Pakistan producers of 'basmati' rice, who fear that the company is trying to lay claim to their rice variety by patenting similar new strains and stopping anyone else from selling them all.

● ORGANIC: With the global spread of 'Green Revolution' techniques, based on an increased use of artificial fertilisers and pesticides, it became much harder to find genuinely organic rice. But such is the recent demand that the range of organic brands is widening and includes *Country Harvest*, *Fior Di Riso*, *Just Wholefoods*, *Watermill* and *Whole Earth*, as well as lots of own-label products.

MEAT AND FISH

Vegetarianism may be on the rise, but the world still eats a phenomenal – and growing – amount of meat and fish. And new technologies have huge implications for both.

These days farmers and cattle breeders are learning to surf through cyberspace to buy and sell cattle – and to find the best bull semen. Breeders can now select semen in terms of a whole range of criteria, including cow stature, rump angle, udder depth, teat placement and 'even central ligament, which is the closest thing you can get to cleavage on a cow'.[88]

It has even been claimed that the days of the bull may be numbered. A new technique would enable farmers to pre-select semen that was likely to produce female calves using artificial insemination techniques, which would dramatically reduce the number of unwanted bull calves slaughtered each year.

It's no accident that meat production is under the spotlight. It ranks second only to cars and trucks in terms of its contribution to environmental damage.[89] Indeed, researchers have concluded that the industrial production of beef, poultry and pork has a significant impact on global warming, air and water pollution, and the loss of natural habitats.

In what follows, we will look at fresh and processed meats, poultry and game, and fish and fish products. We will examine some of the ways that 'new foods' trends – primarily GM and New Organic – could reshape this sector, and we will address some of its more future-unfriendly aspects.

FRESH MEAT

■ **GM:** The first transgenic animal, a mouse, was produced in 1981. Not many people eat mouse, as far as we know, but this was a crucial milestone in the journey towards tailor-making animals.

Ever since, a succession of animals have been genetically

engineered, so far almost exclusively for use in laboratories. In the UK, more than a million animals were produced between 1995 and 1999, most of them mice and rats destined for use in medical research. But government statistics also show that during this period scientists in the UK produced 1,485 GM pigs, 1,472 GM sheep, 200 GM fish, 119 GM chickens and an unknown number of GM cows.

Whatever you may have been told, you cannot yet buy GM meat or fish to eat, but it's presumably only a matter of time.

There appear to be at least four basic reasons why farm animals and fish might be engineered for food in the future:

- *Speed:* To produce animals that grow faster – and reach slaughter age more quickly .
- *Productivity:* To create animals that produce more meat, milk or wool.
- *Health:* To make farmed animals or fish resistant to diseases.
- *Pharming*: To induce animals to make medicines or other valuable products in their milk or other products, a process known as 'pharming'.

◆ FUNCTIONAL: Meat provides absorbable iron and zinc, both good for building up the immune system. But it is high in calories, fat and cholesterol. As more people become vegetarians, for whatever reason, they are looking for alternatives to meat, or at least to red meat. This opens up potentially huge opportunities for producers of appropriate functional foods, designed to bridge the resulting nutritional gaps.

● ORGANIC: Although organic meat still accounts for a small fraction of meat eaten, the quantity and quality of organic production is growing fairly rapidly. The first two supermarkets to stock organic meat, at least in some of their stores, were **Sainsbury's** and **Waitrose**. It's now more widely available, but supermarkets tend still to focus their energies on other organic produce, partly because organic meat is usually much more expensive and has a small customer base.

The production of organic meat is being put in jeopardy by the Government's stringent interpretation of EU regulations affecting small slaughterhouses and meat-processing plants. Small abbattoirs – where most organic meat is dealt with – are being forced to undergo the same checks as big ones, which makes the cost prohibitive. In one case this meant an increase in expenses from £300 per year to

£17,000, equivalent to £180 per tonne of meat compared to approximately £1 a tonne for big slaughter houses. These measures have been introduced since the BSE crisis, with good intentions, but the result could be the decimation of smaller enterprises, which would in turn lead to greater centralisation and the need for for livestock to travel much longer distances. This in turn can lead to stress, soiling and greater risk of food contamination.[90]

Beef

■ **GM**: It is a fact of modern life that almost all non-organic beef in the UK will now have eaten at least some GM animal feed. This is not so much a health risk, as an issue for those who feel that consumers should be offered a clear choice between GM and non-GM foods.

Animal feed

IN THE TROUGH

'Mad cow' disease thrust the animal feed industry into the spotlight of media attention and public concern. Now there is a new issue: it's increasingly likely that any farm animal we eat – unless it has been organically reared – will have been fed on GM food. Although legislation is in the pipeline to change this state of affairs, as yet it's impossible to determine the source of imported feed, which accounts for 20 per cent of what animals eat in the UK.

The main reason for this is that animal feed is a 'commodity'. Commodity markets pool products from different sources, making it practically impossible to trace those products back to particular origins. A number of crops that are in the GM frontline are used to make animal feed, among them beet, cotton seed cakes, maize, rape seed and soya.

These problems are made worse by the fact that rules imposed by the **World Trade Organisation (WTO)** make it very difficult to require animal feed to be labelled either 'GM' or 'GM-free'. For farmers who want to go GM-free, the **Soil Association** (page 45) holds a list of suitable animal feed suppliers.

Even organic meats can legally be taken from animals fed on a small proportion of non-organic feed. The **Soil Association** allows 10

meat & fish

per cent for beef and lamb and 20 per cent for pigs and poultry. But rules introduced around 1997 require that this feed is is GM-free too. Also of environmental concern is the fact that some animal feeds contain fish meal, which may come from processing waste or from industrially caught fish.

UK supermarkets and food manufacturers have combined forces to set up systems that make it possible to remove from their shelves products based on meat from animals fed with GM crops. The companies involved include **Marks & Spencer**, **Nestlé**, **Northern Foods**, **Safeway**, **Sainsbury's** and **Unilever**. The move followed growing concern about the possibility of antibiotic resistance in animals as a result of the use of GM crop ingredients in animal feed. As we were going to press **Marks & Spencer** announced that they planned to be the first high street retailer to remove GM soya and maize from animal feed, initially targeting free-range chickens, eggs and pork. These initiatives were largely spurred by consumer demands for meat from animals fed on GM-free feed, and more will no doubt follow.

◆ **FUNCTIONAL**: American researchers have found that if you chop up sour cherries and mix them with minced beef, the meat is less likely to spoil, and the cherries help slow the formation of cancer-causing substances during cooking.[91] A burger mix including 11.5 per cent cherries produced a 70 per cent drop in the levels of these carcinogens: how long before some switched-on burger-maker starts offering cherry-protected functional beef?

● **ORGANIC**: Nearly half of all cattle industrially farmed are routinely given antibiotics.[92] That's bad enough, but it was the BSE – or 'mad cow' – crisis that really spurred the boom in sales of organic beef. No cases of BSE have been recorded on organic herds since 1985. Even before 1985, the only cases were cows that had been reared conventionally and then transferred into the organic system, which would not have permitted them to be sold as organic beef (to be sold as organic, beef cattle need to have been born to cows reared organically). However, some organic beef producers have been adversely affected by the crisis, as they have been forced to slaughter their cows before they are ready because of indiscriminate regulations designed to tackle non-organic herds.

As far as organic veal is concerned, male dairy calves are now sometimes used, and they have fared well in 'blind tastings' (when consumers test foods without knowing what they are or where they come from). Calves reared for organic veal are allowed to suckle throughout their lives, and enjoy better welfare conditions. The meat tends to be pinker and firmer with a stronger flavour, but it is inevitably more expensive. Organic meat brands include *Eastbrook Farm* and *Graig Farm*.

Beef hormones

GROWTH PAINS

In the USA, beef cattle are routinely injected with growth hormones to speed up the rate at which they put on flesh. This was the main reason behind Europe's not allowing imports of American beef, which – along with bananas – resulted in a bitter international trade war. In June 1999, BBC1's *Countryfile* programme revealed that UK farmers were thought to be illegally importing antibiotics and hormones for use on cows.[93]

There is concern about how these hormones will affect human health, no matter where they enter the food chain. It has been estimated that antibiotics from our food supply account for 50 per cent of our intake, and many in the medical profession are now calling for them to be banned for use as growth promoters in farming. Antibiotics are indiscriminate, wiping out good bugs as well as bad, including those making vitamins B and K in the body. This leaves the field clear for unfriendly bacteria to colonise and, even worse, makes the bacteria increasingly resistant, rendering the antibiotics themselves ultimately ineffective. As serious health problems become untreatable, the effect on human health could be catastrophic.

Europe also argues that hormonal growth-promoters in beef could cause cancer, whereas the USA argues that they are safe. The $64 million question is, whom do you believe?

meat & fish

Lamb and mutton

■ **GM:** There are a number of issues here. First, most non-organic lamb or mutton will probably have eaten GM animal feed. Second, an issue with much more dramatic long-term implications, sheep are now being cloned to create identical animals. They are also being genetically engineered to give birth to more lambs, to shed their wool more quickly and to produce medicines in their milk and blood. To date, however, there is no evidence that these animals are getting into the food chain.

● **ORGANIC:** One of the biggest problems for organic sheep farmers is sheep dipping. Dangerous organophosphates () are widely used for this, but unfortunately, the replacement chemical turns out to be 1,000 times more toxic to aquatic life, and run-off from sheep-dips often ends up in rivers. Organic farmers are permitted to use a veterinary medicine called *Vetrazin* to control maggot infestations.

Apart from the dipping issue, and because sheep are generally allowed to roam freely, up to now there has been less of a difference between organic and non-organic systems than with other animals. But increasingly intensive systems are being used in the conventional sector, with growing numbers of sheep kept inside and fed pelleted food. In some cases, too, antibiotics are being routinely used as growth-promoting agents. As media coverage of such issues increases, it seems that the demand for organic lamb and mutton can only increase in turn.

Offal

● **ORGANIC:** Whether you eat offal from organic or non-organic animals, there is a key issue here to be aware of. Because liver and kidneys are excretory organs, which deal with the toxins in the body, the residues in these organs are generally present at up to three times the levels in other tissues. This fact should be much less significant with organically reared animals, but suggests, nevertheless, that we would do well to ensure that any organic offal eaten comes from properly certified farms.

Pork

Pig farming has changed dramatically in the last 50 years, as pig farmers have competed with chicken farmers to produce ever cheaper meat, available for everyone. For a sense of the scale of their achievement, consider that while the price of a pint of beer has gone up from 6p after the war to about £1.60 in 1999 (over 26 times), the price of a pig remains the same – £60.00!

Clearly, any issues associated with pigs will eventually flow through to a range of products, such as bacon, ham, lard and sausages.

■ **GM**: Pigs have been genetically modified. As yet no GM technology is used directly on pigs entering the UK food chain, except in animal feed (see above). However, porcine growth hormones are used extensively to create larger animals more quickly, and many such pharmaceutical products are now produced using GM microbes.

Note, too, that huge changes have already been made in the pig population by means of selective breeding – without any need for GM techniques. So, for example, the growing public awareness of the dangers of eating fatty foods has triggered a race among pig scientists to use intensive breeding and artificial insemination to produce pigs with less fat. Genetic engineering will simply accelerate this process.

In experiments, genetic modification has already enabled scientists to produce pigs with leaner meat, pigs that will adapt better to intensive farming conditions, pigs that will eat grass (ordinary pigs can't digest grass) and pigs as potential sources of organs for human transplants.

Recently, Canadian scientists have also come up with what they call the 'Enviropig'.[94] They were working on producing a pig that could eat grass like a cow, and stumbled on something else along the way: manure from this GM pig turned out to contain 20–50 per cent less phosphorus than normal, which makes it less polluting. In theory this could mean that pig producers were able to rear 50 per cent more pigs on the same amount of land, because they are currently limited by the concentration of the manure. It's thought that meat from this source might be on the market as soon as 2003.

● **ORGANIC:** A range of chemical issues around pig products will influence the public appetite for organic alternatives, even though they are generally nearly three times more expensive. For example, some 80 per cent of all industrially farmed pigs are routinely given antibiotics, some as growth promoters. Zinc and copper are also added to pig food as growth promoters.

Some people claim that there is an added bonus in the fact that organically reared pigs generally do not smell as objectionable as intensively reared pigs. Non-organic pig farmers dispute this, pointing out that pig-feed often contains compounds from the yucca plant, specifically so as to reduce the ammonia-content of pig dung, and therefore reduce the smell.

Non-organic pig farmers also raise the issue of 'boar taint'. Male pigs (boars) used to be castrated at an early age because it was thought that people could taste this 'boar taint'. Now that pigs grow faster and can be slaughtered for meat before they are six months old – before they have come of age – fewer pigs get castrated. Surprisingly perhaps, organic pigs are usually slaughtered before the age of six months too, except those that are reared for ham and bacon, which need to be bigger. Organic criteria do permit castration where there is a risk of young male pigs getting at underage females which are not yet ready for breeding!

Home-reared pigs are often not organic, because they are fed household waste rather than manufactured, organic animal feed.

There are no fillers or added water in organic hams or bacon, so weight for weight you are getting more for your money. However, sodium nitrite is allowed as a preservative even in organic bacon.

Organic meats

FARM TO PLATE

The organic philosophy is not to push farmed animals beyond their natural capacity for growth, to take account of their welfare, and to rear them in conditions that ensure they are as healthy as possible – so that medication can be kept to a minimum.

Organic farmers often have smaller herds, rear different breeds of animal together and have different requirements in relation to hanging the meat. Although these principles are not stipulated by the

meat & fish

organic regulators, organic meat standards do cover nearly every aspect of meat production and are rigorous.

Antibiotics are only used as and when necessary, and the time between their being administered and an animal entering the food chain is three times longer than for non-organic meat. The organic meat sold in most supermarkets is hung by them in the same way as their ordinary meat and is then vacuum packed; but as with other premium quality meats they sell – and organic is considered to be the premium of the premium – they keep the meat longer to give it more taste. Not everyone is convinced, however, that supermarket organic is as good as fresh organic from a small-scale outlet.

Freedom Food is a system and labelling scheme developed by the **RSPCA** to encourage a higher standard for animal welfare criteria. They have recently been seriously challenged over how rigorous their animal welfare standards really are. Their response was that they needed to be pragmatic if they were to encourage more farmers to adopt their standards. Clearly there will continue to be different opinions about the validity of this approach, but at least they are working for real change.

Richard Guy's **Real Meat Company** also insists on high animal welfare standards and has its own code of practice and inspection system. Although neither of these schemes are organic, they both offer traceability (page 27) and represent a considerable improvement on conventional systems.

POULTRY AND GAME

Chicken and turkey

Selective breeding has already created chickens that are radically different from their jungle fowl ancestors, with varieties custom-bred for egg-laying or meat production.

It also resulted in some broiler chickens, reared for meat, that reach slaughter weight in just six weeks. But it's claimed that around a quarter of these birds are in a significant amount of pain by the time of slaughter.[95] Turkeys also tend to be intensively reared, with modern varieties bred to have super-large breasts.

Something to remember about all birds that are fed industrially produced feed is that it may contain large quantities of fish-meal made from industrially caught fish.

■ **GM**: Of all poultry species, the chicken – followed by the turkey – is probably the most likely to be genetically engineered for the table. A patent has already been applied for, covering a fast-growing GM chicken with an increased lean-to-fat ratio, but it was subsequently withdrawn.[96] In other genetic experiments, featherless chickens were created. As with pigs, work is under way to make chickens better suited to battery farming, to clone them and to create varieties that would be able to eat and digest grass.

● **ORGANIC**: Some 99 per cent of all industrially farmed chickens are routinely given antibiotics. As we were going to press, **Grampian Foods**, the UK's largest chicken producer, supplying about one third of the market, announced that it was dropping the use of growth-promoting antibiotics. But it's worth noting that the company has not ruled out routinely using antibiotics for therapeutic purposes. Indeed it's difficult to see how they might drop these, because of the intensive nature of their production processes.

Expect organic chickens to grow more slowly and therefore eat more and cost more to produce. Remember, too, that up to 5 per cent of the total weight of a non-organic bird can be made up of water injected into the carcass. Organic brands include *Graig Farm*, *Longwood Farm*, *P. J. Onions*, *Springfield Organic Poultry* and *Swaddles Green*.

Pheasant and other game birds

● **ORGANIC**: There is no specific organically reared game, just wild or farmed. Some farmed pheasants are starting to be reared in similar ways to intensively reared chickens, even to the extent that growth-promoters are given to them in their in feed. And wild game is by no means a chemical-free alternative, as the game may be feeding on chemically sprayed crops as they fly around the countryside and forage for their food.

Turkey – see Chicken

PROCESSED MEAT

A GM content in processed meat or poultry products may come from the animal feed or from the additives, such as colourings, flavourings and preservatives. All of these are covered in chapter 3. To date, however, no processed meat products should include any GM animal parts.

Meat pies (including pork pies) and hamburgers

GM: Ingredients in meat pies that may be GM include corn starch, the sugary glaze (which may be made from soya) and soya protein, also used in hamburgers. There are already pork pies on sale, labelled to show that they contain GM ingredients.

Patés

■ **GM**: Thickeners, sweeteners and flavour boosters such as hydrolysed vegetable protein may be used in patés, all of which may be made from GM maize or soya.

● **ORGANIC**: Since patés are generally made from offal, non-organic brands are more likely to contain higher levels of potentially hazardous residues.

Sausages

■ **GM**: Soya flour and protein are both used in some sausages and sausage rolls (see also Pastry).

♦ **FUNCTIONAL**: In Finland, a world leader in functional foods, a company called **Omecol** has come up with a functional sausage. The idea is that sausages are treated to raise the levels in them of unsaturated fats, such as Omega-3, and reduce the levels of saturated fats. The first such product, a spiral sausage called *Balance*, promises to lower your cholesterol levels.[97]

meat & fish

◆ **ORGANIC:** Organic sausages don't contain any artificial flavourings or additives, no preservatives, nitrates, soya proteins, carcass scraps, fillers or added water. Organic brands include *Graig Farms, Taifun, Topas, Viana* and *Wicken Fen*.

FISH AND FISH PRODUCTS

This is an area that has seen a number of exciting recent initiatives. Major campaigns like that launched by the **Marine Stewardship Council (MCS)**, and backed by the **World Fund for Nature (WWF)** and **Unilever**, are helping to put the problems of over-fishing on to the consumer agenda. There are few functional food issues as yet, athough fish oils are an important ingredient, but some potential GM issues. The **Soil Association** has also been developing standards for 'organic' fish.

Farmed fish

■ **GM:** Fish are high on the list of creatures that will be genetically engineered if biotechnology continues along its present track. There are no GM fish currently available for eating, but farmed fish are increasingly likely to have eaten GM crops in their feed.

Farmed fish are more prone to disease because of the conditions they are kept in, which means that they have to be treated en masse with antibiotics and pesticides to keep the diseases under control. Some fish have been genetically modified to increase their resistance to pests and disease. Other experiments are exploring whether new genes might help certain types of fish to adapt to being farmed in colder waters.

Unfortunately, however, when farmed fish enter the wild they can spread diseases, parasites and potentially debilitating genes to wild fish populations. In Norway, it's reported that escaped fish already outnumber wild fish in rivers by an extraordinary five-to-one. The inevitable interbreeding reduces the biodiversity of the wild stock and, very probably, makes it less fit for survival in the wild. As genetic engineering begins to be used, the risk of spreading errant genes to wild populations rises.

Examples of GM work in progress include Scottish salmon which have been injected with a growth hormone from another kind of fish – making them capable of growing up to five times as large as a normal one-year-old fish.[98] These salmon are expected to reach maturity in two years rather than three. The first GM fish on the market, however, may be salmon developed by a Canadian company: they have been implanted with a gene from a flounder that makes them eat all year round – speeding up their growth rate by 400 per cent.

● **ORGANIC:** It was decided to develop standards for organic fish farming in 1989, because while intensive fish farming might prove to be a reasonable alternative to over-fishing, it does raise similar issues to intensive livestock farms. Organic criteria have been drawn up for farmed fish and a number of producers have been certified organic. The criteria cover breeding, environmental impact, animal welfare, water source and quality, treatment of disease, harvesting and, importantly, feed: under organic standards, fish farmers are not permitted to feed fish any of the following: fishmeal from industrial fishing; artificial or synthetic colouring; growth regulators, hormones or appetite stimulants; feed made by solvent extraction; or GM feed of any description.

The **Soil Association** makes it clear that they have only set 'interim standards' to date, because considerable refinement of the criteria is still needed.

Graig Farms do organic certified fish, while **Glenarm** salmon is organically certified on the continent but not in the UK. Nitrites are sometimes used to boost the colouring of non-organic smoked fish, but however much you may want to it's still hard to find organic smoked fish. But things are changing. Orkney salmon farmers, for example, have been leading the charge with organic salmon. Both fresh and smoked Orkney salmon are now available from **Sainsbury's**, and the smoked version is also available from **Waitrose**.

◆ **FUNCTIONAL:** As the value of fish oils is increasingly recognised, so is the concern about fish being contaminated by marine pollution. Alternative ways of producing fish oils are certain to be high on the list of new food innovations.

meat & fish

Farmed salmon

A LEAP TOO FAR?

The new foods menu of the early 21st century is certain to contain an expanding range of fish – and fish substitute – products. One reason why farmed fish are in the spotlight is that one and a half tonnes of fish food can produce one tonne of farmed fish, which is a much better food-to-flesh conversion ratio than can be achieved with animals like cattle. Partly as a result, the fish-farming industry is exploding. During the 1980s alone there was a doubling in the production of tilapia, which originates from Africa and is sometimes described as 'aquatic chicken'. Meanwhile, production of farmed salmon shot up from 23 million lbs (10 million kg) a year to 540 million lbs (245 million kg),[99] and now accounts for a third of the world's salmon.

Once the 'king of fish', salmon is becoming one of the most popular fish dishes. Indeed, it's even appearing on the shelves of fish and chip shops (although it is not the same as so-called 'rock salmon'). Its leap in popularity is almost entirely a reflection of the success of fish farming, which has made it more affordable. At the same time, stocks of traditional fish, such as cod and haddock, are crashing and their prices rocketing.

Among the benefits of salmon are its versatility and its health benefits. It can be poached, baked or grilled – and can be cooked in as little as 10 minutes. It is low in saturated fat, low in calories and rich in beneficial fatty acids. Unfortunately, however, methods of salmon farming also bring a range of problems, most of which apply to fish farming in general. They include the following:

Antibiotics: The routine use of antibiotics in fish-farming is, of course, causing concern, since it may be yet another way in which we're undermining the effectiveness of these vital medicines. It's thought that antibiotic resistance may be transferred to wild fish and, at least theoretically, through the food-chain to humans.

Anti-fouling: Fouling is often a problem with boats and offshore structures. Fish cages and nets are then routinely treated with such compounds as copper and zinc, both of which can be pollutants.

Colouring: It is the natural diet of wild salmon that makes their flesh pink. Farmed salmon tend to have colouring added to their food to create the same effect. Canthaxanthin, the colouring used, is not currently considered a health threat, but it has been banned as a food ingredient (and in suntan pills) because of fears that it might damage the retina.

Disease: Farmed fish are prone to disease, because of the conditions they are kept in. Sea-lice are a particular scourge. The louse starts off by eating the slime coating the fish and can then pretty much eat it alive. A number of chemicals that have been shown to be very damaging to wildlife have been used in the treatment of sea-lice, including organophosphates (see the Organophosphates box earlier in this chapter).

Escaped fish: Escaped farm fish can spread diseases, parasites and potentially debilitating genes to wild salmon populations.

Fish feed: Fish-farmed salmon are often fed on fishmeal made from industrially fished sand eels, which are almost literally 'hoovered' from the ocean depths. These fish are a crucial part of the food-chain for bigger wild fish, such as cod, as well as being crucial to the survival of many sea-birds, including puffins, and of marine mammals such as seals and whales.

Landscapes: Fish farms tend to be found in otherwise unspoiled landscapes, both because this is where fish do best – and because regional grants are often available in remote regions to help counter unemployment.

Wastes: Fish farming can be highly polluting, and is not the clean new industry that many people believe it to be. Waste food and fish faeces from the moored cages fall through the cages into the loch or sea – for every tonne of salmon grown, half a tonne of waste material can settle on the seabed near the cages. It has been suggested that feeding the fish by hand rather than with automatic feeders might reduce the problem. Another idea is to put the fish cages in 'nappies' to catch the waste!

Wildlife: In the 1980s, thousands of birds – such as herons – and seals were shot on UK fish farms. Today, the shooting continues, and other deterrents may be causing equally serious problems for wildlife. It has not yet been established, for example, how marine animals are affected by the high level of underwater sound that some predator-scaring devices generate.

meat & fish

Fish fingers

■ **GM**: The coating for fish fingers could contain corn starch. **Bird's Eye** – whose products include *Crispy Batter Fillet Fish Fingers* and *Chunky Cod in Crispy Batter* – was one of the companies that told us that they were trying to shift away from GM ingredients in their products. **Bird's Eye**, owned by **Unilever** – is also one of the major companies supporting the **Marine Stewardship Council's** campaign for 'sustainable fish'. It will be interesting, too, to see whether the **Soil Association's** emerging standards for organic fish will be applied to fish fingers.

Tinned fish

■ **GM**: Some tinned fish are packed in cotton seed oil, as a substitute for olive oil. The sauces they come in may also contain other vegetable oils derived from GM crops, together with GM corn starch and tomato purées.

◆ **FUNCTIONAL**: Although tuna and sardines have high levels of fatty acids or fish oils, the canning process, which involves severe heating, destroys these. This means that tinned tuna and sardines are not nearly as good for you as the fresh fish.[100]

DAIRY

MILK PRODUCTS

Milk

Although the rest of this section is alphabetical, we start with milk, because it is so integral to all other dairy products, and the issues which affect it, affect all the others.

In the middle of the 19th century, the annual milk yield of a dairy cow was around 1,000 kg[101], but by the end of the 1980s, mainly as a result of selective breeding, annual milk yields exceeded 7,000 kg in some types of cow. The confusingly similarly named BSE and BST controversies (see box below) have helped bring the milk industry into the spotlight.

BST milk

UDDER PERFECTION

It's a bit of a mouthful: BST stands for bovine somatotrophin, a natural hormone produced in the pituitary glands of cows to stimulate milk production. Normally, cows produce just enough BST for their own needs. So the challenge for dairy farmers has been to find a way to boost the amount of this hormone – and therefore milk – produced by each animal. Unfortunately, udder perfection for dairy farmers is not exactly the same thing for dairy cows.

Some years back, genetic engineers worked out how to program bacteria to churn out lots of the BST hormone. They then injected this hormone – the genetic version is known as 'rBST'- into cows. These injections can boost milk production by 10-15 per cent.

The champions of rBST – including the American companies **Eli Lilly** and **Monsanto** – also claim that because rBST helps cows make better use of their feed, it can cut down on the amount of methane they produce and release into the atmosphere, slowing global warming!

Critics, on the other hand, raise a number of issues. They note that some farmers using rBST have found levels of disease rising in their herds. Vets claim that cows' immune systems may be weakened and that the levels of mastitis (an udder infection) may increase. In addition, side-effects include inflammation due to repeated injections, and falling rates of conception and lameness caused by difficulty in walking with swollen udders.

Nor does the saga end there: some of these diseases are treated with antibiotics, which in turn can raise the likelihood of finding antibiotic residues in milk. Worryingly, scientists have found higher levels of antibiotic resistance in BST-treated herds.

And there are other health issues, too. One is that milk from rBST-treated cows contains higher levels of an insulin-like growth factor, IGF-1. BST was originally approved in the USA on the basis that IGF-1 was destroyed in the animal's gut, but it now appears that at least some of it is getting through into the milk. No long term research has been done on any health risks relating to IGF-1, although at higher levels it's thought to be linked with higher risks of breast, colon, muscle and prostate cancer[102] and there are some concerns about the possible implications for infants.[103]

Legal status: The hormone has been used legally since 1994 in the USA, but has been banned in Canada and the EU. The legal status of rBST in the EU is up for review in mid-2000. If it is permitted – which looks increasingly unlikely – milk produced in this way may well be mixed in with our general milk supplies, as it is in the USA. We may already be exposed to small quantities, however, because although milk itself is not licensed for import from the USA, a number of milk products – such as cheese, butter and ice-cream – are imported and could well contain rBST produced milk.

The US **FDA** does not require labelling of rBST milk. In fact where food producers have tried to source rBST-free milk and label their products accordingly, they have faced law-suits brought by BST producers.

Once again, this is an issue of choice. If rBST is cleared in the EU, for example, many dairy farmers will either have to use it or go out of business.[104] The smaller the farm, the more likely it is to go out of business. The American ice-cream maker **Ben & Jerry's** has led the charge in fighting back.

■ **GM**: BST milk is already mixed in with the milk supply in the USA and its introduction into Europe (after a ban through most of the 1990s) is up for review again in mid-2000. Unless they are organically reared, dairy cows will almost certainly have eaten GM crops in their feed. But the involvement of GM techniques in milk production starts even earlier in the life cycle. In addition to selective breeding techniques, the dairy industry has developed a number of ways of boosting how many calves are produced. Artificial insemination, first widely introduced in the 1950s, is now used for the conception of perhaps as many as 85 per cent of calves.

Next in line is the cloning of dairy cows, to producing multiple copies of a given 'superbreed'. If allowed, this will further boost milk production per animal. Moreover, in another field of genetic engineering, cows have already been developed experimentally to produce medicines such as antibiotics or insulin in their milk. Milk from such animals will be banned from normal markets.

Other likely developments include cows resistant to diseases like mastitis or able to produce reformulated milk products suitable for special diets. It's also highly likely that some time soon GM cows will be producing milk that simulates human breast milk, for use in baby foods.

♦ **FUNCTIONAL**: In effect, vitamin-fortified milk was one of the first functional foods available, in part because it's easy to make. In some countries, all milk had to be vitamin fortified in the past. In Denmark, for example, up until the early 1970s all milk was fortified with vitamin D to make up for a deficiency in the Danish diet.

Among the products on the UK market are **Dairy Crest's** *Football Milk* (with added vitamins A and D). More recently, we have seen calcium-fortified milk products, too.

Expect to see some extraordinary functional milk products in future. In Spain, the biggest dairy company, **Puleva**, launched a milk where they had replaced the saturated fat content with fatty acids such as Omega-3. This has been so successful that it now represents 60 per cent of their milk sales. Meanwhile, **Parmalat**, based in Italy, has launched a similar product, named after the company, in several countries and are planning to introduce it in 27 countries altogether.

Vegan: For those who use milk substitutes, among the calcium-enriched vegan products already on the UK market are *Provamel* soya

151

milk (added calcium and vitamins B2, B12, D and E) and **Linda McCartney's** *DairyLike Yogas* (calcium-fortified desserts and soya yoghurts).

● **ORGANIC:** Organic milk is the most popular organic item sold at supermarkets. One reason for its popularity is the fact that pesticides like lindane have been found in some ordinary milk. Unfortunately, however, organic milk is not yet available through most delivery systems.

It's important not to get organic milk confused with 'green top milk', which is unpasteurised and the subject of some debate. Infants, pregnant women and the elderly are advised not to drink this, but regular drinkers see it as the healthy option. Pasteurisation is widely used because it kills bacteria in the milk, denaturing it and therefore making it safer to drink, but advocates of green top milk believe that it also kills the potentially helpful bacteria.

Organic milk, like ordinary milk, can come in pasteurised, unpasteurised (green top), homogenised or long-life UHT versions. Major organic milk brands include *Horizon Organic Dairy*, *Bio H*, *Farmer's Dairy Company*, *Hergest Court Farm*, *Manor Farm*, *Meadows Farm*, *Molkerei Weissenhorn* and *Bio-H*, *Organic Matters*, *Skåne* and *Swedish Farmers*. Most of the major supermarket chains sell organic milk.

Organic vegan milk-replacement products are generally soya based and include: *Bonsoy*, *Granose*, *Granovita*, *Mill Milk*, *Prosoya*, *Provamel*, *Rice Dream* and *Sunrise*.

Rachel's Dairy

SCALING UP

Supermarket shelves are full of fictitious characters designed to make industrially produced foods seem a little more, well, human. Examples include the Edwardian Mr Kipling, with his cakes and pies, and the benign Quaker on porridge oats.[105] But there is a real Rachel behind **Rachel's Dairy**: Rachel Rowlands. And you can now find her organic products on the shelves of most major supermarkets.

Her experience shows just how difficult it can be to meet the demand for organic dairy products. Scaling up over the years, she and her husband were forced to re-mortgage their farm twice, with the first round raising £500,000 and the second £350,000. By

dairy

the time it came to having to raise a third sum, they were delighted when the US organic milk and dairy products company **Horizon** stepped in.

This will help make **Rachel's Dairy** products more widely available, but the question raised by such take-overs of small organic producers is whether their original ideals will be compromised. Rachel Rowlands is determined that, at least in the case of the business she founded, the answer will be no. But, as she says: 'It's early days.'

Butter

See oils and spreads.

Cheese

■ **GM:** Many cheeses – not just vegetarian ones – use rennet made with GM technology (see Rennet box below). Rennet is used in hard and semi-hard cheeses, but not in soft or curd cheeses.

Note that cheese imported from the USA (41 tonnes in 1998)[106] may well contain rBST milk. Some flavoured processed cheese and edible cheese rinds may contain lycopene food colouring. Before long, too, it may be difficult to find hard cheese that is not made with GM rennet.

Rennets

HARD CHEESE

In the process known as curdling, rennet coagulates milk, separating it into curds and whey. It is a powerful enzyme – a single pint can coagulate between ten and fifteen thousand pints of milk. The active enzyme in rennet is called chymosin.

Rennet is normally made from the fourth stomach of new-born calves, although historically it has been extracted from a number of different animals, including kids (goats) and lambs.

It's possible to make vegetarian cheese using a chymosin-like enzyme, produced naturally by a type of mould. The concern with this method is that some claim it can result in bitter off-flavours, which many people do not like. Traditional plant-based rennets are also available, based on fig leaves, melon, safflower or wild thistle.

Meanwhile, genetic engineers have worked out how to produce identical chymosin by transferring genetic material from calf cells into bacteria, which are then used in an industrial fermentation process.

The resulting chymosin is now used to make a range of cheeses, including vegetarian cheese. The attraction for vegetarians is that once the genetic material has been extracted from the original calf's stomach, there should be no further need for the animals.

The GM version of vegetarian cheese has been available since 1992. There is as yet no legal requirement in the UK for cheese producers to label products made in this way, although the **Co-op** do so.

◆ **FUNCTIONAL:** To date, the main thrust here has been towards cholesterol-lowering cream cheeses and spreads. But *Primula Ultra Plus*, introduced in the UK in 1997 is 95 per cent fat-free and has added vitamins A, B6, C, D and E, as well as folic acid and calcium.

● **ORGANIC:** All UK organic cheeses use non-GM vegetarian rennet. Although organic criteria do not normally allow colourings, an exception is made with 'annatto', a natural red colouring traditionally used to make Red Leicester and Double Gloucester cheeses.

Some organic cheeses are now available through selected supermarkets. Organic British cheeses include: *Bradbury, Caerfai Cheeses* (unpasteurised Cheddar), *Franjoy* (farmhouse cheddar), *Llangloffan Farmhouse* (Cheshire style), *Loch Arthur* (hard and soft cheeses), *Lye Cross* (Cheddar and a range of unpasteurised cheeses), *Malthouse Cottage Farm Cheeses* (range of goat's cheeses), *Penbryn* (Gouda), *Pencarreg* (Brie style), *Rachel's Dairy, Staffordshire Organic* (Cheddar style), Sussex High Weald, Welsh Organic Foods and *Whittington* (Gloucester style). Other organic cheeses include: *Cornflower* (Danish), *Hedwigshof* (Dutch gouda type), *Landsby Brie* (Danish brie), *Parmigiano Reggiano* (Italian parmesan), and *Rapunzel* and *Mozza* (German mozzarella).

There are also mail order companies offering organic cheeses, and specialist cheese shops including the **Cheese Shop** (Chester), **Damhead Organically Grown Foods**, **Fresh Food Company**, **Iain Mellis** (Edinburgh), **Longwood Farm**, **Neal's Yard Dairy** (London) , **Organics Direct.**, and the **Real Cheese Shop** (London).

Cream, sour cream and crème fraîche

■ **GM**: Lecithin is often used in UHT and reduced calorie creams. Emulsifiers and vegetable oils may be used in cream substitutes.[107] Thick creams can contain corn starch, although this is unusual in the UK. More likely they will have been 'beaten' until thick.

◆ **FUNCTIONAL**: As with milk, it might be possible to replace unhealthy fats in cream with healthy ones. In the future, for example, might we see a cholesterol-scouring cream product that allows us to gorge as much clotted cream as we like without fearing the consequences? One question about cream: where is all the extra cream generated by the increased consumption of skimmed milk going? We can be sure it is not being wasted.

● **ORGANIC**: Organic cream and clotted cream are becoming widely available. They are high quality and generally delicious. Leading brands include *Elm Farm, Farmer's Dairy Company, Rachel's Dairy* and *Yeo Valley*.

dairy

Ice-cream

There is a world of difference between good quality and poor quality ice-cream. High quality ice-creams use cream, full-cream milk and egg yolks, while, at the other end of the spectrum, cheap ice-creams contain vegetable fats, whey solids and reconstituted milk – and air, the cheapest ingredient of all. Some may contain as much as 120 per cent added air, because ice-cream is sold by volume rather than weight. Good quality ice-creams will weigh considerably more than the cheaper varieties.

In the last ten years there has been a dramatic increase in the different types of ice-cream available. Rich American brands such as *Häagen-Dazs* and *Ben & Jerry's*, and high quality, locally made ice-creams are on offer all around the country, and organisations like the **National Trust**, rather than buy from one national supplier, will quite often sell local varieties.

■ **GM**: Ice-creams can contain a number of possible GM ingredients, including soya oil, lecithin, corn syrup and products made from corn syrup, including dextrose. The UK imported 2,082 tonnes of ice-cream from the USA in 1998[108] and a significant proportion of such imports could be made with rBST milk (see BST Milk box above).

Ben & Jerry's make a point of not using rBST milk in their ice-creams, but some of their products – particularly those including chocolate bits – may contain lecithin. As far as **Häagen-Dazs** is concerned, **Pillsbury** told us that their chocolate-coated stickbars contained soya oil which was not 'identity preserved' (page 27), although it was still definitely 'not from a GM source'.

Ben & Jerry's

DAVID AND GOLIATH

One of the big new food battles of recent years raged between ice-cream makers **Ben & Jerry's** and **Monsanto**, one of the leading producers of the GM dairy hormone BGH (or BST, as we know it in Europe). And, just in case anyone is in doubt, **Ben & Jerry's** played David to **Monsanto's** Goliath. The issue was whether the ice-cream maker could label their products as 'BGH-free'.

In their response to our GM Food Survey, **Ben & Jerry's** told us: 'The campaign we waged in the USA was mostly for the right to label our products as BGH-free. **Monsanto** felt that our labelling our products as BGH-free implied that products from BGH-treated cows were inferior. Luckily, the courts agreed with us, and producers are now allowed to label their products BGH-free if that's accurate.'

Ben & Jerry's produce in five factories world-wide; three are in Vermont, one in Canada (where BGH is illegal) and one in Israel. And all the company's products are BGH-free, but are not organic.

● ORGANIC: Organic ice-creams tend to be at the top end of the quality spectrum. Organic criteria allow 5 per cent of their ingredients to be non-organic, although these must be GM-free. They may include gums, lecithin and pasteurised free-range eggs (organic pasteurised eggs are not yet available). Organic brands of ice-cream are offered by such firms as **Green & Black's**, **Rocombe Farm**, **Swedish Farmers** and **Waitrose**.

Yoghurt

People have eaten yoghurts for thousands of years, partly because fermented milk lasts longer than fresh. In the 1960s, there was a resurgence of interest in this food – with a new focus on health benefits. Fermented foods – including yoghurt – make milk more nutritious, reduce the risk of lactose intolerance and could even have anti-cancer benefits.[109]

■ **GM**: There are at least four ways in which yoghurts could contain GM ingredients. Firstly BST-treated milk (see BST Milk box above) might have been used, but this is unlikely in the UK, unless you are eating imported American dairy products. Secondly, the starch thickeners used in 'thick' type yoghurts could have been made from GM crops. Thirdly, GM organisms could be used in the fermentation process (see Bio-Yoghurt box, below). And the fourth possibility would be for the bacteria themselves (normally *Lactobacillus bulgaricus*) to have been modified. Apparently, no bacteria in UK yoghurts have yet been modified in this way.

◆ **FUNCTIONAL**: Yoghurts have long been understood to have health benefits, partly derived from their high calcium content and top-quality protein; but the growing use of novel bio-cultures is leading to new health claims.

The active ingredients are bacteria, sometimes described as the 'bioculture'. When yoghurts are described as 'live', it means that the bacterial culture is still alive. Interest in the use of 'prebiotics', and 'probiotics' is growing. These terms are better understood in countries like Germany, where products like **Müller's** yoghurt *ProCult* are available. In many products, however, the bacteria have been killed by pasteurisation or other forms of processing. Frozen yoghurts, to which bacteria are added just before freezing, are usually not fermented. And so-called 'yoghurt-dipped' foods generally do not even contain yoghurt; they have just been given a sour taste. (For a detailed examination of probiotics, see the Bio-Ingredients section in chapter 3.)

Because of uncertainties about what effects can be attributed to a particular ingredient or new food, some manufacturers – like the Swedish dairy company **Skånemejerier** – have decided to 'underclaim' and wait for the law to catch up. **Skånemejerier** states simply

dairy

that its *ProViva* 'probiotic' juice drink restores 'the body's natural balance'. Available in blackcurrant and strawberry flavours, *ProViva* also contains oatmeal, to feed the bio-culture. It is apparently suitable for people with milk allergies or lactose intolerance.

Like many other producers of probiotic foods, **Skånemejerier** believes there are real, tangible health benefits, but it worries that there will be a loss of consumer confidence if the industry suffers too many forced withdrawals of functional foods from the market because of claims that regulators might consider exaggerated. The company has also launched three flavoured yoghurts under the *Måväl* brand, which contain *Olibra,* the appetite-suppressant. These foods are sold on the basis that they help reduce the desire to snack between meals and have sold like the proverbial hot cakes, despite being sold at a significant premium.

Bio-yoghurts

THIS PRODUCT'S BUGGED

Yoghurt is made by adding bacteria to milk. Whole or skimmed milk is fermented with a 'starter culture' of bacteria, usually *Streptococcus thermophilus* and *Lactobacillus bulgaricus.* They feed on lactose, the sugar found in milk, to form lactic acid – which, in turn, curdles the milk and gives the resulting yoghurt its tasty tang.[110]

So called 'bio-yoghurts' contain extra bacteria that are found naturally in our digestive systems. The most common of these are *Bifidobacterium bifida*, which has been used in Japan for a long time, and *Lactobacillus acidophilus.* These products tend to be both milder and creamier. As well as the health benefits outlined for probiotics in general (page 90), bio-yoghurts are a good source of protein, vitamins, calcium and other minerals, like the milk they are made from. They are also suitable for people with lactose intolerance

Enthusiasts also argue that bio-yoghurts can be of great benefit to people with lower than normal levels of bacteria in their intestines. These might include those taking a course of antibiotics, which kill both good and bad bacteria, or those undergoing radiotherapy, or suffering from diarrhoea or food poisoning.

When the UK **Consumers' Association** reviewed bio-yoghurts recently, their experts concluded that these added bacteria really can help, 'in certain circumstances'. Reassuringly, none of the experts thought that you could do yourself any harm by eating them. The only issue seemed to be whether particular products have enough of the bacteria to make a real difference.

When *Which?* tested a range of products, it found huge differences in the levels of bacteria in the various brands. *Asda* and *Ski* brand products scored well (with a billion bacteria per gram), while all three samples of *Little Swallow*, **Rachel's Dairy** and **Sainsbury's** bioyoghurts failed to reach the million bacteria per gram mark for one of the strains they contained. Three samples of *Onken* had less than one million bacteria per gram of both bacterial strains.

Conclusion: Don't expect miracles from bio-yoghurts, even organic ones. And, if the health benefits are really important to you, check the likely bacterial content with manufacturers or retailers before choosing one brand over others.

dairy

● **ORGANIC**: Expect to find a lower sugar content in organic yoghurts. Such products should also be free of artificial flavourings and additives. As with some other organic products, organic yoghurts are allowed to use up to 5 per cent non-organic ingredients, which may include pectin or starch in fruit yoghurts.

This has been a boom sector in recent years. Many of the supermarkets now stock organic yoghurts. Among the brands in this category are *Elm Farm*, *Rachel's Dairy*, *Yeo Valley* (same price as non-organic yoghurt); **Rocombe Farm** and **Stonyfield Farm** produce organic frozen yoghurts.

EGGS

Okay, so it seems strange to find eggs under 'Dairy', but our excuse is that this is where many supermarkets put them. And given that an egg features on the cover of *The New Foods Guide*, we obviously need to do it justice.

Once described as 'nature's perfect food', eggs have been under pressure in recent years. They have been damned by health officials because of salmonella contamination, damned by nutritionists because of their cholestererol content and damned by animal welfare activists because of the conditions in which many egg-laying hens are kept.

Nevertheless, eggs are packed with vital nutrients, including protein, vitamin A and riboflavin. There is even a growing debate about whether the high cholesterol content of eggs really has the negative effects that people have attributed to it.

As far as egg-shells go, one golden rule for egg producers and buyers is that the better the quality of the feed, the thicker the shell and the longer the eggs will store.

■ **GM**: Unless eggs are produced organically, the chickens laying them are likely to have been given GM crops in their feed.

◆ **FUNCTIONAL**: The so-called 'super-egg' (see *Columbus Eggs* box below) has a higher vitamin and nutritional content than normal eggs.

Lady Lee also has a new product called *Great EggSpectations*. It is a fat-free and cholesterol-free real egg product which is apparently equivalent in nutritional content to eight large eggs.

dairy

Columbus Eggs
....

BACK TO THE EGG

A new type of egg was introduced in 1998, with the brand name *Columbus*. The producers claim that it offers a number of nutritional benefits: it's rich in protein, vitamins and minerals as well as having extra Omega-3 fatty acid.

If it's not genetically engineered, how do they do it? The answer lies in the feed. It was found that the natural diet of the original jungle fowl, an ancestor of today's hen, was more varied, and included a much wider range of seeds and green vegetation. Feeding a similar vegetarian diet to hens has resulted in eggs with less saturated fat, more polyunsaturated fat and much more Omega-3. It has also given the eggs high levels of the antioxidant vitamin E.

Dean's Farm, the company behind *Columbus Eggs*, have just introduced free-range offerings – and say that they may introduce organic versions at some stage.

● **ORGANIC**: Organic egg producers make their chickens' well-being a priority over the number of eggs they produce. The chickens are given more space, are not de-beaked (clipped to stop them pecking each other), are medicated only when necessary, and are not fed growth-promoting agents, yolk colourants or animal wastes (such as recycled feathers) and GM crops. As a result, organic eggs can be considerably more expensive. And something else to note: all non-organic chicken feed contains yellow colouring, either astaxanthin or castaxanthin, to enrich the colour of the yolk. Organic eggs are therefore likely to be less vivid in colour, especially in winter.

Cherry Tree Eggs, which are organic, are available through specialist outlets. *Martin Pitt Eggs* are not certified organic, but they are produced with extremely high standards all round – and are a prime example of traceable foods. They are widely available throughout the South of England.

In the organic egg world there are signs of a battle looming. While the **Soil Association** certify 70 per cent of UK organic food production, they are not the major certifying body for organic eggs. The **Organic Farmers and Growers** and the **Organic Food Federation**, certify 80 per cent of UK organic eggs. Both organisations are registered with **UKROFS** and operate to their standards. The problem is that in the case of poultry these standards are brief, almost to the point of non-existence. In a particularly interesting twist, the supermarkets are beginning to side with the **Soil Association** on this one and are putting pressure on their own producers to work to **Soil Association** standards.

Free-range: Free-range eggs, unless produced on a small scale, are obviously not a complete alternative to organic eggs. Most free-range chickens are still intensively farmed in huge sheds and there are no extra restrictions on feed or medication. The crowded conditions they are kept in often mean that they don't make use of the access to the outside they are required to have.

dairy

OILS AND SPREADS

COOKING OILS

Vegetable oils are relatively high on the anti-GM lobby's target list because they may be made from GM crops, and it's difficult to tell which oils have been used when eating away from home or eating processed foods.

Most basic cooking oils, such as corn oil, grape-seed, groundnut, rape-seed, safflower and sunflower, are produced by a highly industrialised process, which means that most of the nutrients, particularly vitamin E, are destroyed. Cold-pressing is not what would normally be considered an industrial process, and oils produced this way are more expensive and healthier. Cold-pressed oils such as olive oil maintain their vitamins and aromatic ingredients (which help give oils their flavour).

It is likely that a variety of crop plants will be genetically modified to produce oils similar to cold-pressed ones, but industrially processed. Meanwhile, more work is being done to reduce the fat content of vegetable oils. At the same time, the crop plants from which oils are extracted are also very likely to be engineered to boost resistance to both disease and major pests. Longer term, it might even be possible to produce, for example, fish oils in crop plants. In a decade or two, we may even look out over fields of cod-liver oil, in some shape or form, swaying in the sun.

Coconut oil

■ **GM:** Coconut palms are a natural target for GM scientists, but coconut and coconut oils are GM-free at present.

◆ **FUNCTIONAL:** Coconut oil has been black-listed by many nutritionists, on the grounds that it is stiff with saturated fats and helps harden our arteries. A campaign launched by the soya industry in the 1980s specifically targeted coconut, palm kernel and palm oils, declaring that such 'tropical oils' all boosted blood cholesterol levels in an unhealthy fashion. But coconut oil supporters are now fighting back, claiming that their oils have fewer calories and are more easily digested than other vegetable oils – and that coconut oil is the richest source of lauric acid, an immune system-strengthening substance also found in human breast milk.[111] It seems that lauric acid and substances based on it can destroy a range of viruses and bacteria that can damage our health. Before long, coconut oil may even be back in favour with some food producers.

● **ORGANIC**: We haven't seen it yet.

Corn oil

■ **GM**: GM maize is already permitted for use in corn oil. Although, to date, only a limited amount of GM maize is grown in Europe, it's widespread in the USA, and, in the event that public anxiety subsides, European GM crops are likely to increase dramatically over the next few years.

◆ **FUNCTIONAL**: As long as the focus remains on the health effects of oils, it seems inevitable that a growing range of functional oils will be developed and marketed. Even ordinary corn oil offers some benefits, however. Only around 13 per cent of its fatty acid make-up is unsaturated, compared to 62 per cent polyunsaturated and 25 per cent monounsaturated; and, like oils pressed from cotton seed and olives, it is cholesterol-free.

● **ORGANIC**: Corn oil is likely to be low down the list of oils to go organic, because organic producers may target the higher grade oils, such as nut and olive oils, first.

Cotton seed oil

■ **GM**: More and more of the global cotton crop is being genetically engineered for Bt insect resistance (page 14). Cotton seed oil is a by-product from plants grown for cotton fabric, and there is no segregation of crops that have been GM treated. As a result, any product containing non-organic cotton seed oil cannot be guaranteed to be GM-free.

oils & spreads

163

♦ **FUNCTIONAL:** Food makers like cotton seed oil because it is slow to turn rancid, but it's less good for our health than olive or rapeseed oils. About a quarter of the fatty acids in cotton seed oils are saturated, about half are polyunsaturated and about a fifth monounsaturated. But cotton seed oils do have the advantage of being cholesterol-free.

Linseed oil

■ **GM:** Applications have been made in the UK to produce new varieties of flax (from which linseed oil is made) by means of genetic engineering. But a knock-on problem – one that will no doubt be addressed – is that the modified oil turns out to have lower vitamin E levels than conventional oils.

♦ **FUNCTIONAL:** The linoleic acid in linseed oil has important health benefits. It is a polyunsaturated fat, which is thought to make it more difficult for cancer cells to proliferate, and it plays a roll in reducing blood cholesterol. Symptoms of deficiencies of linoleic acid include stunted growth, hair loss, scaly skin and slow-to-heal wounds.

Olive oil

'Extra virgin' is the highest quality – and highest priced – olive oil. It is made from the first cold-pressing of the olives, using only water (and no heat) to extract the oil. Because of the price of extra virgin olive oil, diluting it even by a small percentage with a cheaper vegetable oil would mean a significant extra profit for the manufacturer. For this reason, traceability is vital. Batches should be tested all along the line to make sure they have not been adulterated.[112]

■ **GM:** No GM technology is used for olive oil at present.

♦ **FUNCTIONAL:** Olive oil has long been recognised as a healthy food. What early promoters didn't know was that olive oil is not only cholesterol-free but positively stacked with monounsaturated fats, which may actively lower blood cholesterol levels.

oils & spreads

● **ORGANIC:** Olives have been produced organically for thousands of years so it's hardly a big jump for many growers, and it is no surprise to find a growing number of olive oil producers switching on to the marketing advantages of organic claims. Organic brands of olive oil include: *Asti, Emile Noël, Essential Trading, Filippo Berio, La Bio Idea, La Terra, Meridian, Midsummer, Suma* and *Sunita*. The leading UK source of quality olive oils is **The Oil Merchant**, in London.

Palm oil

There are two forms of 'palm oil', both from the oil palm. The first is palm-kernel oil, which comes from the kernels of the fruit. The second 'palm oil', comes from the fibrous fruit pulp.

■ **GM:** Oil palms were an early target for biotechnologists, who have already, in effect, churned out oil palm clones. Walk down the rows of oil palms in many plantations and they all throw out the same number of similarly shaped branches at exactly the same point. Weird. And it's going to be hard to judge whether palm oil is GM, because the industry is less regulated in the countries where palm oil is produced – among them Brazil, Honduras and Malaysia.

◆ **FUNCTIONAL:** Watch out for the saturated fats in both palm-kernel oil and palm oil! A stunning 85 per cent of the fatty acids in palm-kernel oil are saturated. This is a major negative factor, given the advice of nutritionists that saturates may do more to raise our blood cholesterol levels than cholesterol itself.

Palm oil is also a problem in this respect, although at a slightly lower level. This beta-carotene-rich, orange-coloured oil is so full of saturates that it usually forms a sludge at room temperature. Something like half of its fatty acids are saturated, compared to 39 per cent monounsaturated and 10 per cent polyunsaturated.

If health is an issue, avoid palm oil. Instead, choose less saturated types such as those derived from olives, rape seed, safflower or sunflower . But there are 'new food' projects under way in this area, too. One focuses on *Olibra*, an emulsion of oat oil and palm oil, claimed to suppress the appetite.[113] If it really works, expect to see it in a growing range of foods aimed at the obese and weight-conscious. It has been licensed both to **Skånemejerier** and **St Ivel**.

oils & spreads

● **ORGANIC:** We haven't seen organic offerings yet, but it may just happen if concerns about the health effects of oils continue to grow.

Rapeseed oil

In North America, rapeseed is known as 'canola'. The name came from the company that developed it and was constructed out of *can* for Canada and *ol* for oil (and *a* to give the word a flourish).[114] The oil is used to stabilise products such as peanut butter and shortenings in cake mixes. Rapeseed oil is most widely used by Indian cooks, and it is also called 'colza' or 'mustard oil'.

■ **GM:** Rapeseed varieties are increasingly genetically engineered for pest and disease resistance. Rapeseed oil imported from the USA and Canada is more likely to be GM than oil produced in Europe. Permission has already been granted for the importation of GM rapeseed into Europe, and it's highly likely that permission will also be given to grow it here, which will make it doubly difficult to avoid.

◆ **FUNCTIONAL:** When it comes to fatty acids, rapeseed oil is extremely low in saturated fats (4 per cent) and relatively high in monounsaturates (55 per cent) and polyunsaturates (35 per cent). But with polyunsaturated fats also now under a certain amount of suspicion, some nutritionists advise switching to olive oil.

Soya oil

A pale, bland oil high in unsaturated fats, soya (or soybean, as Americans would say) oil has been in the spotlight because of the controversy around GM soya in Europe. Because of its high smoke point (the temperature at which it begins to produce smoke), it is also often chosen for deep-fat frying.

■ **GM:** Unless soya oil has been organically produced or it's stated that the product is GM-free it is likely to be made from GM soya crops. Soya oil is often a key constituent of blended 'vegetable oils'.

◆ **FUNCTIONAL:** Only 15 per cent of the fatty acids in soya oil are saturated, with 24 per cent monosaturated and the rest polyunsaturated.

● **ORGANIC**: This would be an obvious area for organic producers to move into, and organic brands to date include *Rapunzel* and *Emile Noël*.

Sunflower oil

An advantage of sunflower seed oil for producers is that it's much less labour-intensive to produce than, say, olive oil. Like soya oil, it has a high smoke point and is therefore a good option for deep-fat frying. Expect to find it in vegetable oil blends as well as in pure sunflower oil products.

■ **GM**: Field trials of GM sunflowers are underway.

◆ **FUNCTIONAL**: Sunflower oil is high in polyunsaturates, second only to safflower oil.

● **ORGANIC**: Sunflower seeds, once seen as 'hippy food', have gone mainstream. But, given their link with health food, it's no surprise to find a number of organic brands on offer. They include *Biona, Huileries du Berry, Meridian* and *Suma*.

Vegetable oil

■ **GM**: Blended vegetable oils are likely to contain soya oil, corn oil or rapeseed oil, which may be made with GM crops. We are told that no GM technology is used on coconut oils, groundnut oil, linseed oil, olive oil, palm oil, safflower oil, sunflower oil and walnut oil, but it seems only a matter of time before this changes.

SPREADS

Butter

For anyone who has ever wondered how they make butters 'spreadable', apparently there is no 'magic' ingredient – just added water.

oils & spreads

■ **GM**: Butter imported from the USA may be made with rBST milk (see BST Milk box above). Otherwise the main issue here is that many UK dairy cows are likely to have been fed with GM crops.

● **ORGANIC**: Hand-made organic butter does not keep well and is expensive. It should be bought fresh and eaten within two weeks of purchase. But commercially made organic butter should keep as well as ordinary butter. Organic butter brands include *Castle Dairies, Carnflower, Harmonie* (same price as some non-organic butters), *Hergest Court Farm, Lye Cross, Longley Farm* (hand rolled), *Thise Dairy* and *Yeo Valley*.

Margarine and other spreads

This butter-substitute has a long history, having first been developed in France during the 1860s. When introduced in the USA in the 1870s, the product caused consternation among farmers. They even suggested it be dyed purple, to stop consumers buying it! By the 1950s, however, margarine was outselling butter in the USA.

Margarines have been in the environmental spotlight because some once used whale fats (long since abandoned) and, more recently, because of the use of oils from industrially caught fish. These days, however, margarines are made mostly from unsaturated vegetable oils – among them corn, rapeseed, safflower and sunflower.

In recent years there has been extensive debate about the merits of margarine versus butter. On the whole people seem to prefer the taste of butter, but think that margarine is better for your health. The evidence is not conclusive. (The arguments are discussed in more detail in the fats section of chapter 3.)

■ **GM**: Soya oil is an important ingredient in many margarine products, potentially raising the GM issue; and lecithin is also used in most margarines as an emulsifier – it helps stop the fat spitting if used for cooking. *Flora* margarine used soya lecithin, but the manufacturers **Van den Bergh** say that it came from stocks made before GM soya came onto the market. They also say that they have been working to remove lecithin from their product entirely. Enzymes and citric acid may also be used in the manufacture of margarines.

◆ **FUNCTIONAL:** All UK margarines are already fortified with vitamin D, and we can expect to see a growing number of products making functional claims in this sector. Omega-3 is added to some spreads. Fat and cheese spreads have also been launched which claim to have cholesterol-lowering properties, such as *Benecol* (page 68), launched in the UK in 1999, and **Unilever's** *Take Control*, on sale in the USA but its European version – *Flora Proactive* – is not yet licensed.

● **ORGANIC:** Because cost is usually a big factor in this area, there has been a limited number of organic margarines on the market. But their number is growing and they include *Biona, Granose, Granovita, Munsterland, Palmaline, Rapunzel, Suma* and *Whole Earth*.

Soynut butter

■ **GM:** Like soya oil, soynut butter is made with soya beans. Unless such products are labelled 'GM-free', there is a good chance that they will be based on GM crops.

oils & spreads

PROCESSED FOODS

In this section, we focus on such categories as baby foods, bakery products, pre-processed foods, and sweet and savoury products. These tend to be the foods containing the most additives, and they may also contain GM ingredients.

BABY FOODS

Children's bodies, it turns out, are much more sensitive than adults'. Babies eat relatively large quantities of a smaller range of foods (children aged between one and five eat around three times more per unit of body weight than the average adult in the UK), yet their organs – their blood, kidneys and liver – are not yet fully able to cope with and excrete complex toxins.

In the USA, following a five-year study, scientists concluded that government pesticide regulations did not go far enough in protecting children against the risks associated with pesticide residues in food. Their fears partly stem from the fact that limits placed on pesticide residues are defined on the basis of adult body weights, rather than children's. It's hardly surprising that some campaigners have focused their efforts on this sector. Apart from the unique vulnerability of children, parents of young children are naturally concerned about the quality of the food the young eat.

The first thing to say about the use of GM for baby foods, is that there is no evidence that they are unsafe. There is a concern that GMOs might result in the unwitting production of a new toxin, which could damage babies or young children[115], but there's no concrete evidence of this. Nevertheless, so great has been the pressure on the industry that even a GM pioneer, **Novartis**, has decided to remove GM ingredients from all the baby foods it makes under the **Gerber** name in the USA.[115] Moreover, as of August 1999, it has added a promise to try to use only organic ingredients.

GET THEM YOUNG

'The guiding principle of *Baby Organix* is that all foods should be simple, tasty and nutritious,' according to **Organix Brands plc.** They told us, 'As well as being 100 per cent organic, *Baby Organix* baby foods are also free of additives, preservatives, added sugar, processing aids and fillers.' In addition, they are labelled 'Guaranteed No GM Ingredients', with all ingredients certified by the **Soil Association**.

Wet and dry baby foods

■ **GM:** GM ingredients that may be found in both wet and dry baby foods include corn or soya flour, crop-derived ingredients such as ascorbic acid, emulsifiers, including lecithin, hydrogenated vegetable fat, vegetable fats and oils, and vitamin E. They may also include GM bug-derived ingredients.

● **ORGANIC:** Brands of organic baby food include *Baby Organix, Boots Organic, Eco-Baby* and *Hipp, Johanus* and *Kallo.*

Baby milk

The contents of baby milks and follow-on milks are tightly regulated. Follow-on milk needs to have more vitamins and nutrients, to fuel the growth of older babies.

Soya-based infant formula milk, used by around 3 per cent of parents, contains isoflavone – a type of phytoestrogen that mimics the female hormone oestrogen. It's alleged that exposure can have adverse effects on infants, particularly on their future fertility and reproductive development. Although the UK Government advises parents to use these formulas only under medical supervision, there is usually no warning to this effect on the pack.[117]

■ **GM:** Products derived from soya are often used in baby milks. Other ingredients that may be GM include ascorbic acid; emulsifiers, such as lecithin; vegetable fats and oils; and vitamin E. There is also concern about the feed given to the cows that produce the milk. **Cow & Gate** say that all the milk used in both their *Milupa* and *Cow*

processed foods

171

& *Gate* brands comes from Irish cows during the spring, summer and autumn, when they are fed solely on grass (non GM of course!).

Most possible GM ingredients in infant formula milk are not subject to legal labelling requirements, so information sent to consumers by some manufacturers states only that the companies comply with legislation and that the products are safe. This may well be true, but it does not guarantee that the products are free of GM crop-derived ingredients or GM bug-derived ingredients.

● **ORGANIC:** Despite the rapidly growing popularity of organic baby formulas, it has only recently become possible to buy them from supermarkets. Brands currently available in the UK include *Baby Nat, Hipp* (the most widely available) and *Eco-Lac*.

BAKERY PRODUCTS

This category of products is particularly likely to show up on the GM radar screen because it depends on flours, which may be made from GM crops. Organic producers have responded accordingly.

Biscuits

Following a high profile **Greenpeace** campaign, **McVities** took the lead in stopping the use of fish oils – which came from industrially caught fish – in their biscuits.

■ **GM:** Biscuits may include corn flour and soya flour. They may also contain sweeteners, which could be made from GM-derived crops, as well as lecithin, lycopene, milk powder and vegetable oils and fats. On the positive side, it's at least possible to imagine a future where oil for use in some companies' biscuits came from GM crops rather than industrially caught fish. *McVities Digestives, Penguin, Rich Tea, Jaffa Cakes* and *Hobnobs* are all made by **McVities** – and are all GM-free.

◆ **FUNCTIONAL:** In the USA they now sell cookies with added St John's wort, to 'help you relax'. Less exotically, **Kellogg** offer *NutriGrain* bars, enriched with calcium.

● **ORGANIC**: Organic brands of biscuits include *Bio Korn, Biona, De Rit, Doves Farm, Duchy Originals, Evernat, Harley Foods, Hawkwood, Kallo, Mrs Moon's, Village Bakery* and *Whole Earth*.

Bread

For most people the bread issue is whether they eat white or brown. Although the consumption of wholegrain bread has gone up dramatically in the past twenty years, for those committed to white bread, making the switch to wholegrain, even though it's universally agreed to be healthier, is out of the question.

■ **GM**: Bread may include corn starch, lecithin, soya flour, vegetable fats or oils. Most wrapped and sliced loaves contain soya flour. At least one GM baking yeast (page 94) has been approved in the UK, but is not yet being used. Again, experience suggests that this is simply a matter of time.

Responses to the GM Food Survey suggested that most bakery companies had not yet got their brains around the GM enzymes issue. For example, **British Bakeries** answered 'don't know' to the question of whether they were using these enzymes for such products as *Hovis, Mother's Pride* and *Nimble*, although the company was clear that it would use such enzymes where they were safe for health and the environment.

◆ **FUNCTIONAL**: It's official, wholegrain breads cuts the death rate. If you eat dark breads, wholegrain cereals or other whole grain products, American research suggests that you are 15 per cent to 25 per cent less likely to die from diseases such as cardiovascular disease and cancer.[118] The evidence also suggests that it's important to eat the whole grain, not just the fibre, if you want to enjoy the full effects. That said, breads with added fibre – usually in the form of bran – represented early functional products.

Burgen Bread was launched in 1997 by **Allied Foods**, who implied it could help women suffering from hot flushes and the menopause. They also claimed that other health benefits of the bread, made with soya and linseed, might include lowering blood cholesterol and 'keeping bones strong'. As with many of these foods, more studies - which in this case should include men and children – are needed before the accuracy of the claims can be gauged.

processed foods

Bread with added folic acid is commonplace in the USA. It's available in the UK, but not widely. **Sainsbury's** offer a folate-fortified own-brand loaf.

● **ORGANIC:** All organic breads must contain at least 95 per cent organic ingredients. A small number of baking agents are also allowed, including ascorbic acid, citric acid, calcium carbonate and raising agents.[119] GM yeasts or other GM ingredients are not permitted.

Organic brands or bread products include *Biona, Bioculinair* (made by **Joannusmolen**), *Doves Farm* (some of their bread is the same price as non-organic bread), *Eghoyan's, Just Wholefoods, Mestemacher, Odenwald, OG Bakery, Sunnyvale, Village Bakery* and *Whole Earth*. There are also organic brands of baguettes, bread mixes, croissants, fruit loaf, pitta bread, pizza breads, rye bread, sunflower bread and wholewheat breads, among other things.

The Village Bakery

BUNS IN HIS OVEN

Founded in 1976 by Andrew Whitley, the **Village Bakery** uses wood-fired ovens and traditional baking methods. Waste wood is the only fuel used for baking because it is renewable, efficient and does not contribute to the greenhouse effect.

The **Village Bakery** sells organic bread, biscuits and cakes all over the country through small retailers and supermarkets, as well as by mail order. And they have a small restaurant at their converted stone barn in the Pennine hills, where they also run bread-making courses.

For special dietary requirements they offer wheat-free, yeast-free, dairy-free, sugar-free, reduced sodium and vegan products.

Cakes, cake mixes and buns

■ **GM:** Cakes and cake mixes may include lycopene, milk powder, vegetable fats or oils, whey powder, and yeast. Cake mixes also sometimes include corn (maize) flour. The sugary glaze on some doughnuts may be made from soya flour.

● **ORGANIC:** Organic cake brands include *Biona, De Rit, OG Bakery, Rapunzel, Saker, Sunnyvale* and the *Village Bakery*. Organic cakes are not yet generally available from supermarkets, but this gap in the market is unlikely to remain open for long.

Flour

Take whole grains and pulverise them. The result is flour. During the industrial era, we developed a taste for increasingly refined flours, many of which were bleached with chemicals such as benzoyl peroxide, chlorine dioxide and acetone peroxide. In recent years, however, we have also seen a growing taste for more natural, unbleached flours.

For Americans and many Europeans, flour usually is made from wheat, but other grains used include rye, corn, soya and even triticale – a relatively new grain hybridised from wheat and rye.

There is concern that the British diet may have been deficient in selenium since Britain joined the EU. In 1974, British bakers had to switch from importing naturally selenium-rich wheat flour from the USA to selenium-poor flour from Europe (where soils have lower selenium levels). As a result, our average selenium intake has almost halved to some 34 microgrammes a day, compared to the optimum levels of 60 microgrammes for women and 74 for men.[120] (Other sources of selenium include offal and Brazil nuts, although in a form that is harder for the body to absorb.)

■ **GM:** Soya flour is a high-protein, low carbohydrate flour. There are three main forms of soya flour: full-fat (about 20 per cent fat), low-fat (about 6 per cent fat) and defatted (less than 1 per cent fat). All forms, however, could now come from GM crops.

We're probably about four or five years from the day when GM wheat, genetically engineered for disease or herbicide resistance, reaches the market. But trials of wheat engineered to have firmer stalks, making them less vulnerable to wind damage, are well under way. Interestingly, this has elicited a reaction from corn dolly makers. They say the stalks are less pliable – and therefore make their job more difficult!

We can also expect GM scientists to come up with new hybrids, between wheat and rice for example.

processed foods

◆ **FUNCTIONAL**: Some flours have been functional for quite a while. Refined flours, for example, have been enriched with various nutrients lost in processing, including iron, thiamin, riboflavin and niacin. The chances are that the range of functional ingredients will expand significantly in future. It's mandatory in the USA to fortify flour and flour-based products, such as pasta, with folic acid but there are no plans to adopt this approach in Europe as yet.

● **ORGANIC**: Flours made from organic crops have similar shelf-lives to non-organic flours. Organic flour brands include: *Allinsons, Doves Farm, Kitchen Garden, Marriages, Pimhills, Stamp Collection, Suma, Swedish Farmers* and *Watermill*.

Pastry

■ **GM**: Pastry is subject to all the same variables as flours generally (see above). More specifically, some pre-made pastries use soya flour and vegetable fats that may be derived from GM maize or soya.

CEREALS

■ **GM**: Cereals may include corn flour, protein isolates, riboflavin, soya oil and vitamins. Many breakfast cereals are fortified with riboflavin (vitamin B2, see XX). Cereals made with maize, such as cornflakes, do not currently use GM sources in the UK. **Kellogg** responded to our GM Food Survey by saying, 'Our products in Europe do not contain genetically modified material.'

As far as the future is concerned, experiments are being carried out to produce cereal crops that effectively produce their own fertiliser (nitrogen-fixing). Research work on this idea tried to transfer the 'self-fertilising' genes from leguminous plants, such as peas and beans, to other crops. But don't hold your breath – this one is going to take a long time.

processed foods

Weetabix

ANSWERING OUR QUESTIONS

One of the most impressive answers we had to the GM Food Survey came from **Weetabix Limited** of the UK. They noted the work they had carried out on 'traceability' and the 'identity preservation' of raw materials and ingredients, and then made the following statement:

'We are in a position to state categorically that no GM materials, enzymes, oils, or processing aids are used in the manufacture of products by Weetabix Limited directly, nor by any of our suppliers, in the preparation of ingredients we may purchase. We have been able to establish this by written confirmation and subsequently by formal audit.'

Whether they use GM ingredients or technology or not, it would be great if all companies could be so clear and concise. But Weetabix are still an exception to the rule that most companies will fudge when pressed on difficult issues.

◆ **FUNCTIONAL:** A number of cereals are being launched with claims about their benefits, particularly in relation to heart disease. Although not permitted to make direct health claims, some companies have been making connections between their products and therapeutic benefits.

Nestlé, for example, linked *Shredded Wheat* with a campaign for the **British Heart Foundation**, hoping not only to boost public awareness of cardiovascular disease but also to build up a database of some 250,000 consumers interested in heart health. What were seen as implicit health claims made by putting a large heart logo on the front of the box led to criticisms from some consumer groups, even though *Shredded Wheat* is itself a very healthy product.

Kellogg promoted their *Start* and *Sustain* brands as particularly good for sports players. Indeed, *Sustain* was endorsed as the official breakfast cereal of the British Olympic team in 1996. But, although a sports dietician confirmed that it was relatively healthy, it was also noted that it did not provide anything unique to the nutritional needs of athletes that competing cereals do not also provide.

Some cereals aimed at slimmers have been challenged because their calorie content sometimes turns out to be nearly as high as

processed foods

non-diet alternatives. In 1996, for example, one big brand diet cereal was shown to have the same number of calories – and double the sugar – of the manufacturer's main brand. The company has bounced back with a range of functional cereals marketed as healthy for kids.[121] They have added vitamins, iron, potassium and zinc, as well as extra vitamin B1, niacin and B6. But critics pointed out that 40 per cent of these products had been used for a long time.

Oat bran, meanwhile, has been shown to help lower cholesterol, but in the end the benefits of eating a low-fat diet far outweigh the importance of eating oat bran in cereals.

● ORGANIC: Organic cereal brands include *Alara, Doves Farm, Familia, Granovita, Hemp Union, Kallo, La Terra, Mornflake Oats, Nature's Path* and *Whole Earth*.

CONDIMENTS AND PRESERVES

On the whole, these are highly processed products. Many contain lots of additives and one or more of the following potentially GM ingredients: aspartame, cornflour or corn starch; lycopene food colouring, and xanthan gum. By far the most impressive response we received from manufacturers of such foods came from **Rayner Burgess**, whose products are sold under the *Rayner, Burgess, Crusha* and private label brands. Their response was very thorough and easy to understand. They are basically GM-free, but it is their committment to transparency that is so reassuring, whether they use GM products or not.

Chutney

■ GM: Some chutneys contain lycopene food colouring. As GM techniques are increasingly used on exotic fruits, expect the proportion of GM ingredients in chutneys to grow.

Curry sauce

■ GM: Curry sauces could contain GM starch and lycopene food colouring.

processed foods

◆ **FUNCTIONAL:** In a sense, curry sauces and powders have always been functional, given that they contained spice-derived ingredients that both promoted health and helped food keep longer in tropical temperatures.

● **ORGANIC: Kitchen Garden** produces an organic curry paste.

Custard

■ **GM:** Cornflour is used for thickening custards, and yellow colouring is also often used. The milk powder in custard products raises all the same issues as milk.

Honey

For most of history, honey has been the only widely available sweetener. The chief concern for most honey buyers of old was knowing which plant's nectar the honey was based on, with the source determining both the flavour and keeping properties of the product. Today, honey is affected by issues linked with both pesticide residues and GM crops. It's also worth noting that most commercial honey is highly processed, having been heated to 70°C to keep it runny – a process that 'de-natures' the product, potentially destroying many flavour ingredients and nutrients.

■ **GM:** There have been claims that honey from Canada has been found to contain DNA from GM oilseed rape. Whatever the truth of the matter, honey produced in the UK is unlikely to have been affected to date, but beekeepers often feed their bees with glucose syrups and other sugars that may be GM, to replace the honey they take from the hives.

As more GM crops are grown, the likelihood of honey containing DNA from GM crops increases, although there is no apparent reason to worry about health in this regard. Where honey is labelled 'product of more than one country', it is even harder to guarantee it is GM-free.

◆ **FUNCTIONAL:** All sorts of health claims have been made on behalf of honey, but the scientific evidence isn't encouraging. While

processed foods

many of us like to believe that something magical happens as bees turn flower nectar into honey, the fact is that – apart from the traces of calcium, iron, phosphorus and potassium it contains – honey is pure carbohydrate.

● **ORGANIC:** Most organic honeys come from a single source, rather than being blended, which should give them a better – or at least a more distinctive – taste. Feeding bees with sugar is forbidden to organic bee-keepers, except in emergencies. Antibiotics and pasteurisation are also not allowed. But probably the most challenging requirement for organic honeys is that wide spaces should be left between the hives and that they should be far from any known GM crop or pesticide usage. This is hard to guarantee with insects that roam up to four miles from their hive in any direction. Expect to hear more about commercial conflicts between GM farms and nearby organic bee keepers whose organic status is threatened.

Organic honey brands include *Allos, Comvita, Equal Exchange Organic, Essential Organic, GFM Organic, Martlet, New Zealand Natural Food Company* and *Tropical Forest. Suma* wildflower honey is also guaranteed GM-free.

Jams, jellies and spreads

Savoury spreads include sandwich spreads, hummus, peanut butter, tahini and a range of vegetable patés.

■ **GM:** GM ingredients could get into jams and jellies via the fruit (although no GM fruit is yet permitted in the UK), the enzymes used to process the fruit, the gelatine (usually from animal tissues), or the sweeteners (e.g. glucose syrup or aspartame). Sandwich spreads could contain aspartame and GM soya oil.

◆ **FUNCTIONAL:** Jams for diabetics have long been available, and there are a number of high quality jams, such as *St Dalfour,* that are high in fruit and low in sugar.

● **ORGANIC:** Organic jam brands include *Biona, Bionova, Bruno Fisher, Meridian, Molenaartje, Suma* and *Whole Earth.* Organic brands of spreads include *Biovita* (sandwich spreads), *Bruno Fisher* (vegetable patés), *Equal Exchange* (cashew butter), *Granovita* (vegetable paté),

Just Wholefoods (hummus), *Kitchen Garden* (peanut butter and other spreads), *Meridian* (peanut butter and tahini), *Nate* (vegetable patés), *Organic Snack Co* (vegetarian pates), *Suma* (vegetable patés and peanut butter), *Sunita* (tahini), *Viana*, *Whole Earth* (hummus and peanut butter), and *Yakso* (vegetable patés).

Mayonnaise

■ **GM**: Mayonnaise could contain corn oil, emulsifiers (such as lecithin) and soya oils.

◆ **FUNCTIONAL**: It's presumably only a matter of time before cholesterol-busting mayonnaises appear.

● **ORGANIC**: Organic brands of mayonnaise include *Meridian*, *Suma*, *Whole Earth* and *Yakso*.

Miso

■ **GM**: Because miso is a fermented product made from soya beans and cereal (barley, rice or other grains), GM is a potential issue.

◆ **FUNCTIONAL**: Once, even miso must have been a 'new food', but its history is now obscured by the mists of time. This heavily salted paste is a product of fermentation. It features in the macrobiotic diet, which is loosely based on traditional Japanese eating patterns. It's certainly tasty and no doubt its mineral content can help those who don't eat animal protein, but there has been a tendency to exaggerate its health benefits.

● **ORGANIC**: **Sanchi** and **Source Foods** make different types of organic miso.

Mustard

■ **GM**: Some mustards may contain lycopene food colouring; and, on the basis of current trends, mustard crops will be largely GM at some point in the 21st century.

◆ **FUNCTIONAL**: Mustards do not provide much in the way of nutrition: they are low in calories and provide only the tiniest quantities of calcium, iron, phosphorus, potassium and vitamins. They also seem to be unlikely carriers for future functional ingredients, since the amounts eaten will tend to vary wildly between people and over time.

● **ORGANIC**: Organic brands of mustard include *Byodo, De Rit, Gordons* and *Kitchen Garden*.

Pickles

■ **GM**: Some pickles may contain lycopene food colouring . Where vinegar is used as a pickling agent, there is also a longer-term possibility that vegetables and the wine- or vinegar-producing organisms will be GM. But these do not seem to be major issues to date.

Salad dressings

■ **GM**: Salad dressings, including mayonnaise, could contain corn oil, emulsifiers (such as lecithin), soya oils and xanthan gum. Other oils might come from GM crops in the future.

◆ **FUNCTIONAL**: **Benecol** has launched cholesterol-lowering salad dressings in the USA and may launch them in the UK.

● **ORGANIC**: Organic brands of salad dressings include *Bionova* and *Whole Earth*.

Salt

We are increasingly aware that salt in our diet can raise our risk of high blood pressure, strokes and related illnesses. But although there is pressure on us to reduce our salt intake, most manufacturers still add large amounts to processed food.

There are a number of different forms of salt on the market:

- *Iodised salt* has added iodine (at about 1 part in 5,000), to eliminate the risk of goitre. As a result, it can taste slightly medicinal – and should not be used for canning, pickling or preserving.

- *Kosher salt* is a term used for all coarse-grained, additive-free salts.

processed foods

- *Low sodium salts* are specially formulated for those who have heart problems or want to reduce their overall sodium intake. **Co-op** has taken the lead in Britain by cutting salt levels, saying that it plans to use a low-sodium salt, *LoSalt*, in reformulating some 500 of its own-brand products. Over time, the **Co-op** plans to extend the initiative to many more of its 4,000 products. Some other manufacturers are now reducing salt levels in their products, and more are likely to follow suit.

- *Rock salt* is mined from deep in the earth, where it was deposited as ancient seas evaporated.

- *Sea salt* naturally contains minerals other than sodium, which is why cooks often insist that it has a better taste.

- *Table salt* is sodium in the form of sodium chloride. It is generally made from rock salt, often with added carbonates, bicarbonates or starch, to keep the grains free-flowing. But, don't use it for pickling, because the additives can make the brine cloudy.

■ **GM:** No GM technology is currently used – or is likely to be – on salt itself, but the anti-caking ingredients designed to keep salt free-running could be a different matter.

◆ **FUNCTIONAL:** Iodised salt (see above) was one of the first functional foods available, although nobody would have used the term then. It was developed in the USA in the 1920s as a way of reducing the incidence of goitre.

● **ORGANIC:** Organic salt is unwashed, unrefined sea salt from unpolluted sources, harvested and evaporated using traditional methods.[122] Organic brands include *Lima*, a range which contains natural coarse and fine salt, *Clearspring* (certified by the **Soil Association**) and *Laguna*, whose products include a herb salt.

Soy sauce

Like miso (see above), soy sauce has long been used in China and Japan, but it has also been popular in Britain for over 300 years. It is even said to be an ingredient in Worcester sauce.

■ **GM:** Soy sauce could be made with GM soya. Barley and wheat are also used in soy sauce – and these could be GM in the future.

processed foods

Sugar

See also the extensive section on Sweeteners in chapter 3.

■ **GM:** Trials are being carried out for herbicide resistance in sugar beet. Meanwhile, genetic engineers in Holland say they have created a non-fattening sugar, and, also in Holland, they are working on GM sugar beet with extra sweetness. Neither of these is yet on the market.

Tate & Lyle noted in its response to our GM Food Survey that GM has never been an issue for cane sugar. The company also owns a maize processing company in the USA and recently stopped it from taking in GM crops for processing. It did not comment publicly about this, preferring to stay out of the GM spotlight.

Silver Spoon/British Sugar

GM NO GO

British Sugar, which manufactures *Silver Spoon*, *Half Spoon* and *Treat Toppings*, is the only processor of UK home-grown sugar beet, buying the entire crop from some 9,000 growers. All growers must purchase approved seeds from **British Sugar**, helping to maintain the integrity of the sugar beet crop in a number of ways.

Selective breeding has long been used to boost the productivity of sugar beet, but **British Sugar** noted in its response to our GM Food Survey that none of the beet it uses is GM. 'Moreover,' it said, 'neither are there any plans to introduce genetically modified varieties in the foreseeable future.'

The company has been monitoring UK trials of GM sugar beet, but says it 'has no involvement in such trials', except to the extent that it operates its own 'rigorous monitoring procedures to ensure that plants grown under these circumstances are ultimately destroyed.'

◆ **FUNCTIONAL:** Artificial sweeteners such as saccharin, sucralose and aspartame are less fattening and less damaging to teeth than sugar, so could be thought of as functional foods. They are covered extensively in chapter 3.

● **ORGANIC:** Organic brands of sugar include *Billington's* and *Ragus* refined white sugar; *Rapadura Sugar*, from **Rapunzel**; *Sucanat* whole cane sugar, *Suma*; and *Syramena* raw sugar cubes. But it's worth noting that organic sugar is going to just as bad for your teeth as conventional alternatives and no better for you in general.

Many organic processed foods avoid processed white sugar, and instead use honey or fruit concentrates.

Tomato ketchup

Variously called 'ketchup', 'catsup' or even 'catchup', the original product was pickled Chinese fish sauce called *ket-tsiap*. British sailors took the name – but not the recipe – home. The Americans soon got in on the act, with a bottled sauce produced by the **Heinz Company** of Pittsburgh.

■ **GM:** GM tomatoes have been approved for use in ketchup in the UK,[123] although it's not clear that they are being used. Ketchup can also contain emulsifiers, starches and vegetable fats.

◆ **FUNCTIONAL:** No-one really claims – at least not yet – that ketchup is a functional food, but all products high in tomatoes are rich in natural lycopene.

● **ORGANIC:** Organic brands of tomato ketchup include *Biona, Bruno Fisher, De Rit, La Bio Idea, Meridian, Seeds of Change* and *Whole Earth*.

Tomato pastes and purées

Because they are more concentrated, tomato pastes and purées contain more beneficial lycopene than do fresh tomatoes.

■ **GM:** The first GM products on the shelves in UK supermarkets were tomato purées, stocked by **Safeway** and **Sainsbury's** from February 1996. The tomatoes, developed by **AstraZeneca**, had increased pectin levels, which made the fruit denser. The result was thicker paste that required less energy for processing.

Both **Safeway** and **Sainsbury's** played it by the book when they introduced the GM purées. They not only labelled the products

processed foods

made with GM technology, but they also provided extensive consumer information and even passed on some of the savings to customers. As a result, the purées proved popular, taking about half the market in those stores. However, **Sainsbury's** subsequently dropped the line because of their 'GM free policy'. **Safeway** also discontinued the product, partly, they say, because of customer concerns but also because supplies had run out. If customers were to ask for it they would stock it again.

GM tomato purée used in other products such as pizzas and pastas, has also been approved for use in the UK. It will be difficult to tell how widely it is used, however, because there is not yet a legal requirement to label products containing GM tomatoes. When they start being used it is likely there will be. Currently grown in the USA, GM tomatoes for purée may well be grown in Southern Europe before long.

● **ORGANIC**: Organic brands include *Bruno Fisher, De Rit, La Bio Idea* and *Rapunzel* tomato purées.

Vinegar

The evolution of wine and vinegar happened hand in hand. In fact, the very word vinegar comes from *vin aigre*, French for 'sour wine'. Beer, ale or wine is soured by bacteria, which turn alcohol into acetic acid.

■ **GM**: If GM brewing yeast is licensed for use on for UK wine and cider, it will affect any vinegar made from these products.

◆ **FUNCTIONAL**: Since ancient times, vinegar has been used as a disinfectant and medicine. Devotees claim that it clears headaches faster than aspirin, stops hiccups in their tracks, eases arthritis, soothes the stomach and prevents food poisoning.[124] Health-giving, maybe, but we have yet to hear of a specifically functional vinegar.

● **ORGANIC**: Organic vinegar brands include *Acetum, Aspalls, Biona, Bionova, Byodo, Clearspring, Hambledon Herbs, Manicardi* and *Martlet*.

PRE-PREPARED FOODS

When the **Food Commission** surveyed up-market diet ready meals in 1995, it concluded that they were no healthier than non-diet products. They were high in salt and fat, but low in fibre.

Desserts

■ **GM**: Ready-made puddings may contain aspartame, cornflour, lycopene, soya oil or xanthan gum. Mousse mixes, for example, are very likely to contain cornflour. Some desserts may also include milk.

Noodles

■ **GM**: Maltodextrin (made from maize) and soya protein can be used in pot noodles and many of these products also contain texturised soya pieces. The sauces on the noodles may also contain GM vegetable oils, soya flour and tomato paste.

♦ **FUNCTIONAL**: It's possible, but not on the market yet – as far as we know.

Oriental style foods

■ **GM**: Such foods could contain corn starch, glucose and monosodium glutamate, any of which could now be GM. Chinese and Japanese dishes also use a lot of soy sauce and soya beans.

Pasta

The generic term for for all forms of spaghetti, macaroni, vermicelli, ravioli and so on, pasta is generally made from durum flour, and fresh pasta also contains eggs.

processed foods

■ **GM**: Today's pasta products will not contain GM wheat, but might contain GM ingredients – for example, through the vegetables used for colour, such as tomatoes for red pasta. Pasta sauces may also contain corn flour, corn starch and tomato purée.

◆ **FUNCTIONAL**: Again, possible – but not on the market yet, as far as we know. One American company, **Organic Food Products**, has plans to sell pasta sauces fortified with Omega-3 (page 65) under its *Millna* brand – an interesting example of an organic functional product. Expect more.[125]

● **ORGANIC**: Organic pasta brands available include *La Bio Idea, La Terra, Meridian, Organico, Orgran* and *the Noodle Company*. Organic brands of pasta sauces include *Go Organic, Kitchen Garden, Meridian, Organico* and *Whole Earth*.

Pies (meat, vegetable or fruit)

■ **GM**: Pie ingredients may include fruit, meat and vegetables, as well as flour and pastry. See individual entries for details. Other possible GM ingredients might include the sugary glaze, which can be made from soya, cornflour, cornstarch dextrose, glucose, soya flour and soya protein. Meat substitutes are also often made with soya.

Pizzas

■ **GM**: The tomato layer in pizzas is not yet made with GM tomatoes in the UK, but approval has been granted for this application, so they may appear in the near future. Sauces may also contain corn flour for thickening. Cheese used for pizza toppings may be made with GM rennet and pizza bases may contain soya flour, corn sweeteners and vegetable oils. GM yeast is permitted for making pizza bases in the UK, but is not yet being used – this is presumably only a matter of time.

Sandwiches

■ **GM:** Ready-made sandwiches are often made with pre-sliced loaves, which are usually made with soya flour. In addition, the bread may contain the ubiquitous corn starch, lecithin, and vegetable fats or oils. Chicken, turkey and ham used in sandwiches are likely to be plumped up using soya protein. For other possible GM ingredients, see separate headings, such as jams, sandwich spread, cheese or tomatoes.

Soups

■ **GM:** In addition to their main ingredients, such as vegetables, meat or poultry, soups may contain colouring, soya flour, soya protein isolates, corn flour or modified starch.

◆ **FUNCTIONAL:** We have heard of soups sprinkled with Echinacea, which is thought to be an immune system booster and cold remedy. But considering the curative properties that have long since been attributed to chicken soup, it seems inevitable that functional soups will appear before long.

● **ORGANIC:** Organic brands of soup include *Barnhouse, Go Organic, Just Wholefoods, Mr Bean, Organic Valley* and *Suma*.

Tofu

Tofu is bean curd that is used regularly in vegetarian cookery. Not only is it loaded with high-quality protein, it's also rich in iron, phosphorus and potassium. At the same time, it's fairly low in calories and saturated fat, contains no cholesterol and has almost no sodium.

■ **GM:** Tofu is made from soya, which – of course – could be GM.

◆ **FUNCTIONAL:** You can also now buy 'Lite' tofu, with 75 per cent less fat and just 35 calories in a 3-ounce serving.[126]

● **ORGANIC:** Organic brands of tofu include *Clear Spot* and *Taifun*.

processed foods

189

Vegetarian meals

■ **GM:** Soya is a common ingredient in vegetarian meals, but because there is widespread concern about GM foods amongst vegetarians there are quite a number of GM free products available.

● **ORGANIC:** Organic brands of vegetarian meat-replacement foods include *Bruno Fisher, Community, Dragonfly, Just Wholefoods, Kitchen Garden* and *Naturemade*. Organic brands of vegetarian dry mixes include *Biosun, Joannusmolen, Just Wholefoods* and *Terrasana*.

SNACKS AND SWEETS

Chewing gum

The basic ingredient in chewing gum is chicle, which is the latex of the sapodilla tree, boiled down until thick, and mixed with flavourings and sugar or sweeteners. It seems to be developing into a popular vehicle for a wide range of claimed-to-be functional ingredients.

■ **GM:** Today's gums could contain aspartame, corn starch, glucose syrup, lecithin and gum made from corn.

◆ **FUNCTIONAL:** Yes, it's here; brain-boosting chewing gum. Such products are enhanced with memory aids, including phosphatidyl serine, gingko biloba or St John's wort.[127] It's not totally clear, however, whether any memory-boosting effects are linked to the active ingredients or to the simple act of chewing, which may help to oxygenate the brain. Don't rely on them to get you through your exams!

Stay Alert, made in the USA by **Amurol Confections**, part of **Warner Lambert**, is fortified with caffeine. It contains some 50 mg of caffeine per stick, equivalent to a 12 oz (350 g) can of soft drink or a cup of coffee. It is seen as suitable for long-distance lorry drivers or soldiers on night duty.

In Finland, the confectionery group **Huhtamäki** offers *XyliFresh*, a gum containing the active ingredient xylitol, designed to cut down on tooth decay. And another Finnish company goes so far as to claim that its chewing gum has aphrodisiac properties. The presumed

processed foods

active ingredients include guarana and extract of reindeer antler. There are two varieties, one for men (which comes in a blue pack) and one for women (in a pink pack). Anyone who relies on this product to make their date a success may be disappointed.

● **ORGANIC:** Organic gum? It seems unlikely, but stranger things have happened.

Chips

See Crisps and Tortilla Chips.

Chocolate

These days, the names of chocolate manufacturers – including **Cadbury's**, **Mars** or **Rowntree** – are some of the first brands we become aware of as children.

Chocolate contains a good deal of fat, much of it saturated, along various trace elements (e.g. calcium, iron, phosphorus, potassium) and small amounts of caffeine. Few foods have a more exotic history (see Drinking Chocolate).

■ **GM:** Lecithin is often used as an emulsifying agent in chocolate and it may also contain vegetable fats. Chocolate syrups can contain xanthan gum.

◆ **FUNCTIONAL:** All solid chocolate is high in saturated fats, but there are some low-fat chocolate bars available, such as *Flyte*. Chocolate also contains caffeine, and a range of more exotic ingredients, among them anandamides, catechins, magnesium, phenylethylamine and theobromine. The catechins, in particular, are through to have a role in lowering cholesterol and cutting cancer risks – ironic since the saturated fats in chocolate are thought to be particularly bad for raising cholesterol.

Ordinary chocolate is already sold as a 'mood food', particularly for women, so it seems very likely that we will see functional versions in future. Chocolate exerts its magic effect by releasing endorphins, which act on the brain in the same way as morphines, helping to ease stress and pain. Interestingly, too, endorphins also increase the taste for sweet foods. There are also those who claim that it has aphrodisiac qualities

In France, you can buy *Carres Memoire*, a bar of chocolate that contains added choline, a compound thought to boost the brain's memory skills and enhance our ability to remember, to concentrate and 'stay vigilant'.[128] We have looked for it, but haven't found it yet.

One of the odder recent claims about chocolate is that it can help you live longer! Moderate amounts of chocolate apparently can help you live up to a year longer, according to Harvard University scientists.[129] After factors like smoking habits were taken into account, men eating chocolate several times a month turned out to have a 36 per cent lower risk of death than non-chocolate eaters. But we don't know how much chocolate they actually consumed.

The researchers suggest that phenolic compounds in chocolate may be responsible for the reduced death risk. Polyphenols act as antioxidants, potentially lowering the risk of heart disease and neutralising the free radicals that can damage our tissues and arteries, but it would be wrong to make health claims for chocolate bars or cocoa, partly because the research is not yet conclusive and partly because these foods also contain less healthy ingredients such as fats and sugars.

● **ORGANIC**: Mass-produced chocolate can contain up to 50 per cent refined sugar, hydrogenated vegetable fats and artificial flavourings. By contrast, organic products are likely to have a much higher content of cocoa solids. In addition, they will have less sugar and no hydrogenated fats.

Green & Black's chocolate is organically produced and totally GM-free. One of the most successful organic products on the market, it is high in cocoa solids, and comes in four varieties: dark, milk, orange spice and white chocolate. Among other things, it's baked into a delicious chocolate and almond cake by the **Village Bakery**. Other brands of organic chocolate include *M & Bee Organic Bars*, *Plamil*, *Rapunzel* and *Traidcraft*.

Confectionery

■ **GM**: Most GM ingredients could be used in confectionery, including aspartame, corn syrup, dextrose, fructose, glucose, lycopene, maltose, protein isolates, vegetable fats and oils and xanthan gum. Textured and flavoured soya is also used in some confectionery as a coconut substitute.

Companies responding to the GM Food Survey tended to be those who had moved furthest to remove GM ingredients. **Mars Confectionery**, for example, makes products including *Bounty, Galaxy, Joosters, Maltesers, Mars bars, Milky Way, Minstrels, Revels, Snickers, Tunes* and *Twix*. It replied: 'None of our products contain any GM materials.'

◆ **FUNCTIONAL:** We already have herbal sweets and a range of strange chewing gums. What's next? One emerging sector focuses on snack and energy bars, see below.

● **ORGANIC:** Organic confectionery brands include: *Bonvita* (soft fruit gums), *Candy Tree* (sweets), *Donna* (lollipops), *Fleur, Free Natural* (liquorice), *Lyme Regis* (marzipan bar), *Molle Skovly, Sano Mio* and *Sunita*.

Crisps and tortilla chips

■ **GM:** Tortilla chips can be made with maize and often include cornflour. Even some imported organic tortilla chips were found to contain GM maize when tested.

Crisps may also be cooked in oils from GM crops, such as cotton seed oil. In the USA, GM potatoes that have a higher starch content and therefore absorb less fat – are already being used for chips. These potatoes may well start to be used for crisps too.

Flavoured crisps often contain hydrolysed vegetable protein, lycopene food colouring and maltodextrin.

Responses to the GM Food Survey suggested that even some major companies did not know whether there were GM crop-derived ingredients or GM bug-derived ingredients in their products. **Golden Wonder**, for example, did not know at the time whether such ingredients had been used in products such as *Golden Lights, Golden Wonder Crisps, Wheat Crunchies, Wild Things* or *Wotsits*.

◆ **FUNCTIONAL:** Low-fat crisps are already being cooked with *Olestra* in the USA. In fact, despite the extraordinary health warnings on the box (see *Olestra* box, page 72), fat-free *Wow! Chips*, made by

processed foods

Pepsi's Frito Lay division, became America's biggest new brand in 1998.

'Happy' tortilla crisps are already on sale in the USA and are due to go on sale in the UK shortly. They contain St John's wort, a herb with anti-depressant properties.

● **ORGANIC**: Organic brands of crisps include *Crucial Crisps* and *Trafo*.

Popcorn

■ **GM**: Popcorn in the USA may be made with GM maize or soya – and GM can appear in toffee coatings. As GM maize will soon be more widespread in Europe, popcorn sold here is likely to go GM too.

Snack and energy bars

Modern fast-track lifestyles mean that these products are on the increase. Snack bars are designed to fill the gap between meals or – like 'breakfast bars' – to replace particular meals altogether. Energy bars, by contrast, are bought by people who want a big nutritional boost when out hiking or cycling.

■ **GM**: Unless it is organic or labelled GM-free, if the product contains dried fruit, flour or sweeteners, the chances are that the bar will have been affected by GMOs at some point in its manufacturing.

◆ **FUNCTIONAL**: *Mountain Lift*, made by **Optim Nutrition**, is a relatively new energy bar product in the USA. Each bar contains 12 grams of soya protein (may be GM) and is fortified with minerals and 100 per cent of the recommended daily dose of twelve vitamins, including antioxidants. And, just in case that wasn't enough, it also contains two 'hot herbs', Siberian ginseng and gingko biloba.

A product that makes interesting claims is the *Califig Fruit & Fibre Bar*, made by **Merck Consumer Health**. Sold in the UK, this fruit-based bar contains figs, plums, apples, oranges, senna and bran, and it's said to maintain intestinal health.[130] Another new cereal bar, called *Preva*, has been launched claiming to exert an anti-cancer effect, as well as helping with osteoporosis, menopause symptoms and cholesterol levels. Amazing.

Some of those who follow the food industry are talking about the dawn of a 'Wild West' period of functional food claims. But we were taken by one energy bar containing the green algae *Spirulina*, which is branded *Spirolight*. In addition to the green algae, this bar contains dates, sunflower seeds, almonds and orange oil. One of us quite liked the bars, the other didn't. But it certainly tastes as though it must be doing you good!

● **ORGANIC:** Organic brands include *9 Bar, Barnhouse, Doves Farm, Granovita Organic, Lite-Jack, Ma Baker, Shepherd Boy, Sunita, Village Bakery* and *Wholebake*.

Sweets

See Confectionery.

DRINKS

HOT DRINKS

Cocoa

See Drinking Chocolate (page 198).

Coffee

Coffee is one of the world's most valuable crops. Almost all of it is grown in the developing world, because it requires tropical conditions to flourish (at least until GM technology creates frost-resistant varieties).

■ GM: No GM technology is yet used in coffee production, although research to make a decaffeinated GM bean is well under way (see chapter 3 for a fuller examination of decaffeination). However, **Nestlé**, which produces *Nescafé*, says it has no plans to use GM decaffeinated coffee beans. Meanwhile, instant cappuccinos may well have added GM crop-derived ingredients, such as colouring, sweeteners or vegetable fats.

Another GM trial already being performed on coffee aims at producing beans with better flavours. Likely GM experiments for the near future include techniques to make the bushes less vulnerable to frost and drought, and coffee crops that ripen simultaneously, thereby reducing waste and the spoilage of the beans' flavour during processing.

◆ FUNCTIONAL: Coffee was an early functional food. The main active ingredient is caffeine. Indeed, it has even been argued that some revolutions started in coffee-houses (rather than bars, pubs or taverns) because the drink is so stimulating to the human brain. Whatever the truth, coffee is a mild stimulant, and it also contains

drinks

196

minute traces of calcium, iron and phosphorus, together with some B-complex vitamins.

There have been many claims that coffee causes health problems (among them cancer, heart attacks, ulcers, infertility and birth defects), but no one has proved that two or three cups of coffee a day are harmful, except perhaps in pregnancy. Drink too much of it, however, and you risk headaches, crankiness, insomnia and even nausea.

The process of decaffeination, where coffee-makers worked out how to extract caffeine from the beans, was a neat trick, but there is evidence that decaffeinated coffee may significantly raise the amount of 'bad' cholesterol in the blood. No doubt GM technologists will come up with other ways of reducing the stimulating effects of coffee.

● ORGANIC: The conditions under which organic coffee must be grown are explained in the Organic Cocoa, Coffee & Tea box overleaf. Organic brands of coffee include *Café Buenaventura*, *Clipper*, *Equal Exchange*, *Mount Hagen*, *Natura*, *Percol* (filter coffee), and *Simon Levelt*. Organic coffee-substitutes include *Joannusmolen*, *Lima* and *Whole Earth*.

Fair trade coffee and tea

PEOPLE-FRIENDLY CUPPAS

The Third-World workers who grow our coffee, tea and other produce rarely get a fair share of the return, and they shoulder a disproportionate share of the risks associated with pesticides. As a result, there is a growing interest in – and demand for – what are called 'fair trade' products.

Working conditions in the coffee growing industry have been notoriously bad. The international coffee trade used to be regulated by the International Coffee Agreement, but this collapsed in 1989, and prices plummeted, leaving millions of farmers destitute. Later, frost and drought in Brazil led to a temporary price boom, but this was short-lived and the outlook for coffee growers remains uncertain.

Against this backdrop, it's easy to see why fair trade initiatives have an appeal to growers. Many operate small family farms of just a few acres, where coffee is grown alongside other crops, such as maize and

drinks

plantain. By working together in co-operatives, aided by fair trade organisations, the farmers can export their own coffee, cutting out the middlemen.

Unlike coffee, most tea is grown on vast estates. The concern here is for workers employed on tea plantations, with the focus on fair wages and decent working conditions. Luckily, it's now possible to find fairly traded brands that are also organic, and vice versa (see Tea).

Drinking chocolate

Like tomatoes and potatoes, chocolate – originally known to the Aztecs as *chocolatl* – was brought back to Europe from South America by the conquistadores. As with many new foods, however, it had a bit of a struggle to catch Europe's attention.

Columbus, apparently, discovered a canoe-load of cocoa beans near Yucatan on his fourth voyage, but found them bitter. It was only when Cortés pushed deeper into Mexico and was invited to share a cup of cocoa with the ill-fated Moctezuma (also known as Montezuma) that the invaders started to take notice. Even when cocoa was sent back to Europe with clear instructions on how to make the drink, it didn't find universal favour until Louis XIII's Spanish-born queen made it fashionable at the French court.[131]

■ **GM:** Cocoa trees are not yet genetically modified, but GM scientists are looking at ways of making them more disease-resistant. Highly processed chocolate products may contain fats and oils, lecithin and glucose syrups.

◆ **FUNCTIONAL:** The anti-ageing properties of chocolate, identified in a recent Harvard study (see Chocolate, above), should be greater in cocoa because it is a rich source of the relevant antioxidants.

● **ORGANIC:** The conditions under which organic cocoa must be grown are explained in the box below. Organic brands of drinking chocolate and/or cocoa include those made by **Equal Exchange**, **Green & Black's** and **Hambledon Herbs**.

drinks

Organic cocoa, coffee and tea

HOT TOPICS

Demand for organic hot beverages has been growing fast, and these days the quality of the products is often excellent. Among the key requirements set by IFOAM for those producing such beverages are the following:

- The cocoa, coffee or tea should be produced as part of a sustainable farming system
- The whole farm should be organic
- Any land clearance should not damage the environment or adversely impact the local population
- Any demand for fuelwood should not lead to deforestation
- By-products should be recycled back to the fields
- Natural – rather than chemically assisted – fermentation processes must be used
- Crops should be residue-free, with samples tested regularly.[132]

Tea

This, apparently, is the oldest caffeine drink known to man. All tea comes from the same resinous, ever-green Asian shrub. According to legend, the idea of making tea first occurred when tea leaves drifted into a cup of boiling water being prepared for the Chinese Emperor Shen Nung in 2737 BC.[133] In Britain, the afternoon tea ritual was launched by Anna, the seventh Duchess of Bedfordshire, and some 185 million cups are now drunk every day.

What determines whether a tea is green or black, for example, is the way it is processed. The most natural is green tea, which accounts for about a quarter of world's tea production. Black tea, which takes more processing, contains a bit more caffeine, but both forms of tea have roughly half the caffeine found in coffee.

There are a growing number of fairly traded teas, which are intended to help promote better working conditions on tea plantations (see Fair trade Coffee and Tea box above).

Herbal teas are becoming increasingly popular and varied.

■ **GM**: The same GM techniques now being developed for coffee are also being considered for tea. High on the list of priorities are disease

drinks

199

resistance and improved flavours. Some instant teas may contain GM ingredients such as dried glucose syrup and vegetable oils.[134]

It's a little known fact that some producers of herbal teas use gums to stick flavours to their teas. Some producers use acacia gum, but most use a maize-based gum, which may be GM.

◆ **FUNCTIONAL**: Tea has long been thought to have health-promoting effects. William Gladstone extolled its virtues thus: 'If you are depressed it will cheer you, if you are excited it will calm you.'

Recently, nutritionists and the tea industry have been getting in a tizzy about the possible cancer-fighting powers of both green and black teas. Chinese research has shown that women who neither smoke nor drink and sip green tea regularly can lower their chances of getting oesophageal cancer by a startling 60 per cent (and men by 57 per cent).

Some American researchers also believe that green tea may help prevent, and even cure, cancers of the lung, skin and stomach. The current thinking is that it works by blocking the development of the new blood vessels that are required by a tumour if it is to survive and grow. Work with black tea is beginning to suggest that this may be just as effective.[135]

So what are the magic ingredients in tea? The industry is focusing on a range of tannins, such as catechins, which are antioxidants. The race is now on to isolate these substances, to combine them in new ways and to create new food products with real health benefits. Argentina is jumping on the functional teas bandwagon with a new promotional campaign for maté (see box below), which it bills as the 'green tea of South America'.

Herb tea made with St John's wort by **Heath & Heather** is available from many health food shops, as are teas to combat stress (including **Dr Stuart's** *Tranquility*), insomnia (including **Celestial Seasonings'** *Sleepytime*), colds, stomach upsets and constipation.

Maté

ANYONE FOR 'SEXIER SEX'?

Is Argentina's national drink, the bitter herbal infusion maté, the next star of the functional drink world? The country certainly hopes so and has launched an aggressive marketing campaign aiming at nothing less.

drinks

Made from a type of holly, and once drunk mainly by the country's cowboys, or *gauchos*, maté is now available through vending machines and even appears – via The **Republic of Tea** in the USA – (blended with cocoa and almonds) as 'Maté Latte'.

Along with a host of minerals and vitamins providing inumerable supposed health benefits, the key active principle in maté is mateine. Although similar to caffeine, matteine also helps induce sleep.[136] One American company that sells the drink, **Jaguar Maté**, lists 'stress release', 'spirit energy' and 'sexier sex' among 21 reasons for drinking the infusion. Interestingly, this company – which is targeting health food stores and university campuses – only sells organic maté.

One of the authors used to drink maté in the 1960s, from an authentic silver-lined gourd, or *bombija*. It's certainly a stimulating drink, but one more stimulus was hard to discern in the midst of the general excesses of youth! Clearly, too, this 'new' food is more of a resurrection than a new-born.

● **ORGANIC:** Organic brands of black teas include *Clipper, Equal Exchange, Hampstead Tea and Coffee, Luaka, Ridgeways, Seyte, Simon Levelt, Topqualitea, Traidcraft* and *Twinings*. Green tea brands include *Equal Exchange, Qi* and *Topqualitea*. Organic herbal tea brands include *Floradix, Hambleden Herbs, Kitchen Garden* and *Piramide*.

SOFT DRINKS

Children under five have doubled their consumption of soft drinks in the past fifteen years and in the USA they now account for 27 per cent of everything drunk (including water)![137] Not surprisingly, the war to get recognised brands into particular outlets is intensifying, with the **Boys and Girls Club of America**, for example, apparently being paid a staggering $60 million to ensure that one big brand product is sold in their clubs.

Some soft drink products – like fruit juices – are healthy, but others are decidedly not. Indeed, they are sometimes described by Americans as 'liquid candy'. The main problem with many commer-

drinks

cially produced soft drinks is that their sugars and acids can erode the teeth. They can also dull the appetite, encouraging children to eat less natural food and more junk food.

Energy drinks

See Sports and Energy Drinks

Fizzy drinks

It's now hard to imagine a world without fizzy drinks, but we only worked out how to carbonate water in 1767. Since then, the number of carbonated drinks has exploded, and the industry has been extraordinarily successful in boosting consumption, both through advertising and by steadily increasing container sizes. In the 1960s, a 6.5 oz (175 g.) bottle was the standard, whereas now we even see 64 oz (825 g.) 'Double Gulp' containers. Gulp.

Carbonated drinks are the single biggest source of refined sugars in the American diet. They are mainly (around 92 per cent) water, sweetened by natural means (e.g. corn sugars or syrups) or with artificial sweeteners (e.g. aspartame).

In addition to having carbon dioxide gas pumped into them to make the bubbles, most soft drinks are made even more acid by the addition of citric, fumaric, malic, phosphoric or tartaric acid. Their flavours and colourings are usually (but by no means always) artificial.

'Supercarbonation' is another food trend bubbling under. In the USA, for example, a drinks firm appropriately called **Excuse Me** has launched a supercarbonated soda called *Belcher!* Each can of *Cherry Cola*, *Gastro Grape*, *Loogie Lime* or *Obnoxious Orange* comes with its own 'belch gauge'. Probably resistible, unless you're under 14.

And just in case you wonder whether parents are needlessly worried, surveys of teenagers show that heavy soft-drink consumption tends to go along with a low intake of magnesium, ascorbic acid, riboflavin and vitamin A, and a high intake of calories, fat and carbohydrate.[138] None of them criteria for a healthy diet!

drinks

■ **GM:** Many GM ingredients (of various descriptions) could pop up in fizzy drinks, among them aspartame, citric acid, colourings, corn syrup, dextrose, fructose, glucose, maltose, sucrose and vitamins, including riboflavin (vitamin B2).

Reading Between the Lines

THE CLINTON DEFENCE

GM-produced enzymes are used to make some of the sweeteners used by soft drink makers. So what are we to make of the following statement made by one big brand cola supplier in its response to the GM Food Survey?

'Ingredients used in our products are not derived from genetically modified sources and no genetically modified organisms are used in our soft drink manufacturing process or in those of our ingredient suppliers in Europe.'

Suspicious minds might just read between the lines that GMOs are used by American suppliers. If so, why not say so? And what about this response from a much smaller UK soft drinks maker.

'We do not knowingly use any ingredients in the production of soft drinks which contain genetically modified organisms as described under European Council Regulation EC No. 1139/98.'

This reliance on very specific definitions is more than slightly reminiscent of President Clinton's line on oral sex. Compare the style of these responses to that of **Weetabix** (page 177).

◆ **FUNCTIONAL:** Some soft drinks have added caffeine. If you were cynical you might see the commercial benefit of including a mildly addictive ingredient to a product.

● **ORGANIC:** At least one American company has launched a range of high quality carbonated drinks such as lemonade, ginger ale and a range of fruit lemonades. These are made with carbonated, filtered, well-water, organic juices, cane juice and flavourings. In the UK, **Free Natural** do *Kicking Cola* and *Lively Lemonade*, **Voelkel** offer *Orange Soda* and *Bitter Lemon Soda*, and Prince Charles's **Duchy Originals** is known for *Lemon Refresher*. **Santa Cruz** and **Natur Frisk** also do organic fizzy drinks.

drinks

Fruit juices

Like most fruit, fruit juices are good for us. So, for example, there is growing evidence that drinking purple grape juice, which tends to be rich in antioxidants, reduces 'bad' cholesterol in the body and therefore helps prevent – or perhaps even treat – heart disease.[139]

We're also seeing explosive growth in the UK in the area of 'fruit drinks' – including squashes and concentrates – although the distinction between fruit juices and squashes is becoming somewhat blurred (see below).

■ **GM:** Some fruit juices contain corn starch, and savoury drinks, such as tomato juice, may contain hydrolised vegetable fat. It's not unlikely that a number of GM fruits, such as the pipless orange, will be used for juices in the future.

◆ **FUNCTIONAL:** Fruit juices are almost the perfect carriers for functional ingredients. Indeed, we have already seen calcium-enriched orange juice (*Tropicana*, made by **PepsiCo**)[140] and even products containing the herbal 'aphrodisiac', damiana. To date, however, such fortified juices have not been a great success in the UK. A vitamin-fortified juice from **Roche Consumer Health** produced disappointing sales, and **Del Monte's** *Extra* fortified juice and **MD Foods'** Pact juice with calcium are both now history. *ProViva* fruit juice containing probiotic bacteria can be found in **Safeway**, **Sainsbury**, **Tesco** and **Waitrose**.

Smoothies: Herbal and vitamin-fortified 'smoothies' are also becoming popular in the UK. Aimed at the young and style-conscious, these are chilled, 100 per cent fruit juices, with no added sugar, and, in the case of *C Monster*, boosted with 300 per cent of the recommended daily dose of vitamin C. Another smoothie, *Get Your Vits!*, is a blend of oranges and mangos, with a cocktail of vitamins (A, B1, B3, B5, B6, B12, C and E, plus guarana extract).

As an example of the range of smoothies now on offer (and some of the claims made), here is a partial list of the smoothies on offer at **Squeeze**, in London's Kensington High Street:

- *British Burner* – which 'burns fat and increases metabolism'
- *Dr Squeeze* – 'double immunity boost'

- *Girl Power* – contains added 'female boost', including iron, folic acid and calcium
- *Marathon Powerboost* – powered by all five 'boosts' (see below)
- And each of a total of 17 smoothies can be further fortified with *Energy Boost* (with ginseng, ginko biloba and bee pollen), Fibre *Boost* (added dietary fibre), *Immunity Boost* (including Echinacea and vitamin C), *Protein Boost* (contains soyabean-based vegetable protein) or *Vita Boost* ('100 per cent of the recommended daily intake of 19 critical vitamins and minerals').

We have no idea whether these things do what they say, and they are fairly expensive. But we have tried them and they are certainly delicious.

Ben & Jerry's also seem keen to get in on the smoothie act. They are said to be planning to launch a range of *Frozen Smoothies*, featuring a blend of herbal ingredients, fresh fruit, yoghurt, vitamins and minerals. As usual, they seem to be going for weird names, among them *Strawberry Banana Man* with chamomile, *Tropic of Mango* with Echinacea, *Raspberry Renewal* with ginseng, and *Chai Tsea Latte*, with five spices.[141]

In Australia, California and New Zealand, smoothies are now being made with the green algae *Spirulina* as a main ingredient (see chapter 3, page 103, for a detailed look at the rise of *Spirulina* as a new food).[142]

Another trend is for juices which 'detoxify' the body, after a hard night's drinking. **Juicemoose**, in London sell products with names like *Detoxifier*, with ingredients including fruits such as apple and grapefruit and vegetables such as beetroot, carrot, celery, parsley and spinach. Those who have tried them say they taste vaguely medicinal, but still wonder whether they live up to their claims.[143]

Pepsi had to drop one of its prized products, *Josta*, because it didn't meet the expectations they'd had that it would win a market worth $500 million. This was a soft drink laced with guarana.[144]

A small Swiss-run company, **Biotta**, has introduced an organic range of specially formulated vegetable juice, as a dietary tonic and for use in cancer therapy.

● **ORGANIC:** Organic brands of fruit juices include *1066 Country, Aspalls, Biona, Biotta* (vegetable juices), *Crones, Eden, Grove Fresh*

drinks

(fresh juice), *Organic Food Company, Robinvale, Sunland, Vitalia, Vitamont, Voelkel* and *Whole Earth*.

We're also seeing the start of a new trend, in which mainstream companies like *Libby's* (a brand of **Gerber Foods Soft Drinks**) are producing a widening range of organic products. These include apple, grapefruit, orange and tomato juices. Excellent products, but note that several are made with concentrated juices, rather than – by contrast with many speciality organic products – juices from a single source. Traceable they aren't.

Sports and energy drinks

The industry may be able to distinguish between an 'energy' drink and a 'sports' drink, but we can't. Both tend to be stuffed with ingredients designed to make you work harder, run faster, jump higher or whatever. Both also tend to be relatively expensive and, we suspect, unlikely to turn you into an Olympic athlete in seconds.

■ **GM:** Energy or sports drinks may contain the same ingredients as fizzy drinks, and can also contain soya protein isolates.

◆ **FUNCTIONAL:** The idea of these drinks is to pump up energy levels in ordinary consumers or in athletes so they can give of their best. Such drinks are generally supplemented with herbs, vitamins, minerals and amino acids. It's still not clear that they have a direct functional effect on most people, although they certainly pumped up this sector of the soft drinks market: the size of the American market grew from $10 million to $50 million in a single year, between 1997 and 1998.

Typical ingredients include green tea, long touted for its antioxidant properties; herbs like ginkgo biloba, a memory improver; St John's wort, a natural mood raiser; the non-essential amino acid taurine, to detoxify the body; ginseng, a traditional energy booster; and caffeine.

The claims made for such drinks vary widely. The packaging for **Celeste's** *Pro'Elixir*, for example, claims that it 'enlivens and fortifies for today's busy environment'. **Purdey's** *Gold High Energy* is described as 'a unique formula of pep-u-up herbs and vitamins blended with complex carbohydrates for a sustained energy boost'. And **Red Bull's**

Stimulation Drink – containing taurine, among other things – presents itself as 'especially developed for times of increased stress or strain'. *Gusto Sparking Herbal Drink* contains guarana, an 'energising herb' and Siberian ginseng, 'the immune-boosting herb'.[145]

A long-standing brand of energy drink in the UK is *Lucozade*, which has been re-launched recently by **SmithKline Beecham** with nationwide advertising using the **Sony Playstation** cyber action woman Lara Croft. *Solstis* is a new energy drink addition to the *Lucozade* range, targeted at attracting people with extremely busy lives, particularly students and people working in the financial sector. 'Our consumer research shows that among 18–25-year-olds across the world there are very similar trends,' said the product's marketing manager. 'Eighteen-year-olds feel insecure, but they need to look confident – and they use brands to demonstrate that confidence.'

But the company is not relying simply on hype to sell *Solstis*. The product is based on glucose, which the company says the brain uses 'almost exclusively as a source of energy'. The drink also contains caffeine, vitamins (B1, B2, B6 and B12: page 86), and panthothenic acid, all at 20 per cent of the recommended daily amounts.

According to *Which?*, however, so-called 'energy' drinks are unlikely to be more stimulating than a cup of coffee or tea with sugar. The 'healthy' energy boost in **Purdey's Gold**, for example, comes from the glucose syrup. Tests showed that a single bottle contained the equivalent of more than ten teaspoons of sugar, while the **Red Bull** product contained nearly six. Meanwhile, the caffeine present in many of them actually slows down the absorption of sugars.

Some of the major sports drinks targeted at American athletes also sound exciting, with their implied promise of boundless energy and endurance. But most of these are no more than water, sugar and two so-called electrolytes (sodium and potassium), plus various colourings and flavourings. You may be quaffing a product stuffed with vitamins and amino acids, but remember that sugar content.

The scientific evidence suggests that for most people (the average person, children, and those exercising for less than 30 minutes at a time) these drinks are no more useful than drinking water. The exceptions are athletes exercising their bodies to such an extent that they need to replace the electrolytes that play such a vital role in nerve function and the proper functioning of muscles.

drinks

And the overall *Which?* verdict: don't buy sports drinks. They often cost twice as much as most cans of drink – and fail to deliver the results they appear to promise.

Squashes and cordials

■ GM: A lot of squashes and cordials contain citric acid and aspartame.

◆ FUNCTIONAL: Many squashes are promoted as containing essential vitamins, implying that they are beneficial to health. But even without added sugar they are usually acidic and contain natural sugars such as sucrose which means they can contribute to tooth decay.

The undoubted soft drink star of 1998, for example, was *Sunny Delight*, made by **Procter & Gamble**. The product appeals to parents who are keen to cut their children's consumption of colas, and the fact that it contains fruit juice reinforces the healthy image, as does the 'vitamin enriched' copy on the label. It has added vitamins B1, B6 and C. But, for all that it is stocked in supermarket chillers alongside 100 per cent juice products, it contains only 5 per cent fruit juice and it has high levels of sucrose.

Ribena Toothkind is approved by the British Dental Association[146] but its claims are being challenged by **Action and Information on Sugar**.

● ORGANIC: Organic brands of squashes or cordials include *Bionova*, *Ekoland*, *Meridian*, *Moulin Valdonne*, *Swans*, *Voelkel* and *Rocks*.

Water

The discovery of traces of benzene in **Perrier** products dented the entire market for 'designer waters'. But now it seems to be bouncing back, although **Perrier's** market share has not made it back to its previous levels. The company did react well, however, with very public demonstrations of its commitment to dealing with the problem – including a bulldozer being driven over a heap of 'contaminated' bottles. Among the new products on offer is the *O+* (*Eau Plus*) range from **Aqua Libra**, in such subtle flavours as 'Mandarin with a hint of

Lemongrass' and 'Lime with a hint of Cactus'. Clever, and, at less than 10 calories per 100ml attractive to those who like taste without calories, but it's still an expensive way to buy water!

■ **GM**: An increasing number of flavoured water products contains aspartame.

◆ **FUNCTIONAL**: One American company offers slightly flavoured, unsweetened drinks with added high-tech aromatherapy. They are said to be infused with fragrances that 'reach the sensual side and quench the deepest thirst within you'. There is also now Serenity, a herbal fortified water containing St John's Wort and made by **Smart Water**. And **Tesco's** has a range of waters flavoured with herbs and fruit juices: *Soothing* with chamomile, *Revitalising* with ginseng, and *Harmonising* with jasmine.

One recent product launch focused on so-called *Liquid Oxygen*, an oxygenated water packed in a gleaming silver bottle with a sports top.[147] Basically a still spring water, the product was claimed to have 'up to' 10 times the amount of oxygen found in normal bottled water. Again, an expensive way to buy your water, but still probably a lot better for your health than many other soft drinks – or alcoholic ones, come to that.

ALCOHOLIC DRINKS

Alcohol has been used for thousands of years, and by a wide range of cultures, largely because of its intoxicating effects. It is produced by fermenting raw materials such as fruit juices, grapes, malted grain, potatoes or rice. Many different reactions take place in a single fermentation process, which helps give the final product its unique combination of flavours, colour and other characteristics.There are different types, but ethyl alcohol is what gives most alcoholic drinks their kick. Some people also drink methyl alcohol, or 'meths', but usually only if they are desperate (because it's cheap) and this is definitely not recommended!

People have been ingenious in producing an ever-growing range of alcoholic drinks, from low-alcohol beers through to 50 per cent alchohol spirits like some whiskies. Moderate drinking can have

drinks

some benefits, including a reduced risk of heart disease and even, among non-smokers, of the common cold. However, there are also a range of diseases linked with alcohol consumption, particularly over-consumption. They include cancers of the mouth, tongue and throat; liver damage and disease; nervous system disorders; heart and circulatory system disorders; and mental disorders like depression. And some of us are more at risk than others. For example, even moderate drinking can increase the risk of breast cancer in women, while pregnant women – or those planning to conceive – are advised not to drink alcohol at all. Meanwhile, anyone downing large quantities also risks depleting their body's reserves of vitamin B1 and magnesium.

Beer and ale

■ **GM:** Some products may contain aspartame, caramel colouring and protein isolates.

Although at least one GM yeast has been approved for use in the UK, brewers claim not to be using it. Again, it's presumably only a matter of time. GM strains of barley are already under development, engineered for resistance to crop diseases.

◆ **FUNCTIONAL:** Asked which was better for health, apple juice or beer, most people would say apple juice. But beer can also have positive health effects.[148] Men and women who drink moderate amounts have a 30–40 per cent lower rate of coronary heart disease than people who don't drink beer at all. The antioxidants (polyphenols) in beer apparently make it as effective as red wine in combating heart disease. Much of the positive effect comes through the boosting of 'good' cholesterol.

Starch-digesting yeasts could eventually help reduce the beer belly that regular drinkers acquire. One yeast (*Schwanniomyces castelli*) breaks down starches, dextrins, lactose and other substances that boost a beer's calorie content. Unfortunately it also makes poor beer. The GM solution is to take the traditional brewing yeast (*Saccharomyces cerevisiae*) and add to it some useful genes from the starch-digesting yeast. Again, brewing scientists found the 'improved' beer had off-tastes. But GM techniques have helped pin-

drinks

point the genes responsible, so that they can be removed. The potential result: a drinkable, low calorie beer.

● **ORGANIC:** There is a limited supply of organic hops in the UK. Most conventional farmers and seed merchants focus on developing high yield crops, with the help of chemical fertilisers. Chemicals used by conventional hop growers include nitrates and organophosphates, as well as herbicides and fungicides. On top of that, funding in the UK for growing organic hops has been cut back. There is more enthusiasm, however, in Germany.

There are only two UK organic brands of regularly produced beer. One is *Golden Promise* produced by Edinburgh's **Caledonian Brewery**. The brewery buys the entire crop of hops from the only British grower, and *Golden Promise* is widely available in supermarkets and off-licences. The second brand is *Organic Best Ale* from **Samuel Smith** in Yorkshire, which imports its organic hops from New Zealand. This beer is available from selected branches of **Waitrose** and some wholefood shops. Other UK organic brewers, such as the makers of **Pitfield's** *Eco Warrior,* cannot source enough organic hops to meet demand.

German organic ales, beers and lagers are produced by, among others, **Pinkus Müller**, one of Germany's best-known brewers. Other continental organic brands include **Castelain's** *Jade*, **Dupont's** *Saison*, **Öko Krone** (wheat beer), *Pilsner, Rapunzel,* and *Weisse Wheatbeer.*[149]

Spirits

■ **GM:** Some spirits contain caramel colouring.

◆ **FUNCTIONAL:** Whisky drinkers will be pleased to hear that Scotch whisky raises the body's levels of health-promoting antioxidants. Recent research indicates that whisky is even more beneficial in this respect than red wine.[150]

● **ORGANIC:** There is only one certified organic whisky to date: *Dàmhìle*, a 'Millennium Malt', for drinking as the century turns. It's available from **Vinceremos** and Planet Organic. Organic Calvados – apple brandy – and vodka are also available. For G&T drinkers, Sainsbury's has just launched Juniper Green organic gin, along with organic tonic water.

drinks

Wine

■ **GM:** Trials for a GM wine yeast were successfully carried out as long ago as 1979, but it is still not used on a commercial scale. Although some people in the industry are keen to use such yeasts, their introduction is being hampered by negative feedback from consumer groups.[151]

The wine industry may have been relatively slow to catch on to the GM revolution, but research well under way in the USA, Australia and France suggests that it's only a matter of time. Given the impact of vine pests like phylloxera, viruses such as fanleaf, and diseases like mildew, disease- and pest-resistant varieties will probably be the first targets of GM scientists. Other goals are modifying vines to make them more productive and, perhaps, able to produce good red wines in the colder climates of England or even Sweden.

In the longer term, it may be possible to use so-called 'flavour triggers' to produce particular styles of wine in a wider range of climates and on different soils. So, for example, it might eventually be possible to mimic the unique tastes of Sancerre, Hunter Valley Sémillon or claret almost anywhere in the world.[152] (Which raises the interesting question of whether real wine experts would be able to taste the difference.) Grapes could also be modified with flavours from other fruits, such as gooseberries or raspberries.

The idea of using GM processes to spread existing wine types to other soils and climates might mean that wine production moved to where labour was cheapest, which could hit European producers hard. Smaller wine-makers would be particularly undermined, as wine became more of a commodity. 'We are dialling up the death of the wine industry,' warned one leading Australian winemaker. 'We could be about to destroy regionality and the idea that vineyard location matters, the very things which makes wine so special.'

● **ORGANIC:** Organic wines *(biologique* in France) – usually contain lower levels of the preservative sulphur dioxide. This may be the reason why people claim to suffer less intense hangovers when drinking organic. The average German currently drinks five times as much organic wine as the average Briton does.

Conventional wine production is a chemical-intensive business. Vineyards, accounting for 10 per cent of farmed land, use over 75 per cent of the chemical pesticides and herbicides used. Many wines contain fungicide residues and will also have used a cocktail of chemicals during production, as well as 'fining agents' used to filter out impurities, which may be made from blood or other animal products. Organic grapes, on the other hand, are grown without artificial fertilisers and synthetic pesticides. Vine varieties are chosen for their suitability to their environment and disease-resistance rather than for high yields. The organic wine list is growing and the wines are now widely available, generally costing around 5–10 per cent more.

Major suppliers of organic wines include the **Organic Wine Co**, **Sedlescombe Vineyard**, **Vinceremos** and **Vintage Roots**. They all sell by direct mail too. Most of the mainstream supermarkets and wine merchants now stock organic wine. Worth a tipple.

CHECK-OUT TIME

And now your supermarket trolley's full. None of us can make all the relevant decisions and choices every time we go shopping, but perhaps this time around you have picked out one or two products on the basis of their future-friendly appeal. And maybe one or two products have stayed on the shelf. This is an area where we are all on a learning curve.

Since many shoppers are buying for families or households, members of which may have very different tastes or needs, we will now look at some of the ways in which new foods can help – or hinder – us in our pursuit of the perfect (or at least well balanced) diet.

drinks

5

PERSONALISED MENUS

Good For You

No one diet is right for everyone. As Lucretius put it in 50 BC: 'One man's meat is another man's poison.' Except that it's usually more subtle than that.

The scientist who discovered vitamin B5 (pantothenic acid) argued that there are huge differences in the way that different individuals absorb proteins, vitamins and minerals.[153] Each of us, he argued, is born biochemically unique. One study showed a thirty-fold range in vitamin levels in the blood of people fed the same diet.

As our recent interest in the health effects of particular foods has evolved, modern diets have reflected an exploding spectrum of appetites – for energy, fun, health and principles. Indeed, if today's trends continue most of us will soon have our very own personalised diets and menus.

FOODS FOR THOUGHT

Soon food manufacturers, supermarkets and Internet retailers will have far more details about us than are already attached to our loyalty cards, and the overriding focus will be on health. They might even have key elements of our medical records, with details about our genetic susceptibility to different diseases, as well as personal details about our lifestyles and the stages of life we are at. One customer profile might read something like this: a middle-aged woman, with three teenage children, who works from home, is into sport, and has a tendency to thrush, a family history of breast-cancer and occasional bouts of migraine.

What will these companies do with this information? And why might we let them have it in the first place? The answer to both questions is that we will be buying not just food and groceries from the supermarkets but also personal services tailored to our specific needs. And the companies to which we will give our custom will be those who learn to know our tastes and needs perhaps even better than we do, like a good butler. In the not-too-distant future supermarkets may help us plan our weekly menus, making sure that we get a good nutritional balance for each family member, amusing party fare for a lunch we are planning, a special (but not too unhealthy) treat – and something to help with pre-menstrual syndrome.

Eventually we might even have a service that involved talking packaging. We might press a panel on the pack relating to heart disease and it would tell us how the product measured up. Some supermarkets might have teams of health experts on hand to give us regular check-ups – so they can report back to us on how we are and give us their recommended diets and menus.

In the meantime, the best advice is something that most of us have heard many times before: eat a balanced diet. And here are the well-rehearsed ground-rules:

- Eat lots of starchy foods, such as bread, cereals, noodles, oats, pasta, potatoes and rice.

- Eat plenty of fruit and vegetables. They boost your intake of fibre, minerals and vitamins, including antioxidants.

- Eat moderate amounts of milk, cheese and yoghurt, but cut back on butter and cream to reduce the amount of saturated fat in your diet.

- Unless you are vegetarian, eat some lean meat and lots of oily fish. Lean meat is a valuable source of iron, although meat fat can be a problem. Oily fish is highly recommended and a range of fish oils are now being added to some new foods.

- Go easy on fatty foods, particularly crisps, chips, biscuits and chocolate, but don't cut back too far. Some fat is essential for health. Indeed, there have been cases of children who were given so much low-fat food that they did not develop properly.

- Cut right back on foods with high levels of added sugar. There will be plenty of natural sugars in your diet from fruit and vegetables. Added sugar is a key factor in tooth decay and may also increase the risk of diseases like diabetes.

True, some people are now challenging even these basic guidelines. They say that since our traditional diets – and thus our digestive systems – were established when we were hunter gatherers, we should avoid all foods that come from farming, like grains, because they are hard for our bodies to process. Instead we should eat meat and lots of fruit and vegetables. But they are a good start.

Now let's take a look at what's in, what's out and what's new for children, for pregnancy, for cancer prevention, to help combat flu or to boost the immune system. This is not an exhaustive list of conditions and ailments, but a sample of some of the areas where new foods are or may soon be offered. We have taken a light-hearted approach and should point out that anyone planning to cut or replace a particular food in their diet should consult a doctor, dietician or nutritionist first.

Much of the information here about nutrition and health comes from *The Food Bible: the Ultimate Guide to All that's Good and Bad in the Food We Eat*, by Judith Wills, *The Optimum Nutrition Bible* by Patrick Holford and *Which? Online*. We recommend them as comprehensive and accessible reference publications. Where particular ingredients or foods are mentioned there will generally be more details to be found in chapter 3 or 4 (see index).

Ageing
ELIXIRS OF YOUTH

Throughout history, people have looked for elixirs that would postpone ageing and even grant immortality. Generally, although it made for great myths and legends, it proved a fruitless task. However, life expectancy in some parts of the modern world has extended considerably, particularly over the last century, and there are a growing number of clues to foods and diets that may well extend it even further.

Unfortunately it seems that the best way to live longer is to eat much less food. If you could bear to restrict your calorie intake to between 30 per cent and 70 per cent of normal levels, research on species as different as fruit-flies and monkeys suggests you might extend your life expectancy by anywhere between 20 per cent and 50 per cent. Even so, it's hard to see most people choosing that option.

Anti-ageing foods and drinks, both real and imaginary, are already on offer; products with extra calcium, for example, to help prevent or delay osteoporosis, or snack bars with blue-green algae, an ingredient originally used by the Aztecs as a possible cure for ageing. And more will be discovered about existing foods, such as whether olive oil really does have brain-boosting properties, whether red wine might help us smooth out the wrinkles, or whether Icelanders live longer because of their diet of fresh seafood.

While the elixir of eternal youth will probably remain beyond our grasp, there is now a real buzz around the anti-ageing benefits of antioxidants. Found in many fruits and vegetables, particularly dried fruit like prunes and raisins, they will become an added extra in more and more manufactured or GM foods.

Allergies
REACTING BADLY

People seem to talk a lot more about allergies these days than they once did, particularly in cities. Although it's still not fully under-stood why some allergies seem to be increasing, foods can certainly play an important role, either in causing the problem in the first place or in controlling it once it is unavoidable

Food allergies are often difficult to diagnose, but once they have been identified – and appropriate steps taken – a person's health can improve dramatically. Note, however, that food allergies are much less common than many of us might believe, indeed only 1-2 per cent of people are actually allergic. And doctors have warned that some people risk making their (or their children's) lives miserable by insisting on a strict diet when it's not absolutely necessary.

The most common foods that provoke allergic reactions include milk, eggs, nuts, soya, wheat, fish and shellfish, which together account for some 90 per cent of all food allergic reactions.[154] Food additives, like certain colourings and preservatives, have been blamed for triggering allergies, but there is now strong scientific evi-dence to suggest that, while people may have 'intolerances' to addi-tives that can give rise to rashes, for example, they generally do not cause food allergies *per se*.

If you are looking for a diet that can help cut allergic reactions, avoid – or at least cut back on – alcohol, dairy products and wheat. It's believed that foods rich in vitamins B6 and C, calcium, magne-sium and zinc can all help. In particular, vitamin B6 and zinc help rebalance histamine levels, while vitamin B5 may even help reduce the symptoms.[155]

As we've indicated above, anyone planning to drop specific foods from their diet should consult an expert (doctor, dietician or nutri-tionist) first. Even replacing foods with similar products can have undesirable and unexpected side-effects. There have been recent warnings about replacing cow's milk with goat's milk, because those allergic to the one may well be allergic to the other.

Take the case of coeliacs, who are allergic to the protein gluten found in such grains as wheat and rye, as well as to similar substances found in barley and oats. Gluten appears to damage the lining of their intestines. Expect GM techniques to be used to grow gluten-free – or more likely gluten-reduced – crops. For the present, a number of gluten-free products are available, among them biscuits, bread, cakes and cereal.

As GM technologies become more widely used in food, the fear is that there will be all sorts of genes and gene products in the food we are eating that we will not know about, and will therefore not know to avoid. This would add a complicated dimension to any exclusion diet, which is one of the ways that people find out what may be the trigger behind an allergic reaction.

But GM techniques are also being used to help allergy sufferers – for example, scientists have developed non-allergenic GM nuts, but they are not yet on sale. And in Japan work is underway to produce non-allergenic rice. GM scientists have also worked out how to remove lactose from milk, an innovation that may be welcomed by millions of Africans and Asians, who often develop an intolerance to lactose (and therefore cannot drink much milk) in adulthood. One possible side-effect, though, which is unlikely to be taken into consideration, is that if more Africans and Asians start drinking milk, the increased demand will mean that dairy farming starts to encroach on large areas currently left open for wildlife.

One of the weirder stories to come out of the GM world suggested that relief might be on the way for hay fever sufferers now that 'sneeze free' flowers are being developed.[156] Scientists have managed to come up with pollen-free flowers – and are also planning to look at ways of producing pollen-free pasture grasses. The sheer number of pollen sources would suggest that this approach was almost doomed to failure, but is representative of the recent spate of 'advances' announced by the GM industry in its attempts to persuade a sceptical public to give it a freer rein.

Anaemia
BEYOND THE PALE

We become anaemic when we have too few red blood cells. This can be caused by some forms of heavy bleeding, such as heavy periods, ruptured piles and stomach ulcers.

The key to tackling anaemia is iron – and lots of it. The richest source of iron is red meat, whose iron is more easily absorbed than that from vegetable sources. This means that vegetarians (and vegans) may be more vulnerable, unless they are take care to eat enough vitamin B12.

Enthusiasts say that organic vegetables have higher iron levels than non-organic, but we have yet to see the proof of this. If you are taking iron tablets, the vitamin C in fruit and vegetables helps you to absorb it, while caffeine should be avoided as it slows down absorption. Folic acid is also thought to help ward off anaemia, so folate-fortified flours and breads might be helpful.

Arthritis
PAINS IN THE JOINTS

Arthritis is a potentially crippling disease, involving intensely painful inflammation in one or more of the body's joints. The affected joints gradually stiffen and, in osteoarthritis, the bone can become roughened and knobbly.

A small number of arthritis sufferers have a bad reaction to dairy products, and saturated fats are generally not recommended. Other possible problem foods include coffee, nuts, fruits with pips, and red wine. For some people members of the nightshade family – such as potatoes, tomatoes, aubergines and peppers – seem to aggravate their symptoms.

Traditional food cures have included vinegar and apples, while garlic and ginger are thought to have anti-inflammatory effects. Sunflower oil is recommended for cooking and gelatine is apparently good for joint pains. Vitamins A, C and E are all helpful, too. Indeed, one American study suggested that people who ate higher levels of vitamin C were three times less likely to see progression of the disease than those eating the lowest levels. These people may be attracted by the growing range of products with added vitamin C. But remember that citrus fruits, which have high levels of vitamin C, also have pips (see above).

Other new food products that may suit arthritics are those with added boron, calcium, magnesium, selenium and fish oils such as Omega-3. In this respect, a high-fish diet should be helpful, as both selenium and helpful oils are found in fish.

Asthma
BREATHING DIFFICULTIES

Anyone who has had – or slept next to a child suffering from – asthma knows how terrifying it can be. This is a lung condition that can lead to coughing, wheezing and shortness of breath. It affects about two million people in the UK and is generally something you are born with.

Preservatives and other food additives containing sulphites are known to be common triggers for asthma attacks. They are most likely to be found in squashes, wines, beers, cider, vinegar, dried fruits, quick frozen shellfish and some pre-prepared salads. Salt, too can make you more prone to an attack. Organic criteria rule out the use of sulphites.

Foods that can help include those rich in magnesium, such as nuts, rice and green vegetables. And fish oils, antioxidants, selenium and vitamins C and E may also boost the body's defence mechanisms against asthma attacks. Research suggests that people who don't eat fruit and vegetables regularly are more likely to suffer from asthma than those who do. Interestingly, British scientists now believe they have the makings of an asthma vaccine, based on an African soil bacterium.[157] Watch this space.

Brain and Memory
THOUGHT PROCESSES

Think about it. As we move into a knowledge economy, our brains become ever-more important. And as more of us live for longer, the demand for products that boost brain-power seems set to grow dramatically. But we will need to know a great deal more about how our brains work (see the Brakes and Accelerators box below) before we can safely use some of the more sophisticated products.

There are already some simple things that can be done to help our brains and memories function better, such as cutting down on alcohol intake. Drinking can damage both short- and long-term memory. Eating organic may also help, because pesticide residues are thought to damage memory, especially organophosphates.

Other things that may slow our brains down include too little vitamin B1, excessive carbohydrates (as opposed to proteins), and maybe even dieting. Tests have revealed that some dieters performed worse than non-dieters in tests of their memory, ability to sustain attention and reaction times.

If, on the other hand, you want to stimulate your brain, caffeine really does help you concentrate. It stops the brain chemical that tells your brain to 'put its feet up', so a cup of coffee helps offset that post-lunch dip in energy levels.

Below are some types of brain-food whose active ingredients may turn up in future new foods:

- *Arachodonic acid:* An essential fatty acid that aids brain development and is naturally found in cod liver oil and shellfish. GM scientists say they will soon be able to mass-produce this fatty acid in crop plants.[158]

- *Bananas:* These are rich in potassium, which can help combat fatigue and post-meal drowsiness.

- *Fish oils:* They always said that fish was good for your brain. Now it turns out that the fish oil DHA, one of the Omega-3 series, is linked to brain development in infancy and is good for the adult brain, too.

- *Olive oil:* Italian researchers have discovered that monounsaturated fatty acids, a major component in olive oil, may help guard against the effects of ageing on the brain. One possible reason: extra-virgin oil contains high levels of oleic acid.[159]

- *Vitamin E:* An American study found that vitamin E can slow the progress of Alzheimer's disease.

- *Wine:* A French study suggests that drinking three or four glasses of wine a day (red or white) actually decreases the risk of developing Alzheimer's.

Available on the Internet, but not elsewhere, is *Brain Gum*, which contains a fat called 'Phosphatidyl Serine' or PS, derived from soya. Claims that the gum 'switches on the brain' are based on the fact that PS plays a role in regulating the functions of brain cells. The manufacturers recommend chewing two pieces of gum, three times a day for three weeks and then cutting down to one piece a day thereafter. And they claim the gum is particularly helpful for older adults already experiencing a decline in memory.

Some experts in the field are sceptical about the product, but if it proves to be effective – or popular (not always the same thing) – we will probably see a lot more products of this sort. Gingko biloba and ginseng are already being used in a growing range of products – including 'smoothies' (see the section on Fruit Juices in chapter 4) – as 'brain boosters'.

Brakes and accelerators

L-TYROSINE vs L-TRYPTOPHAN

Some things speed our brains up, other things slow them down. In fact it turns out that two amino acids compete to control the way our brains work. L-tyrosine is used by the brain to make substances that are critical to feelings of alertness, to clear, quick thinking, and to long-term memory. L-tryptophan, on the other hand, is used to make serotonin, which slows down our reaction times, makes us feel full after a meal and induces sleep.

Natural sources of L-tyrosine include protein-rich foods like meat, poultry, seafood, beans, lentils and tofu; and L-tryptophan is found in bananas, milk and sunflower seeds. L-tryptophan supplements have been under a cloud in recent years (see XX box in chapter 3), however, and they are no longer available in the USA.

If L-tyrosine reaches the brain before L-tryptophan, it will prime the brain to function at top performance levels all day (or all night, depending on when you eat your meal). But if L-tryptophan gets there first, your mental performance will start to ebb and your brain will start to shut down – even if it's the middle of the day.

Cancer
THE BIG C

There are many different forms of cancer, with many different causes. It's possible to imagine a world in which our knowledge of genetics makes it much easier to know exactly who is at risk, from what and with what implications. In the process, some of us might have to worry more about specific cancers, others a lot less.

Meanwhile, the links between diet and cancer are increasingly highlighted. If present trends continue, literally every food and drink product will be suspected of cancer at some point in the 21st century. In Asia, for example, breast cancer strikes one in 40 women, compared with one in 12 British women. Genes presumably play some role, but increasingly, scientists are thinking that diet is crucial too.

Among the many foods suspected of causing cancer in at least some people are alcohol; barbecued or over-cooked meats; BST milk; some artificial colourings, preservatives and artificial sweeteners; coffee; salt; and saturated fats.

Foods and ingredients thought to help fight cancer include antioxidants; bio-cultures; blue-green algae; calcium; fatty acids, including fish oils; dietary fibre; fruit and vegetables; green and black teas; phytochemicals, although they work both ways; prebiotics and probiotics; yoghurts; wholegrain foods; and moderate wine drinking.

One possibility is that soya, which contains the phytochemical, genistein, is a powerful cancer-fighter. Genistein can also be found in flaxseed.[160] 'Anti-cancer' cereals bars are already being promoted because they contain this ingredient – and other similar food products are likely to follow.

Among other foods – or ingredients from them – likely to be targeted as anti-cancer aids are:

- The brassica family, including broccoli, cauliflower and other similar vegetables that contain indoles or glucosinolates

- Carrots and all red, yellow or dark green vegetables that contain carotenoids, thought to boost the immune system

- All citrus fruits, with their antioxidant flavonoids

- Low-fat dairy products, including spreads containing Omega-3 or Omega-6 fats

- Olive oil – indeed one Greek study has suggested that a daily dose of olive oil lowers the risk of breast cancer by 25 per cent

- Soyabeans, thought to help with menopausal problems and the prevention of breast cancer

- Tomatoes, thought to be most effective against cancers of the prostate, lung and stomach[161]

- Vitamin E, with recent American research suggesting that those taking vitamin E supplements were some 40 per cent less likely to die from cancer

- Wine, with grape skins containing reservatrol, a cancer-fighting chemical.

A challenge facing those trying to eat an anti-cancer diet is the complexity of foods and diets. No single food is going to be a panacea for cancer prevention, but some may help against one type or another. What is certain is that eating a balanced diet helps and that still more research is needed.

Candida
SILENCING THRUSH

This is an uncomfortable vaginal infection, caused by a yeast-like fungus. It often attacks when the immune system is depressed, which might be caused by a lack of vitamins and minerals.

Symptoms may also be provoked by foods containing yeasts (including fermented foods like alcohol, bread, blue cheeses and vinegar) and high-sugar foods, because the problem fungi feed on the excess sugar.

Traditional food remedies include garlic, with its wealth of phytochemicals. Some people also swear by bio-yoghurts. Their pre- and probiotic contents help to boost the numbers and health of beneficial microbes in the intestine. Bio-yoghurts are also recommended as a lotion to be applied to the affected area.

Children
GROWING UP

Children cannot be viewed simply as miniature adults. What they eat differs from adults most notably in both quantity (they eat more for their body-weight) and in the types of foods they need: the right foods for growth.

Children are often much more sensitive to contaminants such as pesticide residues, largely because their immune systems are less developed. There have been long-standing questions over the possible effect of some food additives, such as colourings (linked to hyperactivity) on children, but these have not been confirmed.

It's quite likely that the new range of functional foods will throw up its own set of worries for parents, since to date each functional food tends to be tested on its target audience, which generally does not include children. But manufacturers of cholesterol-lowering spreads, for example, point out that their spreads are unlikely to be eaten by children, partly because they are expensive; and they add that it would not be a problem if they were. Nevertheless, as more of these foods become available children will be eating more of them. To know that they had also been tested with children in mind would be reassuring.

Problems have already arisen when children have been fed inappropriate foods. Weight-conscious households, for example, may be giving children skimmed or semi-skimmed milk, rather than whole milk. Or, even worse, replacing the milk in their diets with fizzy drinks, to avoid the fat. Not so obvious is that if children under the age of five are given too many high-fibre foods, they may feel too full to eat the right foods that will satisfy their energy needs.[162]

One of the most controversial recent GM debates has been over the issue of Professor Pusztai's experiments on rats. The accuracy of his conclusions aside, he helped to expose a significant weakness in GM research to date. Pusztai pointed out that he was doing his tests on *young* rats, whose immune systems were still developing, to see if the effects were different than on adults. Specific testing for the safety of GM food ingredients on children had been virtually non-existent.

Kids mean big bucks for food-manufacturers. Indeed, many products are targeted directly at the young, encouraging them to use 'pester-power' to persuade their parents to buy. Some, such as the unsuccessful 'chocolate-flavoured carrots' mentioned earlier, actively try to encourage them to eat more healthily. But parents are also being beguiled into thinking that drinks such as squashes are less harmful because they have added vitamins, or that sugar-coated cereals are a healthy choice because of the minerals they contain.

New foods, with their array of new claims, are going to make choices for children even more complicated. But we should never lose sight of how crucial the diet we choose for our children is. It can shape their tastes, eating habits and health in later life.

Colds and Flu
SNEEZING AWAY

Although colds are the most common human disease, no effective cure has yet been found. This is partly because colds and flu are caused by hundreds of different viruses. Each time you catch a cold you become resistant to that particular virus, which is why young children are more susceptible than older people: almost every virus they meet is new. But these viruses are so clever at changing their appearance, they can make it hard for our immune systems to recognise, detect and destroy them.

At the moment, the best anti-flu strategy is to eat a diet including lots of fruit and vegetables. There is no good evidence that taking mega-doses of vitamin C prevent colds or flu, but taking vitamin C tablets once a cold has arrived in order to decrease its severity has both its supporters and detractors. Zinc is also recommended, but not alongside vitamin C.

Once infected, some people find it helpful to avoid foods like dairy products, chocolate, eggs and excessive meat or soya, all of which can be mucus-forming.

On the positive side garlic, fresh thyme, ginger and chillies are natural decongestants. Surprisingly, too, 90 per cent of those taking part in one medical trial showed a complete recovery from a flu virus within three days when taking elderberries, while those not eating the berries took an average of six days to recover.

Echinacea is billed as a useful cold remedy and immune system booster. It's already being added to yoghurts and confectionery. Worth trying, but don't count on it working miracles.

Constipation
BLOCKED PIPES

If you suffer from constipation, food is nearly always a major part of the solution. A diet high in fibre is recommended, as is at least a litre of water a day, preferably between meals. Include linseeds, oats and prunes in your diet, and remember that refined foods like sugar, white breads, white rice, cakes, biscuits, refined cereals and white pasta contain much less fibre than their unrefined counterparts.

On the new foods front, it really all began with the 'whole foods' trend and bran-fortified breads and cereals. The soluble fibre psyllium has even been used in *Ribena Juice & Fibre*, although this product is no longer on the market. Psyllium is now being put into a growing number of probiotic yoghurts, however, extending their beneficial effects on the gut to include regular bowel movements.

Cystitis
WATER WORKS

Cystitis can be a very painful bladder infection. At the onset of an attack, it's essential to cut out tea, coffee and alcohol and to drink plenty of water. A fundamentally healthy diet, low in refined sugar, can help prevent infection.

Some research suggests that drinking cranberry juice is an effective remedy, but no-one seems to know how it works. Vitamins A and C can help protect against such infections, while vitamin C can be helpful in tackling infections once they have started.

As yet there seem to be no 'new foods' targeting cystitis sufferers, although sales of cranberry juice have probably increased as this remedy has become better known. If and when a novel active ingredient is identified, food scientists may try to transfer it to a host of functional drinks – while GM scientists try to make other crops produce it in huge quantities. Another possible treatment is grapefruit seed extract.[163]

Depression
FEELING LOW

One reason why Finland has become such a hot-bed of functional food research is that its inhabitants are particularly at risk of dying of heart disease. They are also among the world's greatest depressives, some say because of the long winters spent without sun; and perhaps another factor to be taken into account in Finland is the high consumption of alchohol – a product that is almost guaranteed to cause depression when taken in excess.

On the bright side, all of this may mean that the Finns will develop new types of functional foods purpose-designed to cheer us all up. In the meantime, here are some mood enhancing tips.

- Research suggests that people who do not eat enough of the B complex vitamins are less happy than others and more prone to mood swings.

- Magnesium is also important for mental health.

- Vitamin C is depleted faster when your body is under stress – which it is if you are depressed.

- Fresh and dried fruit may help mild depression by releasing tryptophan, which your digestion can convert into a mood-enhancing compound.[164] Bananas, milk and eggs are also rich in natural tryptophan.

- It may be no coincidence that many people crave sweet foods when they feel depressed – like healthier carbohydrates, they release tryptophan as they are digested.

As for the traditional advice on depression, we are encouraged to cut down – or avoid – sugar and refined foods, and on stimulants like alcohol, chocolate, coffee, cola drinks and tea.[165]

New food offerings include foods containing Gingko biloba extracts or St John's wort, which are now being marketed as mood-lifters. And Omega-3 is also thought to be helpful with depression. In one trial of its effects on depressives, the results were so impressive that after four months those patients taking a placebo were given the real thing.

Digestive Problems
STRONG STOMACHS

Whatever form digestive problems take, they usually have a food solution. A growing range of foods and novel food ingredients – from bran to blue-green algae – are now on offer as keys to digestive bliss.

Among the more traditional remedies for an upset stomach is chamomile, because of its phytochemicals, some of which seem to block the formation of cancer-causing chemicals during the digestion of our food.

Some new foods are tailor-made to tackle digestive complaints like lactose intolerance. Others, including *Olestra*, are meant to alter the way in which key foods in our diet are digested. And still others, like blue-green algae and prebiotics and probiotics, are putting a new spin on some pretty traditional approaches to nutrition.

Fatigue
TIRED OUT

Many of us suffer from – or know people who suffer from – bouts of fatigue. In some cases it may even shade over into what is known as 'chronic fatigue syndrome', where the problem can last for six months or more.

Among the symptoms of chronic fatigue syndrome are memory or concentration problems, sore throats, tender lymph nodes, muscle pain, joint pains, headaches, poor sleep and prolonged fatigue after exercise.[166] Sometimes, this syndrome can be linked to a chronic back pain condition called fibromyalgia, which affects mainly women.

Normal fatigue can be addressed in a range of ways, including exercise, more sleep – and a diet that is strong on foods that counter stress and boost energy levels and the immune system.

For chronic fatigue, magnesium is thought to help. Although alcohol and caffeine may perk you up (in different ways) in the short term, they may well contribute to chronic fatigue. High-sugar and poorly balanced vegan or vegetarian diets low in iron or B complex vitamins may be other triggers.

Fertility
PRE CONCEPTION

There is a fairly long list of foods to avoid if you are having problems conceiving a child or bringing one to term. Alcohol would be high on anyone's list of must-avoids and caffeine can also be a significant problem.

Male fertility can be boosted with an adequate intake of zinc and a diet high in vitamins B6, C and E, fatty acids from fish oils, selenium and zinc. New evidence suggests that polyphenols in tea can boost fertility. Remember, too, that an organic diet can help both sexes avoid residues and other potential problem ingredients.

Flatulence
WIND CONDITIONS

We all suffer from flatulence at one time or another, but some people have more of a problem with it, especially when they eat pulses and other gassy foods. Beans (particularly baked beans) are always thought to be the gassiest food, but dieticians and nutritionists tell us that raw apples, onions, cooked cabbage and sprouts are worse for many people.

Bananas, particularly unripe ones, can boost stomach gas by as much as 50 per cent, and apples and raisins can double it. Other culprits include caffeine, beer and other fizzy drinks (not surprisingly), high-fat foods (such as cream and pastry) and fresh bread.

Some new foods – such as *Olestra* – are thought to make matters even worse. But bio-yoghurts can help the condition, and a growing range of foods, among them lentils and soya beans, are being genetically modified to make them less gas-producing. If these products ever get to market, it will be interesting to see how the public respond to 'fart-free' or 'low fart' foods. Perhaps they will go like the wind over the Net, where no-one can see what you are ordering.

Fun
THE F FACTOR

Food should be fun. Indeed, some Disney-like people even talk about 'eatertainment'. Be that as it may, the fun factor is always going to be part of the appeal of new foods. Many of us love trying something new, something different, which is how the human diet has developed into such a complex thing over the course of history. By now, we are probably genetically programmed to experiment with new foods, and if the manufacturers of new food products offer us the prospect of having our cake and eating it, chances are we'll love them for it.

Imagine not just talkative packaging but also foods that actually say 'Snap, Crackle and Pop' – or sing nursery rhymes – as you spoon them into your mouth. You heard it here first.

Hay Fever
POLLEN COUNTS

See Allergies.

Headaches and Migraines
BRAIN ACHES

Huge numbers of people suffer regularly from headaches, and many of us have also felt the full force of a migraine. It's not fully understood how particular foods help trigger migraines or headaches, but trials have shown that as many as 70 per cent of migraines in adults are caused by food, although the relationship between food sensitivity and migraines is complex. Two of the main triggers are dehydration and a drop in blood sugar. So the first bit of advice is to avoid long periods without food. Make sure you drink water regularly, but avoid sugar and stimulants.

Among the foods and food ingredients that can provoke headaches or migraines are alcohol; bakery products made with brewer's yeast; cheeses – the real 'head-bangers' seem to include Brie, Camembert, Emmenthal and Stilton; coffee; fruit (e.g. apples, bananas, citrus fruits); monosodium glutamate; some herbal remedies; pesticide residues; pickled, preserved or marinated food; various types of beans; and, back in the alcohol department, red wine.

Food that can sometimes help prevent or treat headaches and migraines are, oddly, coffee and cocoa (new information suggests that two cups of strong coffee taken just as migraine strikes can help some sufferers!);[167] herbal teas; feverfew, a herb similar to chamomile; nuts and seeds (Brazil nuts, pine nuts, cashew nuts, hazelnuts and walnuts are all high in magnesium, as are sunflower and sesame seeds); fish oils; and vinegar.

Heart Disease
CLOGGED ARTERIES

Heart disease is a major killer in the western world and diet is one of the main things that dictates who the victims are going to be. Among the foods that can contribute to heart problems are: alcohol; animal and other saturated fats; caffeine, which can lead to heart palpitations; calcium; the wrong types of cholesterol; salt; and some sweeteners.

As saturated fats are such a key factor in heart disease, a vegetarian diet may be one of the best preventative approaches. One study found that vegetarians have somewhere between 24 per cent and 45 per cent less risk of dying of coronary heart disease than meat-eaters.[168]

Some of the foods and ingredients that can help prevent, delay or treat heart disease include moderate consumption of alcohol; antioxidants; cereals; soluble dietary fibre; fish oils, including Omega-3 oils; flavonoids; folic acid; fruit and vegetables; liquid vegetable oils (corn, olive, soya, sunflower); nuts; potassium; selenium; and vitamins B6, C and E.

Cholesterol-lowering products are major players on the new food scene. Whether it's plant sterols (used in *Benecol*), the soluble fibre added to yoghurts, soya beans or soya milk to cut blood levels of LDL cholesterol, or the prebiotic and probiotic yoghurts, growing numbers of products are targeting heart disease.

Immune Systems
RUN DOWN

If you want a prediction of where the cutting edge of 21st century medicine will go, it's easy. We already see intense interest in the human immune system, which can only intensify. Diseases like AIDS have spotlighted just how complex our immune systems are – immune-boosters and anything to do with them are likely to rocket up the food industry's agenda.

Simpler ideas that already work include avoiding substances that can depress the immune system like alcohol, coffee and strong spices.[169] That said, we're also likely to see rapid growth in the number of products featuring antioxidants, beta-carotene, bio-cultures, extracts of plants like Echinacea, St John's wort and ginseng, other phytochemicals, such as catechins, vitamins C and E, and perhaps also coconut oil-derived lauric acid.

Insomnia
SWEET DREAMS

In these stressed-out times, insomnia is more common than ever. Although chemical solutions, such as sleeping pills, may be tempting, there is much that can be done on the dietary front.

Most obviously, drinks containing caffeine – among them coffee, tea and some soft drinks – keep many people from sleeping. Foods eaten late – including cheese and meat – can spark bad dreams in some people. It's better to eat at least three hours before going to bed; and, while it may seem like a good idea at the time, alcohol can produce a state of semi-unconsciousness rather than true sleep.

Calming foods that may help bring on sleep include potatoes and other carbohydrates; hot milk drinks (milk contains calcium, known as 'Nature's tranquilliser'); nuts and seeds, both rich in calming magnesium; and lettuce. People who sleep badly in winter, but not in summer, may be suffering from low serotonin production. Foods rich in tryptophan help boost serotonin levels. They include hot milk, digestive biscuits, bananas, low-fat cheese, bread and peanut butter.

Menopause
CHANGE OF LIFE

As women continue to live longer – and expect a higher quality of life – we will see a burgeoning of foods designed to prevent or moderate the problems linked with the menopause.

It is important to keep a sensible weight throughout menopause, and the best way to do this is to eat healthily and cut back on junk foods. Some women find that a hot drink or drinking alcohol can also trigger hot flushes. Traditional foods for reducing PMS are useful during the menopause, helping to avoid fluid retention, a common problem in both. Fluid retention is provoked by foods with high salt content and helped by natural diuretics such as asparagus, celery and parsley.

Mood swings and depression can be helped by bioflavonoids, B complex vitamins, magnesium, zinc and St John's wort, which is now being added to a number of new foods. Selenium may also help improve hair and skin condition.

A vegetarian diet can help moderate oestrogen-linked problems (an issue in menopause) – and is actively anti-carcinogenic, unlike hormone replacement therapy (HRT). Vitamin E is said to help minimise hot flushes and counter vaginal dryness.

Interestingly, Chinese and Japanese women tend not to suffer from hot flushes and other significant symptoms of menopause. This has been put down to the fact that they regularly eat soya-based foods, such as tofu, which contain powerful phytoestrogens, alongside other oestrogen-rich foods such as yams, linseed and bean-sprouts.

It seems likely that we will see something of a gold rush in this area, with food manufacturers racing to design functional foods to tackle menopause symptoms. Products with added antioxidants, blue-green algae, added calcium, new dietary fibres, fatty acids like Omega-3, probiotics and vitamin E are already beginning to hit the shelves.

One product, already on the market is *Burgen Bread*, launched in 1997 by **Allied Foods**, which has been promoted on the basis that it can help women suffering from hot flushes. The stated health benefits of the bread, made with soya and linseed, included lowered blood cholesterol and 'keeping bones strong'. But an Australian study concluded it was too early to make any such links.

Another new cereal bar, called *Preva*, has been launched. Its manufacturers say it is formulated to exert an anti-cancer effect, as well as helping with osteoporosis, menopause symptoms, breast health and cholesterol. Breathtaking claims.

Mood
SWINGS AND ROUNDABOUTS

The drug industry is pouring out a growing range of products designed to alter our moods, from *Prozac*, billed to tackle depression, obsession and bulimia, to *Paxil*, which promises to address shyness as well. Many of these drugs target the brain chemical serotonin, which seems to govern mood.[170] Too little serotonin, and we feel negative about ourselves and the world around us. Those feelings can express themselves in different ways, as anxiety, depression, kleptomania, obsession, phobias, pre-menstrual mood swings, eating disorders, the list is endless. These new mood drugs work by keeping serotonin levels under control.

And where drugs go today, new foods may well go tomorrow. Low-tech 'mood foods' include coffee and chocolate, while carbohydrates can relieve depression and high-protein meals increase alertness. Both serotonin and tryptophan – our body uses the latter as a building block for making serotonin – are the magic ingredients in effective mood foods. St John's wort has also emerged from the medicine cabinet and can now be found in so-called 'happy crisps', amongst other things. But, remember, one of the best mood-lifters is – and will remain – healthy exercise.

Obesity
FAT FIGHTERS

See Slimming.

Osteoporosis
CRUMBLING BONES

Bones are strongest and thickest in early adult life. Thereafter, they gradually become thinner with age, through the progressive loss of protein and calcium. Exercise is usually the best way of keeping your bones strong, so immobilising diseases like rheumatism or arthritis can boost your chances of suffering from 'brittle bone syndrome'. Sex hormones can also play a role, which is why women are more vulnerable than men to osteoporosis in later life, after the menopause.

For young women, the most important time to boost calcium intake and bone strength is during their teenage years, when they are still developing. Yet surveys show that two-thirds of teenagers are more concerned about how much fat there is in their food than about its calcium content. As a result, the head of nutrition at **Nestlé** recently warned of 'a potential osteoporosis epidemic 50 years from now', as the number of elderly people increases.

Foods to avoid include alcohol (heavy drinkers often suffer from' low bone density, because alcohol can reduce the absorption of calcium); caffeine-rich foods, which also slow calcium absorption; and salts and other sodium-rich foods (sodium causes increased excretion of calcium in the urine).

Some experts believe that magnesium is as important as calcium in bone formation, along with fish oils and vegetable oils, which are also good for absorbing calcium. Other pieces of the healthy bone puzzle include vitamins B6, C, D and K, folic acid, potassium and zinc.

New foods already on offer include cereal bars with extra soya, which are not a good source of calcium but are thought to contain beneficial phytochemicals; flour fortified with folic acid; and fruit juices and other products enriched with calcium.

Pain
NERVE ENDINGS

No-one needs to be told what pain is, although the forms it can take are almost as various as the number of people on the planet. Many of the diseases profiled here – among them arthritis, various forms of cancer, and osteoporosis – can cause great pain in sufferers. What relatively few people know is that foods can help fight many types of pain.[171]

We have already mentioned several ways in which pain can be relieved. Gelatine-based products may help with pain in the joints, for example, and ginseng can provide pain relief during cocaine withdrawal. But these facts simply represent the tip of an iceberg.

It is now known that many of us feel pain more acutely after we have eaten sugar, and less pain after we have eaten wholegrain foods. Spicy foods are also powerful pain fighters, because they block the abilities of the nerves to transmit pain signals. And the same low-fat, high-fibre diet used to treat heart problems has been found also to ease back pain.

Research has shown that rice or peppermint oil can soothe the digestive tract. Ginger and the herb feverfew can prevent migraines, and coffee can sometimes cure them once they have started. Natural plant oils can reduce the pain caused by arthritis. And vitamin B6 can increase your overall resistance to pain.

Pregnancy
GREAT EXPECTATIONS

What you eat during pregnancy can make a great deal of difference to the health of your baby. Most mothers are now well-informed about foods to avoid, which include alcohol – even moderate drinking during pregnancy can affect the baby's development; caffeine – research suggests that as little as one and a half cups a day can significantly increase the risk of miscarriage; green top milk; and any food likely to be contaminated by listeria bacteria, such as patés and soft cheeses.

Many women take folic acid supplements prior to conception and during the first few months of pregnancy. This apparently reduces the chance of having a child with spina bifida. Because so many women were lacking in folic acid in the USA, all flour is now fortified with it.

Obviously all the general advice about a balanced diet applies particularly during pregnancy, but one thing prospective mothers may not be aware of is the particular benefits of fish oils. DHA, a component of Omega-3, is an essential building block for the brains of the unborn and newly born. If levels of DHA in pregnant mothers is low, the baby will use what there is and leave the mother lacking. And studies in Australia show that breast-fed babies whose mothers have adequate levels of DHA in their diet may enjoy a 10-point IQ advantage in later childhood.

There are already a number of supplements designed for pregnant women. Expect more, with a new food spin. But let's say it again; nothing beats eating a balanced diet, with lots of fruit and vegetables.

Pre-Menstrual Syndrome (PMS)
MONTHLY BLUES

One of the most common complaints linked to periods is pre-menstrual syndrome (PMS). The symptoms include weight gain, fluid retention, bloating, food cravings, breast pain, irritability, tiredness and depression. All of these can appear a few days before a woman's period and disappear a day or two after it has begun.[172]

Among foods to avoid prior to menstruation are alcohol, caffeine, fats (cut down by eating leaner cuts of meat and drinking skimmed milk) and salt. Fluid retention partially caused by such foods can account for 7 lbs (3.25 kg) of extra weight before a period, but reducing salt intake can help lessen the bloated feeling. A recent study suggested that reducing vegetable oils is helpful because a dramatic reduction in fat can curtail the hormone swings that influence the severity of menstrual pain.[173]

Foods and food ingredients for dealing with PMS include bananas (rich in potassium and vitamin B6, recommended for breaking down oestrogens); drinks like water, low-fat milk, fruit and vegetable juices, and herbal teas; yeast extract, whole grains, and fruit and vegetables (particularly leafy vegetables); iron and iron-rich foods; tryptophan, found in fresh fruit, vegetables, hot milk, digestive biscuits, bread and bananas; vegetable oils, fish oils, nuts and seeds; and vitamin E. In short, a healthy, balanced diet.

Scientists hope to engineer crop plants like sunflowers and linseed to produce commercial quantities of products like gamma linoleic acid (GLA). Better known as evening primrose oil, GLA is now a popular medicine and health supplement and PMS is one of the conditions it is used to treat. Recently, scientists in the UK said they had managed to double the levels of GLA in crops such as tobacco – and forecast they would boost levels further.

Commercial varieties, it is claimed, are less than five years away; but such products are much more likely to be offered as pharmaceuticals than as functional foods, at least to start with.

Sex
BASIC APPETITE

Many of the conditions and diseases reviewed here link – directly or indirectly – to our sexual health and energies. If we are depressed or anxious, for example, our sexual drive is likely to be lower than normal.

Scientists in the USA have even speculated that vegetarian and vegan diets are not good for the libido because the higher levels of zinc found in meat and eggs boost energy levels. They say that up to half the vegetarians they surveyed reported they were too tired to make love when they got home from work.

Other scientists, unsurprisingly, have trashed these claims, noting that zinc also appears in vegetarian foods (e.g. wheatgerm, *Quorn*, cashew, pecan and pine nuts, seaweed, and poppy, pumpkin, sesame and sunflower seeds). They also point out that vegetarians are less likely to suffer from atheriosclerosis, which can be linked to impotence.[174]

Among possible new food solutions for low sex drive are Maté for 'sexier sex', and anything fortified with vitamin E. But in our view the brain, in the end, is still the sexiest organ by far.

Skin
OUTER LAYERS

Our skin can be an excellent indicator of our health, and a healthy diet is always going to be better for skin than a diet rich in junk foods, fat and sugar.

The causes of skin problems like acne and eczema are complex, and they will rarely be cured by a simple food switch. Nevertheless, there is still some useful nutritional advice for acne sufferers: avoid fatty foods, chocolate and salt. Instead, eat plenty of fresh fruit and vegetables, particularly those rich in beta-carotene, including carrots, apricots, sweet potatoes and broccoli. Also important, particularly for healing wounds, is zinc, found in foods such as shellfish, lean meat, eggs and nuts, and sulphur, found in foods such as eggs, onions and garlic.

Vitamin A, which is synthesised from beta-carotene, helps boost the immune system. The B complex vitamins are helpful, as is vitamin C, which helps the body fight infections, and skin healing can be promoted by foods rich in vitamin E, including vegetable oils, nuts and seeds. Both sunshine and selenium can help, but avoid supplements containing iodine, which may make matters worse.[175]

Foods commonly reported to cause or worsen eczema include milk, cheese and eggs, citrus fruits, food colourings and preservatives, nuts, tomatoes and fish. Eczema sufferers often find that the condition improves if they adopt a diet low in saturated fats but high in essential fatty acids.

Some new foods – like aspartame – are suspected by some to cause skin problems, but there is also a range of new food solutions including bio-cultures and novel fats and oils. Possible candidates for future fortified foods include vitamins A and B2 and niacin. Deficiencies of linoleic acid, which is found in fish and vegetable oils, such as cottonseed, linseed and safflower oil, can cause scaly skin, suggesting that it may also qualify. And green tea is promoted as a preventative for skin cancer, raising some interesting functional food prospects.

Slimming
WEIGHTS AND MEASURES

Unfortunately, people who are obese are more likely to develop arthritis, high blood pressure, heart disease, diabetes and gallstones. In America, more than half the adult population – nearly 100 million people – are now considered overweight. For a few people, this is simply a matter of their genetic inheritance, but for most it's a direct result of eating too much for too long – and of not exercising enough.[176]

Obvious foods to cut down on include butter and other saturated fats and oils. Although eating fats makes you feel full, they generally take some time to release sugar into the bloodstream, so we tend to overeat them before noticing any 'satisfying' effect.[177]

When you eat sugary foods you get an almost immediate boost to blood sugar levels and a subsequent surge of energy and feeling of fullness. So far so good. But the body then metabolises the excess blood sugar, which makes you feel hungry again. The net result is that sugary foods can add to your fat quota and leave you feeling hungry.[178] Cereals, potatoes and beans, by contrast, are high in carbohydrates and fibre, so they absorb water and fill you up without piling on the pounds. Fruit and vegetables will provide most of the nutrients you need, without loads of calories. And it is worth noting that beans, pulses and grains are almost fat free.

On the new foods front, we see growing numbers of products designed to allow you to eat more without getting fat. One of the longest-running new food sagas focuses on *Olestra*, now used in a growing range of deep-fried foods in the USA. We're also seeing new products – like *Benecol* – designed not only to cut down on our fat intake but also actively to scour our bodies for harmful cholesterol.

It's sensible to avoid most 'meal-replacement' products, as the sort of crash diets they are designed to help are not at all healthy. It is no longer permitted for food and drink products to state that they lead to 'a reduction in the sense of hunger or an increase in the sense of satiety'. Nor is it permitted for products to make any claims relating to the weight loss that might result from their use. Some products making such claims proved to have high sugar and fat contents. They are not recommended for most slimmers, because they make it easy to return to poor eating habits and can encourage unhealthy 'yo-yo' dieting.[179]

One new product in this area is *Skåne Dairy Måväl*, which includes an ingredient said to suppress appetite, but the manufacturer does not make the claim that it will help people to take off weight.

There are also interesting moves afoot to develop products that send more powerful 'I'm full' signals from the stomach to the brain. **Amgen**, a leading American biotechnology firm, has been working on a new drug, based on a protein called leptin, which would persuade the brain to switch off the appetite sooner than normal.

This is a different approach from existing anti-obesity drugs (not foods) that work either on the brain or on the gut. **Roche**, for example, manufactures an anti-obesity pill – *Xenical* – that inhibits the enzymes in the intestine that are responsible for breaking down fat. Others, some of which have proved to have worrying side-effects, act by boosting levels of the brain chemicals that suppress the appetite.

Food companies are fascinated by this work. **General Mills**, the American food giant behind brands like *Betty Crocker* dessert and *Yoplait*, has an agreement with the Scottish biotechnology company **Scotia** covering the latter's *Olibra* appetite suppressant. The compound, which could be used in everything from soups to salad creams, hoodwinks the brain into thinking that the stomach is full when it isn't.

Scientists have discovered a gene that, if modified in humans, could allow them to eat as much as they want and still stay thin. Scientists do not yet know how the gene works, but tests on GM mice show that they stay the same weight, while other mice fed the same high-fat diet double their weight. Before you get too excited, however, consider that one unexpected side-effect for the thinner mice was that they aged faster![180]

Sports
FIGHTING FIT

The sports industry is booming around the world, and with it the demand for new sports drinks and energy bars. Some of these products may genuinely help, but the consensus seems to be that most are over-priced and fail to deliver on their promises.

The vogue for rippling physiques – in part inspired by stars like Madonna – has been tempting growing numbers of athletes to take a muscle-building food supplement.[181] Indeed, the number of people taking creatine supplements has jumped four-fold in the past five years. The supplement provides a massive daily dose of 30 grams of amino acids, producing creatine levels equivalent to eating 25–30 steaks. The two leading UK manufacturers sell about a fifth of their products to women, mostly by mail order. But this isn't like an anabolic steroid, and it only really works if you take lots of exercise. As with so many other short-cuts, there are reasons to be careful. Creatine may impose extra strain on the kidneys, which have to work harder to dispose of the waste products, and any side effects may only begin to surface decades in the future.

Stress
OVERLOADED

All sorts of things can cause stress: over-work, too little sleep, moving house, a new job, bereavement. Obvious symptoms of stress include eating disorders, fatigue, migraine, heartburn, impotence, insomnia, irritable bowel syndrome, memory problems and muscular pain.

Beware of the temptation to treat the symptoms, rather than the root cause. But if you are suffering from stress you will need to be careful about what you eat because stress weakens the immune system and depletes the body of certain vitamins and minerals.

Vitamin B is largely responsible for the smooth running of the nervous system and can be severely depleted by chronic stress. Increased levels of vitamin C are needed, and of zinc, which is important for the immune system. Magnesium, too, which is excreted in greater amounts when one is under stress, should be boosted.

Avoid alcohol, if possible, because it can further deplete the body of vitamins B and C, and can hinder the absorption of other vitamins. Recognise, too, that the increase in adrenaline caused by stress can raise the level of fats and cholesterol in your blood, increasing the risk of heart disease.

Fruit and vegetables are good sources of vitamins B and C, magnesium and zinc. And the carbohydrates in fruit and whole grain will help the brain to calm down by triggering the release of serotonin. Bio-yoghurts may help and products containing St John's wort claim to bring benefits for the stressed. The key steps are to slow down, eat a healthier diet, take exercise and try to find ways to relax.

Teeth
STOPPING THE ROT

Hey, you know all this. Brush and floss regularly. We all know that eating sweets is bad for teeth. In fact, all sweet foods and drinks – including honey – increase acidity and contribute to tooth decay. This can happen within 5–10 minutes of exposure to the sugar-loving bacteria! But not everyone knows that eating hard cheese at the end of meals can help stop tooth-damaging acid formation.

Foods containing sugar are part of a healthy balanced diet, but obviously it's better to eat them as part of a meal, rather than continuously throughout the day. Fizzy drinks and squashes often have particularly high sugar levels. And drinking sweet drinks from a straw – or beaker – can be particularly damaging, because this means your teeth may be under focused 'sugar attack' for longer periods.

Good-for-teeth foods include almost anything rich in calcium, although beware of calcium-fortified soft drinks, with added sugar; fluoride-fortified water and toothpastes; phosphorus, vitamins A and D; and, up to a point, artificial sweeteners that give you the impression of sweetness without the sugar attack.

Ribena Toothkind, although supported by the **British Dental Association**, came under attack because, while it may have been less bad than competing products, it was definitely not actually *good* for children's teeth – which the name might seem to suggest.

Vegetarians
EATING GREENS

There are all sorts of reasons for becoming a vegetarian. The ethical issues, like animal welfare, are obviously high in many minds; and the fact that if the world switched to a vegetarian diet overnight many of our most serious ecological problems would disappear obviously feeds into the equation. But there are plenty of selfish reasons too.[182]

For example, large-scale research studies have shown that vegetarians suffer from up to 30 per cent less heart disease, up to 40 per cent less cancer, 20 per cent less premature mortality, less obesity, lower blood pressure and better health on many other fronts, too.

As with any diet, it's important for vegetarians to include as many different foods as possible, since no single food contains all the nutrients required for good health. Vegans, in particular, need to research their needs carefully to make up for the lack of meat, eggs and dairy produce. If a vegan eats an unbalanced diet, there is a real risk of problems like anaemia and chronic fatigue.

So what does a balanced vegetarian diet contain? Here are some key elements:

- Plant-based protein, with grains such as wheat (which are poor in the essential amino acid lysine) mixed with legumes (beans, peas), which are rich in lysine

- If you can add in egg or milk products, the protein quality increases considerably

- Margarine or dairy products, to supply essential fats, calcium and vitamins A and D

- Improve iron absorption by eating fruits rich in vitamin C (e.g. blackcurrants, grapefruit, guava, kiwi fruit, oranges), or drink a large glass of fresh fruit juice with each meal

- Wholegrain cereals provide a rich source of B vitamins, other than B12, as well as being a good source of dietary fibre

- Phytic acid, found in whole grains, can cut mineral absorption, but is broken down by yeast. This means that bread is particularly important to the vegetarian diet.[183]

In addition to traditional foods based on soya beans, among them soy sauce and tofu, we see other novel foods feeding into the market, including products containing blue-green algae, chymosin and – that minor miracle – *Quorn*.

And what about the impact on the vegetarian's sex life? A storm in teacup, we suspect, or perhaps a salad bowl.

Now, before launching our New Foods Manifesto in chapter 7, and spotlighting the New Food Stars, we explore some of the deep trends and big issues likely to shape our diets over the first couple of decades of the 21st century. They range from the constant tension between population numbers and food supply to the question of how we can make all our food chains not only more productive but also more transparent and future-friendly.

6

FOOD FIGHTS

Behind the Scenes

Most of us threw food around as children, many of us even got involved in food fights in the nursery or at school. But now the world of food is being rocked by food scares and virtual trade wars between the superpowers. The EU and the USA have recently locked horns in a series of hard-fought food disputes over bananas, beef hormones and GM foods. In the fallout, the USA has threatened to boycott European products as diverse as chocolate, motorcycles, salami and woollen clothing.

Why is all this happening now? We will look briefly at some key issues that are defining the future of food. In doing so, we will move from questions with global significance (such as the continuing tension between feast and famine) to the sort of concerns that people ordinarily worry about: Is 'natural' food better than processed? Should I stop eating meat? Is fast food always unhealthy? And, finally, where can I find future-friendly food that will help ensure that today's children enjoy healthier food and tomorrow's enjoy a healthier environment?

Feast vs Famine
HOW MUCH IS ENOUGH?

Famines have devastated different parts of the world throughout history. When we took the New Foods Time Machine back to the year 1,000, for example, there had been repeated recent famines. Even today, an estimated 19,000 children die every week from hunger and diseases related to poor nutrition. That's equivalent to a jumbo jet full of children crashing into the ground every hour and killing everyone on board.

We live in a world of extremes. While hundreds of millions of people struggle to find enough food to survive, many millions are also now overweight to the point of obesity. In England alone, a staggering 9.5 million people were recently found to be obese – 16 per cent of men and 18 per cent of women. And another 45 per cent of men and 34 per cent of women were found to be overweight.

Whether we like it or not, functional foods designed to combat obesity will probably bring their manufacturers ever-fatter profits. Indeed, the central aim of many functional foods is to allow the wealthy world to eat more of what they like without getting fat or unhealthy in the process. It may not be stretching it too far to see this as the modern equivalent of the Roman vomitoriums where wealthy Romans went to eat, regurgitate and eat again. In the face of mass starvation, this trend might appear to be rather grotesque.

On the other hand, new food technologies are also being offered as a means of feeding the starving. We should be in no doubt that a great deal more food will be needed as the world's human population soars from its current 6 billion to an estimated 7.5–10 billion by 2050. If we are to feed up to twice as many people world-wide, and do so without putting every last acre of the planet's surface under the plough, we will have to intensify agricultural production still further.

The GM food industry, in particular, claims that its products will help feed the world's poor. Most GM food companies say that their technology will simultaneously boost the productivity of farms and cut the costs of production. But their critics, including many aid charities, urge caution. They warn that if peasant farmers become totally dependent on hi-tech solutions offered by giant corporations, the risk of mass starvation could grow rather than lessen. GM companies and food companies have fought back with highly pessimistic forecasts for organic production. The chairman of one big food manufacturer, **Northern Foods**, has even predicted that 'an organic global food chain would create instant catastrophic famine'. The organic movement hasn't accepted that attack lying down. The head of the UK's leading organic certification organisation, the **Soil Association**, counter-argued that 'organic or low-input systems can produce just as much as intensive systems, if they are well managed.'

The uncomfortable truth remains that the organic farming industry is still small, fragmented and struggling to scale up production without sacrificing its standards along the way. Organic production has huge potential, but it has a long way to travel if it is to become a major player in the market. It receives minute subsidies and financial support from governments compared to the vast sums invested in developing more intensive systems such as those based on GM crops, and this imbalance will have to be rectified if the potential of organic food production is to be realised.

In the end, though, feeding the world will not simply be a matter of either GM or organic, but of both/and.

Price vs Quality
IS FOOD TOO CHEAP?

How many of us, when staggering back from the supermarket with the week's shopping, think our food should be more expensive? Almost none of us, of course. Yet there is a strong argument for believing much of our food is too cheap. The pressure to make food ever cheaper is forcing every part of the food chain to cut its costs, a process massively reinforced by the buying power of the supermarkets. Unfortunately, cutting costs can often also mean cutting corners and therefore standards, and all sorts of environmental, social and ethical problems have surfaced around the world as a result.

Hedgerows are ripped up to create ever-larger fields for bigger farm machinery, promoting soil erosion. Heavy applications of fertilisers are used to ensure greater productivity, causing widespread water pollution. Single crop monocultures proliferate, boosting the need for pesticides. And animal welfare standards are too often compromised in the quest for more meat or eggs per 'unit' of space or food.

Perhaps the most dramatic example of the damage that such cost-cutting could wreak surfaced with the BSE (bovine spongiform encephalopathy) crisis. The media dubbed it 'mad cow disease', but this was a very man-made madness. The current consensus is that the BSE outbreak was caused by cows being fed the remains of diseased animals. But it still is not clear if the feed was contaminated because it contained dead animals that were diseased, or whether it was because some of those dead animals had been injected with contaminated growth hormones. Experiments carried out in the 1980s took hormones from dead animals and injected them into live ones, to create larger cattle. Recent research suggests that some of these hormone-containing extracts may have been contaminated with a new variant of Creutzfeldt-Jakob disease (CJD). And therefore when cows which had been used in the experiment were turned into animal feed, it's thought that they may have passed on the contamination.[184] Another theory is that the immune systems of cows may have become weakened by the use of organophosphates, a pesticide used against warble fly.

Whatever the explanation turns out to be, one thing is clear. The experiments were largely driven by pressures to cut the costs of producing food – and of animal feed. As one farmer put it, 'If the first priority of consumers is cheap food, it may not be entirely coincidental that the same objective is adopted all the way up the food chain.'

Now we see the American chain **Wal-Mart** taking over **Asda** in the UK, with the implication that the price competition will soar to dizzying new heights. While there will be undoubted short term economic benefits for many consumers, the environmental (and social) costs could be considerable.

It is too easy to blame farmers. They are only supplying what we – and, as a result, the major food retailers – demand. Recent laws, for example, have forced UK pig and poultry farmers to adopt the highest animal welfare standards in Europe, because of strong animal welfare concerns here. And what has happened? Most British consumers won't pay the higher prices, preferring the cheaper meat from abroad on offer in the supermarket. When it comes to food scares, however, organic farmers are on strong ground. They do not cut the same corners as most mainstream farmers. As a result, their produce and products are often – although not always – significantly more expensive. The evidence, though, is that growing numbers of us will pay for quality in at least some of the food we buy, for example free-range chickens, organic fruit and vegetables, or fairly traded coffee.

Even the more conservative supermarkets now stock such products, and some, like **Safeway**, **Sainsbury's**, **Tesco**, **Waitrose** and **Marks & Spencer** are investing considerably in this area. As they do so, economies of scale switch on. Prices fall, overall quality and availability improve, and packaging and presentation become more competitive. It's no coincidence that sceptical consumers who felt they were 'paying more for less' are beginning to be won over.

And where do functional foods fit in? Well, they are potentially big earners for the food industry. While companies can charge more for processed foods than for fresh produce, functional foods will allow them to charge more again. But here's the catch: these higher prices will be no guarantee that the functional foods have been produced in a future-friendly way or that they will be better for you than eating a healthy balanced diet, with lots of fresh fruit and vegetables.

Natural vs Hi-Tech
CAN WE EAT OUR WAY BACK TO EDEN?

We have always had a tendency to over-dramatise the way that hi-tech will change our lives. In the 1970s, TV advertisements for *Smash* instant mashed potato featured robots laughing at human cooks. The robots found it hilarious that we still peeled potatoes using metal knives and then 'smashed' them to bits. The message was that all the food of the future would be hi-tech, but, while such convenience products do sell well, consumers today are more likely to buy pre-prepared peeled potatoes rather than powders.

At the other end of the spectrum, there have been the intermittent protest movements encouraging us to move back to the land, 'back to Nature'. The hippies were one such movement, 'dropping out' to grow their own food and re-establish their roots in the soil. Although the flower power period of the late 1960s faded, the interest in food intensified in the 1970s. This is the wave that some of the smaller pioneers rode, among them **Doves Farm**, **Rachel's Dairy**, the **Pure Food Company**, the **Village Bakery** and **Whole Earth Foods**.

For years, many of these pioneers struggled to make a living, but the high-profile food scares of the 1990s, including those triggered by food additives, food contamination (particularly BSE) and GM foods, have boosted public fears of hi-tech food production. The appeal of the 'natural' is something many food manufacturers already try to exploit, offering products dressed up as if they were natural and traditionally produced. But there are no laws about the definition of the word 'natural' in this context. And in the wider context it doesn't mean 'safe', either. The natural world is full of perfectly natural toxins designed to protect plants against pests or animals against predators. When Arctic explorers gorged on perfectly natural polar bear livers, many died.

This is the background against which functional foods are being introduced. Such products are often made by big manufacturers with large advertising budgets, but you can be sure they won't use this particular F-word in their ads. Instead, expect them to steer clear of hi-tech images and to play up what we might call 'super-natural' health claims.

The challenge is not to opt for either exclusively natural or exclusively hi-tech foods, but to take on board the lessons that nature is trying to teach us as we create our new farming systems and food products. And the interesting thing is that growing numbers of consumers understand that.

When asked, 'what type of food would you say is the healthiest?', people interested in healthy eating put fresh organic produce at the top of their list. Further down the list come processed organic foods, ahead of fresh non-organic produce. Functional foods come next, ahead of other processed foods, then fresh GM produce, and very definitely last, processed foods that are both GM and functional.[185]

For new food manufacturers wanting to sell in the UK, the consumer message is clear. Health conscious consumers want organic products, as long as they are affordable and well presented. They welcome functional foods cautiously, but are inclined to reject GM foods. Here, at least, natural wins out over hi-tech. But in other parts of the world the balance will be different.

Global vs Local
HOW MANY FOOD MILES HAVE YOU GOT?

As we collect 'air miles', are we also now being asked to collect 'food miles'? No. The idea behind the food miles campaign is not to encourage us travel more, but to make us aware of how far our food travels before we get to eat it. German researchers have shown that the various ingredients in one kind of strawberry yoghurt had travelled thousands of miles before the finished product landed on the table. Nor is that unusual. Refrigerated container ships and jet aircraft now crisscross the globe. Freight lorries speed from one end of the continent to the other. Even within the UK, food now travels 50 per cent further than it did just 15 years ago.

The effects of globalisation can be seen wherever you go. In Mongolia, a country that has survived on local milk products for thousands of years, you find mainly German butter in the shops. In Kenya, butter from Holland can be half the price of local butter. In Spain, the dairy products are often Danish. And in England butter from New Zealand is often considerably cheaper than most locally produced brands, even though it has been shipped from the other side of the world. Peas from Africa, strawberries from California, apples from Chile or new potatoes from Cyprus – absurd, perhaps, but people are becoming increasingly dependent for their every day 'needs' on food produced far away. And summer, autumn, winter or spring, there is now little difference in what is available on the supermarket shelves.

There are many benefits, of course, but most people, faced with what looks like a growing diversity of foods on offer, are unaware that this consumer choice is achieved only with a considerable narrowing of the varieties of any particular fruit or vegetable. All over the world, crop varieties are now picked for their size, ability to travel and for their shelf-life, rather than for their taste. Consequently, the number of, for example, varieties of pea, carrot or potato that are available to us has shrunk dramatically.

Many local varieties are becoming altogether extinct. This is partly because it has become illegal to sell them unless they are officially registered, and registration requires a fee. In the UK, the **Henry Doubleday Research Association's** (**HDRA**) Heritage Seed Fund campaigns to protect fruit and vegetable varieties that may be of interest only to small-scale gardeners because, for example, they taste good but do not have a long shelf-life.

The cultural impact of food giants with world brands are another concern, as their operations spread around the world. Such companies not only operate by driving local, more diverse suppliers into bankruptcy, but their products help reprogram the values and lifestyle expectations of whole societies.

And GM foods, of course, are the very epitome of globalisation. Some claim that the trade wars between the USA and Europe have really erupted because the USA wants to force world-wide acceptance of their GM technology. Rich world consumers worry that globalisation means their foods often come via commodity markets. Commodity markets can make it almost impossible to tell where particular food ingredients have come from. A high proportion of GM crop products have already been produced on a commodity basis and then mixed in with non-GM versions. The answer, say campaigners who want greater consumer choice, is segregation of GM from non-GM.

Organic and functional foods are at the other end of the spectrum; the companies behind them want, albeit for very different reasons, to ensure that their products are clearly branded when they reach supermarket shelves. But while organic food companies pay a great deal of attention to where their raw materials come from, functional food makers are likely to be less particular. In terms of food miles, most functional foods are highly processed and, even if they start off in particular countries like Finland or Japan, will often be developed as global brands. If they work, or if they become fashionable, they will be shipped around the world.

Meanwhile, although organic produce is often sold locally through farmers' markets or organic box schemes, and although many organic food companies would prefer to keep food miles to a minimum, increasingly large volumes of New Organic produce are now shipped to Europe from far-away places like California, Israel or Australia. People eating foods supplied by the organic sector could be piling up food miles almost as fast as those eating normal foods.

Fast vs Slow
MUST WE EAT ON THE HOOF?

However much we may want things to slow down, to stop the world and get off, the signs are that our lives will continue to be lived in the fast lane. Whatever we may say, our actions speak louder than our words. The amount of time most of us are prepared to spend on cooking is always shrinking. Just before the Second World War, for example, most Americans spent over two hours a day preparing meals. That figure has now dropped to as little as 15 minutes!

Tesco, the leading supermarket chain, has summarised these changes as follows: we are 'time poor' but 'cash rich'. We no longer want to spend time shopping for ingredients and preparing meals from scratch. There has been a correspondingly sharp decline in our cooking skills, and a dramatic increase in single person households.

In the UK alone, some two billion pre-packed sandwiches are now eaten every year. The attractions of fast food are obvious. It's convenient, often tempting and usually affordable. But many fast foods are not particularly healthy. Happily, high quality fast foods are also becoming available. Whether the focus is on high street takeaways, supermarket ready-meals or even pre-prepared ingredients for home cooking, fast food is becoming available to people with more discriminating tastes who are willing to pay a premium. Surprisingly, perhaps, New Organic could be a major winner here. In Sweden, even **McDonald's** – that temple of fast food – has found it necessary to offer organic milk and coffee in all of its outlets.

Functional foods are also already beginning to make an appearance in this area. If people want to go on eating 'junk food', then these will be obvious targets for the extra nutrition and health benefits that functional foods have to offer. GM foods, meanwhile, will turn up right across the culinary spectrum, but if discriminating consumers continue to avoid GM products, they are perhaps most likely to appear in fast food, where people pay less attention to what they are eating.

McDonald's

THE McLIBEL AFFAIR

One of the most symbolic clashes between fast food culture and the world of slower food came when the American fast food giant **McDonald's** announced its plans to open a new burger restaurant on the Champs Elysées. Parisians, who have long had a love-hate relationship with the Americans, were incensed.

But a clash on an altogether bigger scale began when **McDonald's** slapped libel writs on five campaigners in 1990.[186] Accused of writing a libellous leaflet entitled 'What's Wrong with McDonald's', the five quickly became two, Dave Morris and Helen Steel. The pair decided to fight on – and the case entered legal history.

It was England's longest ever court case. There were 313 days of evidence and submissions, 18,000 pages of court transcripts, 40,000 pages of documents and witness statements, 28 pre-trial hearings and 180 witnesses.

Denied a jury trial and finding themselves ineligible for legal aid, Morris and Steel were forced to defend themselves. The court case soon became the ground for a battle between those who believed in the merit and inevitability of capitalism, globalisation and fast food – and those who did not. For two years, the debates raged over issues such as animal rights, deforestation, nutrition, advertising, litter and recycling. And despite **McDonald's** having employed top libel lawyers to present their case, the hamburger chain did not emerge as the all-out winner. Apart from being found at fault in a number of respects, they also managed to attract a great deal of negative publicity. This PR problem was given a fierce spin by the launch of a now famous website, 'McSpotlight' (www.mcspotlight.org), which enabled millions of people to sift through every shade of criticism of **McDonald's** and the fast-food culture.

Vegetarians vs Meat-Eaters
HOW MUCH FLESH?

This issue comes very close to home. One of the authors is a long-term non-carnivorous omnivore, the other a keen meat-eater. But both of us believe that most intensive livestock farming is not good for animals – and often not good for our health or the environment, either.

There is no doubt that meat will stay on the menu, but vegetarianism is now on the rise in many countries. People are choosing vegetarianism for religious reasons, taste, or concerns about cruelty to – or the killing of – animals. A growing number are also choosing to eat plants because they are lower down the food chain, which means less land is needed to produce them. For example, it takes 7 kg (nearly 16 lbs) of soya beans or grains and 22 litre (about 25 gal) of water to produce 1 kg of beef. Fully four-fifths of the world's agricultural land is used to feed animals – these are sometimes called 'ghost acres'. And, as a result, some parts of the meat industry are heavy contributors to the destruction of fragile habitats, including rainforests.

On the health front, too, vegetarians are winning out. Although they need to make particularly sure they are eating the right combination of foods, a balanced plant-based diet can be healthier. Among other things, it is lower in cholesterol and other animal fats – and richer in carbohydrates, vegetable fibre and roughage. Some claim that vegetarians are less prone to a range of health problems, including coronary heart disease, high blood pressure, diabetes, obesity, arthritis, rheumatism, constipation and kidney disorders, although this is by no means universally agreed. But vegetarian does not necessarily mean anti-GM. Many vegetarians happily eat products made with GM rennet rather than rennet made by an enzyme from a calf's stomach (page 153), although the organic movement does not support this. **The Vegetarian Society** does approve this, but has recently taken a stand against GM crop and crop-derived ingredients in products carrying their symbol. Clearly, there will be 'food fights' even within the ecological movements.

Expect some functional foods to be increasingly appetising for those on non- or low-meat diets as well. Nutrient-enhanced foods could help give vegetable-based products the nutritional value of meat-based products. Indeed, a number of new foods have already helped to extend the range of options available to vegetarians and those trying to cut down on meat.

Longer term, the resolve of some wavering vegetarians could be tested. For example, it is at least conceivable that genetic engineers might come up with animals 'happy' to tolerate factory farm conditions. They could also produce wingless chickens that don't peck – and can live in cramped conditions and still produce an egg every day, regardless of the season. But would this be seen as progress by most people? Surely not.

Other GM breakthroughs could include ways of ensuring that only female dairy calves are born for milking or female chickens for laying eggs. As with the GM rennet, there would be clear benefits for some ethically minded consumers, but by no means for all. As GM technologists move into such areas, the number of ethical issues to be resolved is surely going to increase at an exponential rate.

Healthy vs Naughty
CAN GOOD FOOD BE FUN?

Remember the TV advertisement showing someone taking a mouthful of an oozing, sumptuously creamy bun? The strapline read 'naughty but nice!' By contrast, too many health foods seem worthy, insipid, boring. They may be good for you, but they are most definitely not sexy. How often have we seen parents stuffing their children with junk food and saying, 'well, they just won't eat anything else'?

Most of us have a large appetite for foods that are not particularly good for us in excess. Part of the problem is that over several million years we have evolved to like some foods – such as sweet, salty and fatty foods – and dislike others.[187] Children, in particular, are often devoted to crisps, fizzy drinks and sweets, and so-called 'fun foods' for kids are being given fresh impetus. Mainstream brands are linking up with cartoon shows and featuring other children's heroes, such as Action Man, Barbie, Noddy, Postman Pat or Thomas the Tank

Engine. Another marketing wheeze is to use names such as *Fun Pots, Bags of Fun, Mega Foot Gummi* or *Uncle Ozgood's Microwave Popcorn Corn on the Cob*.

Most of these products are not yet promoting healthy eating, but some do try to combine the 'fun' approach with health claims. Nor are adults immune to the appeal of novelty foods. Some people in the food industry even use terms like 'snackitecture' to describe the art of devising ever-more ingenious foods for jaded palates.

Whether GM, functional or organic products win out, the pressure to make food healthier can only grow. The challenge for the 21st century will be to develop healthy foods that also taste great and are pleasing to the eye. Chocolate-flavoured vegetables didn't win as great a market as their developers hoped, but – as the Victorian hymn-writers might have put it – why should the Devil have all the best tunes? Good food should be good fun.

Secrecy vs Transparency
WHY SHOULD WE EAT IN THE DARK?

Most supermarkets have not encouraged consumers to look at where their food is made and produced. Given that price and quality have been the top consumer concerns, this would have seemed like an unnecessary complication. But issues like pesticide residues, salmonella contamination, animal welfare, BSE and the dioxin contamination in Belgian pigs and poultry have dramatically spotlighted some of the ways in which our food is produced.

We are now seeing new interest in what is sometimes called traceability (see 'Identity preserved' products box, page 27). Some types of food – like the kosher and halal food insisted upon by Jewish and Muslim communities respectively – have long offered versions of food chain transparency. Jews and Muslims need to know that the meat they are eating, for example, has been slaughtered in the way they approve of. Now the trend is spreading. For example, **Martin Pitt's** eggs have his name stamped on each egg. Similarly, the owners of Suffolk-based **Broadside Farm** were keen to preserve the identity of their brewery-fed pigs, because they were thought to have superior flavour and therefore attracted a premium price.

The GM food issue has highlighted how, with commodity markets, the source of today's food ingredients is quickly obscured, which is why we so often see labels like 'product of more than one country'. But we can be 100 per cent sure that as soon as the GM industry comes up with products that have a real added advantage for consumers – 'functional GM'- it will exert every effort to ensure they are carefully segregated and labelled throughout the food chain.

Ultimately, there is absolutely no reason why we should be forced to eat in the dark, and companies like **Weetabix** and **Yakult** are showing how big companies can work with increased transparency. But it is the New Organic sector that leads this movement, since a key part of the value offered to consumers is the reassurance that products have been grown and processed according to strict standards. Indeed, organic traders (and some supermarkets, too) can often trace produce back to the farm – even field – where they were grown.

The mainstream food industry could learn a good deal from some parts of the organic sector about how to ensure transparent food chains. Some supermarkets have already begun producing annual environmental reports, explaining what they have been doing to clean up their stores and food chains. Some, too, have been pioneering in the way that they label their products – among them the **Co-op**, **Out of this World**, **Safeway**, **Sainsbury's** and **Waitrose**. Several have been experimenting with 'identity preserved' products.

Before long, perhaps, supermarket trolleys could be equipped with TV screens telling customers the story behind the products on the shelves. For food retailers worried about people slowing down in the aisles to see where their carrots or peppers came from, it is worth remembering that the Internet is ideally suited for providing greater transparency. How long will it be before supermarkets go the way of the online booksellers **Amazon.com** and offer consumers detailed on-demand information about their foods and how they have been produced?

Conclusion
WHO'S FOR FUTURE-FRIENDLY FOOD?

We say 'future-friendly', the experts say 'sustainable', but the sense is the same. We need to produce, buy and eat foods that are healthy, fairly traded, cruelty-free and environmentally friendly. Many trends, however, are moving in the opposite direction.

Take fish. We have been taking too many fish out of our waters. Almost 75 per cent of the world's fishing areas and 70 per cent of major fishing species are at peak production or already in decline. If we are going to continue to eat 'wild fish', the fishing industry will have to implement major changes. Some companies are beginning to wake up to this threat. Look at **Unilever** and its joint enterprise with **World Wide Fund for Nature** (**WWF**) in setting up the **Marine Stewardship Council** (**MSC**).

Our farming activities are also having a massive impact on land-based ecosystems. Nearly 1,000 agricultural pests – including insects, plant diseases and weeds – are today more or less immune to commonly used crop protection chemicals. In the USA alone, pest resistance is now thought to cost $1.5 billion a year.

The New Organic sector has its answers for these problems – and others. Environment and animal welfare criteria are key factors when farming organically. And organic producers also tend to employ more people and take account of fair trade principles, too. The main questions are: just how fast can this sector scale up production to meet demand? And can it do so without sacrificing its principles along the way?

Time is running out for the old 'future-unfriendly' ways of producing food, but how can we speed the necessary changes? Well, for a start, we can support the relevant campaign groups and vote for enlightened political parties or leaders. Ultimately, however, positive change in this area will depend on what we demand as citizens and consumers. We have already seen the phenomenal changes that supermarkets and food manufacturers have been forced to make as a result of worries about GM foods. If we demand future-friendly, we will increasingly be offered future-friendly.

7

FUTURE FOODS
What's Next On The Menu

Now, back to the future. Having worked through the major developments and trends in the food industry, let's pull out our crystal ball. The main question is: where will new foods take us next? We offer our own answers in this final chapter – and propose a 10-point New Foods Manifesto. The manifesto spells out some of the things we think the food industry and governments should be doing to make tomorrow's food more future-friendly.

THE NEW FOODS TRIO PLAYS ON

Our first conclusion is that GM, functional and New Organic foods will all remain on the menu.

This will not be a popular conclusion in some quarters. Many anti-GM campaigners remain adamant that they want an end to the whole GM industry. They have been extraordinarily successful in getting publicity for their cause – and, for the moment, have won overwhelming support from the British public. Some financial analysts have even begun to question the long term profitability of some parts of the GM foods industry. So why do we think GM is unstoppable? And, if it is, have the campaigners simply been wasting their time?

As the steam engine, the internal combustion engine, the jet engine, radio, TV, nuclear reactors and personal computers all did in their time, GM products are initially raising major concerns. They threaten the interests of all sorts of people, and they pose very real health, social and environmental risks. Consequently, GM is being fiercely challenged, and rightly so.

But, as with earlier technologies, at least some GM food approaches and products will survive the storm. Like all pioneer species, they will adapt and then, very likely, spread rapidly around the world. Like it or not, that is how new technologies have always behaved. That message will perhaps be music to the ears of many in the GM foods industry, but there is a real sting in the tail. If the GM foods industry goes on trying to railroad (a term that itself reflects the impacts of an earlier technological revolution) its new products through to a sceptical public, it will run a very real risk of destroying its commercial prospects for the future.

Biology is different

We have worked with people and companies in the GM industry. Most readily accept that there could be major problems associated with the introduction of at least some future GM products. For their products, however, they consider these risks are worth taking. But their critics, sensibly, note that something significant has changed. We have begun to build an industrial revolution around biology, they say, rather than the physics or chemistry used in the past. The industrialisation of physics gave us everything from massive train crashes to Chernobyl, while the industrialisation of chemistry gave us everything from DDT to Bhopal.

What will the industrialisation of biology bring? Many good things, to be sure, but these new technologies involve the engineering of life – and, ultimately, of ourselves. If the BSE crisis, which has cost the UK £4 billion and may have claimed as many as 40 lives to date, proves to have been wholly or partly caused by experimental hormone injections for cattle in attempts to breed new super-cattle , the implications for the GM industry could be profound. Whether or not GM techniques were in part responsible, the saga suggests what can happen when we start to manipulate biological systems without fully understanding what we are doing. We would be mad to rush forward without thinking things through very carefully indeed.

None of this will stop the GM revolution, however. Too many people want it to happen. Investment funds (many of which hold our pensions) and companies around the world have now pumped billions of pounds – or dollars – into GM science and technology, and real progress is being made.

If you visit hospitals and clinics around the developed world, you will find patients are readily accepting GM drugs, if they offer an effective treatment or cure for AIDS, cancer or some other, otherwise incurable, disease. In the early years of the 21st century, GM health-care innovations will grow at unbelievable rates. As they do, it seems very likely that our willingness to accept GM in other areas of our lives will also grow.

Business views

AFTER THE STORM

Most companies responding to our GM Food Survey were trying to keep their heads down, not surprisingly; but some were aggressively optimistic about the longer-term prospects for GM foods, developed and introduced in the right way. Let's hear from one Swiss-based GM company, **Novartis,** and one UK food manufacturer, **St Ivel**:

'In the future, genetic modification will be able to produce food ingredients with improved nutritional value and food quality. With an appropriate, transparent regulatory framework to protect human health and the environment, these advantages can be harnessed to benefit agriculture, the environment and quality of life.' **Novartis Nutrition**

'We are not opposed to the use of GM technology provided that it can be shown to have consumer benefit and food safety and quality are not compromised.' **St Ivel Limited**

These are big 'ifs', of course, but that's now the essence of the 21st century challenge for the GM foods industry.

The GM spotlight shifts

Some GM applications are already an integral part of the food industry and it's almost inconceivable that they would be abandoned. It was no accident, for example, that food manufacturers and retailers found it so hard to answer our question about GM enzymes. These are now second nature to many parts of the food industry. Our forecast: particular enzyme applications may hit speed-bumps, but GM enzymes are very much part of future food – and future food chains.[188] GM crops, on the other hand, together with the products made from them, are likely to have a rougher ride. Anti-GM protesters in the UK have made GM crop trials almost impossible. In Germany, Austria and France there have also been fierce protests.

But, so far at least, the reaction has been significantly different in other European countries. In Spain there has been extensive plant-ing of GM crops, with almost no opposition – at the time of writing, 5 per cent of the Spanish maize crop was expected to be GM by the end of 1999. And in China, there is now a burgeoning GM industry, which is developing largely in secret. Indeed, published statistics on the area under GM crops around the world exclude China, because the information is impossible to get hold of. Yet, although it may be out of the spotlight at the moment, China is exporting GM food ingredients, such as citric acid, onto world markets. Meanwhile, Chinese media reports – anti-GM campaigners point out – sound like 'the regular bulletins of the Mao era'. They talk about the spectacular success of Chinese scientists in growing grapes on persimmon trees, apples on pear trees or crossbreeding pigs with rabbits![189]

Whatever the Chinese may claim, however, the USA is the GM leader, and the country where GM foods are now most widespread. Opposition was originally sparked in the 1970s by fears about GMOs being accidentally released from laboratories. Now, although public concern lags behind that in the UK, the resistance to GM crops is building rapidly. The issue of the monarch butterfly (page 14) played a crucial role in raising American public awareness.

Many Americans, however, like many Europeans (even after the media storms), remain totally unaware of the use of GM technologies and their implications for health and the environment. In part, this is because of the high level of confidence in their main regulatory body, the **FDA**. By contrast, in Europe, there is no overall body equivalent to the **FDA**, and each country draws up its own set of rules.

Resistance spreads

However and wherever it happens, the anti-GM movement will continue to grow, as more countries around the world become aware of the implications of the new technology. The power of individuals and small groups to hold even giant companies to account will grow enormously with the evolution of the Net.

Many Third World countries are alarmed. In India, for example, there has been real fear about the prospect of foreign multinationals taking control of Indian food chains, with terrible impacts on small peasant farmers. A campaign organisation called **Monsanto Quit India** has been set up, and now has the support of more than 1,000 groups. That these same big companies are becoming more powerful than many nation states is a fact that can only fuel these worries and help them spread.

Brazil is another country that has found itself at the centre of the GM storm. On the one hand, Brazilian farmers are the biggest suppliers of GM-free soya to the growing European market. On the other, the USA has been bringing intense pressure to bear on Brazil to introduce GM soya and other crops. Different Brazilian states have been taking different views on which course to take.

And in Japan, now heavily dependent on GM crop imports from the USA, we are starting to see the anti-GM snowball growing. A major Japanese importer has said that it will be setting up systems to segregate GM and non-GM crops and food products. Interestingly, the same company has large contracts to grow GM-free soya for traditional vegetarian products such as miso and tofu.

In the end, of course, if enough people demand GM-free products they will get them. Our sense is that after a period of tremendous controversy, which could profoundly reshape the GM foods industry and sink some major companies without trace, many consumers will be won around to GM foods. But only if they are presented with clear, reliable research findings and offered real choice in the matter.

The long organic boom

As the GM foods industry came under ever-greater pressure, the UK and international organic movements produced their best results ever. While the benefits of pesticide-free food were already being embraced by a significant number of consumers, GM-free benefits added to the appeal of going organic, and helped create a real organic boom. Some organic foods companies have long been anti-GM campaigners in their own right.

Although the organic movement itself will inevitably attract criticism – and may even have food scares of its own – it's unlikely to slow down any time soon. Apart from anything else, more major supermarkets and food manufacturers will want to move into organic products, if they are not there already – and to expand their range if they are. One clear implication is that there could be even greater pressure to compromise on – or to dilute – organic standards and criteria. People will want to buy organic, but many will also demand food that lasts longer, travels better and looks succulent. The worst that could happen is that these pressures could lead to a split in the organic movement, with 'purists' sticking to strict and rigid organic criteria – while 'reformers' adapt their criteria to meet mass consumer demand.

The mainstreaming of the New Organics sector, which is so

important if a growing proportion of world food production is to be organic, may well accelerate this trend. The politics of food will simmer away for some time to come – and will periodically boil over. But, in the end, we all have a strong vested interest in future-friendly food.

Lessons from the anti-GM snowball

Whatever happens, the food industry has a number of important lessons to take on board in the wake of the anti-GM backlash and this boom in demand for organic produce and products. One lesson for big GM manufacturers and GM food companies is to pay more attention to what campaigners and – indeed – ordinary people are thinking. Supermarkets in the UK were concerned about the introduction of GM soya as long ago as 1996, but they didn't make much of a fuss because they had no idea how big the issue would eventually become – or how much it would eventually cost them.

Early in 1997, the **British Retail Consortium**, representing many leading retailers and supermarkets, warned that consumers might not accept GM foods. They pointed out that if the USA proved unable (or unwilling?) to segregate GM from non-GM soya, its attitude might actually threaten the introduction of all agricultural biotechnology – and what the consortium described as 'its huge potential for good'.

Despite such warnings, at least one American company decided to plough ahead, hoping that Europeans would 'come to their senses'. Americans hadn't made a fuss about GM foods, so why should Europeans – and particularly Britons – be so agitated? Surely this was one more case of media-driven hysteria? To some extent it was. But the hysteria was feeding on something important – and that was the denial of choice. This was clear to many European companies (see Supermarket voices box below), but not to their American counterparts. The Americans repeatedly expressed their determination not to change their distribution systems to segregate GM from non-GM crops. As a result, the consumer backlash hit far harder than anyone could have predicted.

WE WANT CHOICE

Many supermarkets feel that the American agribusiness has bounced them into banning products that they believe to be absolutely safe. Indeed, chains like **Safeway** and **Sainsbury's**, which had done so much to build consumer support for their GM tomato purée products, could have been excused for feeling more than a little aggrieved. Companies try to stick together in times like this, but you could hear the real issues echoing beneath the surface of many replies to our survey:

'Unfortunately, this introduction of genetically modified soya and maize has compromised this fundamental right (of choice), a situation we have worked hard to address.' **Safeway**

The principle of consumer choice is supported by most supermarkets:

'We have always felt that food which contains GM ingredients should carry labelling, so that customers can make an informed choice.' **Sainsbury's**

Many retailers support the idea of segregating GM from non-GM crops:

'An insistence on traceability of both soya beans and processed products is essential if consumers are to regain their right to choose.' **Co-operative Wholesale Society**

Most retailers have also found it expensive and time-consuming to move out of GM foods:

'For the future, we are in discussion with the industry to find ways to achieve segregation of raw materials used in the production of animal feed to provide non-GM alternatives. Realistically, this work will take some time to complete.' **Marks & Spencer** (M&S have now committed themselves to doing this)

Iceland Frozen Foods was the first of the mainstream retailers to break ranks. It did so publicly, saying it was going to remove GM ingredients from its own-brand products. It started with the removal of all ingredients where GM protein or DNA was present. Then, it moved on to ingredients from GM crops where no GM protein or DNA was detectable. Third, it began to look at GM processing aids, with the intention of removing these wherever possible. And finally, it plans to tackle GM animal feeds, once traceability systems are in place. Other retailers started to notice the writing on the wall. Within months, all the major UK supermarkets had taken a public stand and were removing GM foods from their shelves.[190]

By the time we launched our GM Food Survey, most retailers and food manufacturers were well aware of the problem, but still at sea in terms of what to do next. Before long, food giants like **Nestlé** and **Unilever** were also announcing plans to go GM-free, at least in the UK. And the snowball continued to roll. There was fierce competition to get GM products off the shelves as quickly as possible, and **Asda** hit the front pages with their announcement to move out of GM foods entirely. **Marks & Spencer** were the first chain to report that they had achieved GM-free status across the board, because they sell 100 per cent own-brand products (where they have direct control over what goes into the product).

Behind the scenes, however, there was often confusion. There were long queues for the services of the small number of testing houses that could find out if food products contained any GM protein. The supermarkets and manufacturers, having made their GM-free promises, now had to work out what those promises really meant. They discovered that the first thing they would all have to do was drop any GM ingredients that the proposed new EU rules required to be labelled. In most cases, they also decided not to use GM crop-derived ingredients. But it has taken more time for companies to understand to the need to investigate whether the meat or milk they sell comes from animals fed with GM crops. Even now, companies are finding it hard to move away from these products because animal feed is not yet labelled accordingly.

And then there was the question of the GM technology used in food processing. Only the **Co-op** has labelled vegetarian cheese – and many other cheeses – to say they contain GM enzymes. But even they have not, to date, made any public commitment to label other foods that might be made with GM enzymes. Perhaps retailers are simply hoping that the storm will blow over before they need to embark on this next expedition of discovery.

GM goes functional

Governments clearly have a crucial role to play in all of this, but some have allowed themselves to be blown all over the map. Nor is it hard to see why they are finding it difficult – consumers who are anti-GM are also likely to be voters who are anti-GM at some point. But our political leaders see the potential economic rewards from GM being at least as great as they have been from information technology – and they want their countries and industries to share in the wealth.

One politician who spotted the emerging challenge was American agriculture secretary Dan Glickman. 'With all biotechnology has to offer,' he warned, 'it is nothing if not accepted.' A real breakthrough was his argument that GM foods could no longer rely simply on providing benefits to farmers and to industry. The focus would need to start shifting on to the real benefits to the consumer.

This means that GM foods will be going functional in future, with a growing focus on direct nutritional or health benefits to consumers. So, for example, we might see GM potatoes with anti-ageing antioxidants. The chip that keeps you young! Or GM bananas designed to combat pre-menstrual tension and GM apples that prevent migraine.

But even functional foods – which are in their infancy – are not getting an easy ride. Some critics see such products as evidence of a cunning plot to shift mountains of junk foods onto our plates. Others protest that some functional ingredients or foods could have unexpected health effects if used in the wrong way. It's clear that the boundaries between food and medicine are going to be blurred at dizzying speed. We are already being offered foods with something approaching medicinal effect, while existing laws make a clear distinction between food and medicine – and set the standards accordingly. Pharmaceutical companies are required to spend literally millions of pounds on rigorous testing for safety – and to back up any claims they make. Meanwhile, food companies are not supposed to make medical claims, and are not subject to the same testing requirements.

As more products begin to offer real medical benefits, two things are likely to happen. The first is that the laws relating to testing and claims will have to be revised and tightened. Second, more effective functional products will start turning up on the supermarket shelves. Whether or not they are GM, these foods will definitely be in the media spotlight. Some of them will be genuinely worth having. But functional food makers will try to play on our health concerns, as have the vitamins and supplements sectors before them. They will encourage us to think that we need a whole range of 'added' extras. Even at their best these products are unlikely to be any more effective than a healthy, balanced diet.

Hair-raising cocoa?

By 2020, we forecast, there will be many more kinds of GM produce and processed foods on our shelves. But they will more rigorously tested and clearly labelled.

In many of these cases – but far from all – the big food companies will also be using exactly the same 'identity preserved' segregation methods (page 27) that they have fought so hard against in recent years. They will do this as soon as they have something of their own to protect, something quite specific to offer us (such as anti-cancer carrots or, an outside chance, hair-boosting cocoa). And, commerce being commerce, they will want to secure the highest possible price for their branded functional products.

The organic sector will try to steer its own course in all of this, but may find it increasingly difficult to do so. Its own expansion will force some parts of the sector to adopt large-scale production and processing systems that will begin to nibble away at the gap between New Organic and mainstream foods. Some parts of the organic movement will dilute some of their criteria along the way, perhaps even starting to offer functional organic products. But of one thing we can be almost certain. GM organic is unlikely to happen within the next decade in Europe. Evel Knievel may roar across some fairly big chasms, but large industries don't find such daredevil jumps quite so easy.

THE NEW FOODS MANIFESTO

To end, let's look at what needs to be done next by the food industry if it is to ensure future-friendly food in the 21st century. The New Foods Manifesto which follows now represents a realistic agenda, thanks largely to the work of the anti-GM campaigners. They may not have pushed GM off the map completely, but they have certainly ensured some major changes in how GM foods are regulated, grown, shipped, processed, tested and marketed.

Finally, and perhaps their ultimate contribution, the campaigners are helping to ensure that we all have a choice in what we eat and in how it is produced. Few things are more important – and many campaigning groups really do deserve our full and continuing support. But the real question now is whether each of us will be prepared to make the right choices in our daily lives to ensure future-friendly food.

We hope *The New Foods Guide* has given you at least some starting points for the journey. Good luck!

THE NEW FOODS MANIFESTO

There are 10 points in this Manifesto, each addressing one or more of the concerns and trends identified in *The New Foods Guide*. The 'New Food Stars' that follow provide real-world models of how to put some of this into practice.

1 CHOICE

RESPECT OUR RIGHT TO CHOOSE!

Companies that lobby or act against consumer choice are arguing against what people want, which raises real questions over their own futures. GM foods, at least as currently presented, threaten to undermine key options.

- Food manufacturers and retailers should offer consumers real, informed choices in relation to GM, functional and organic foods. Where consumers do make choices, they will want regular feedback on the progress achieved.

- The segregation of GM crops is essential and GM producers should pay for it, even if most of these costs will ultimately be passed on to the consumer. The news that one of the world's largest exporters of soya and maize – the US company **Archer Daniels Midland (ADM)** – has said that it would move to segregation is a major coup for those who argue for greater choice.[11]

- Organic producers should be protected from the GM contamination of their crops. This will be difficult to arrange in areas where both GM and Organic crops are grown, but the benefit of the doubt should always be with the Organic producers.

2 TRANSPARENCY

TELL US MORE!

People are demanding more openness, or transparency, whether it is from governments or companies or from each other. Companies or industries that try to resist this trend will usually find the strategy backfires. Successful businesses will be those that make sure they know, understand and support all the processes that go into the food they produce, and they will make this understanding work for them in the marketplace, by informing consumers and labelling products accordingly.

- It should be compulsory to label all foods made with GM crop ingredients or GM crop-derived ingredients.

- Governments should ensure that the definitions used for GM ingredients – and for the term 'GM-free' – are appropriate, clear and well understood.

- All food producers should be able to tell us about all the ingredients in their products. They will need to know where the crops were grown, how they were grown, what processes they have been through (including enzyme processing) and where they are likely to turn up in our food.

- As shopping on the the Internet becomes more popular, companies should provide full information about the products they are selling through the Net.

3 TESTING

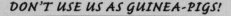

DON'T USE US AS GUINEA-PIGS!

Food safety commands an enormous amount of government time, attention and resources, particularly when they get it wrong. But there is a strong sense that the introduction of GM foods has proceeded on the basis of inadequate testing.

- Testing for new foods should be at least as rigorous as testing for new pharmaceuticals, particularly since we are likely to be exposed to far greater quantities of food products.

- More tests should be carried out to verify that food and food ingredients are safe specifically for children.

- Foods with ingredients – functional or GM – not previously consumed by humans should be tested even more rigorously than others.

- A moratorium should be declared on the planting of GM crops so that industry and government can consult and agree how to proceed with field trials safely.

4 LAWS

GIVE THE REGULATORS REAL TEETH!

In the end, governments and political leaders are responsible for making sure we are properly protected. To do this they need to set up clear and effective rules that the food industry are able and willing to comply with and that can win back public confidence.

- For a time, at least, GM foods should not be allowed onto the market simply on the basis that they are 'substantially equivalent' (page 20).

- Regulators need to revise and update the laws relating to both food and medicine, to speed 'good' functional foods onto the market and derail 'bad' ones.

- Whether or not an effective Food Standards Agency is set up in the UK, the European Commission should now form a European equivalent of the US **Food and Drug Administration (FDA)**, with real powers and real teeth.

5 HEALTH

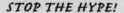

STOP THE HYPE!

Most of us are all to easily seduced by foods that make credible health claims. But knowing whether or not particular foods (or supplements) are really going to make us healthier is often difficult.

- All manufacturers should be required to back up any health claims made – or implied – in relation to their products.

- Government should ensure that unhealthy food products are not permitted to make health claims on the basis of one specific ingredient, if the overall product is likely to be unhealthy.

- Food retailers should give more user-friendly advice to consumers on how to achieve a balanced diet without resorting to 'miracle foods'.

6 PURITY

GET RID OF RESIDUES!

The contamination of our food chains, whether from pesticides, packaging or people, will be on the agenda for the foreseeable future. People will want food that is as close as possible to how nature 'intended' – and, if processed, that has no more ingredients than the manufacturer intended! It is not acceptable, for example, for the government to issue regular health warnings telling us that we should peel or wash fruit before we eat it.

- The government should do more to ensure that the fruit and vegetables we eat are as close to residue-free as is humanly possible.

- The government needs to be stricter on food importers. For example, they should not be allowed to import produce sprayed with chemicals banned for use in the UK.

- All major food processors and retailers should test regularly for pesticide residues and publish the results.

- The use of organophosphates (page 126) should be banned.

- The routine use of antibiotics should be banned, particularly as growth promoters in pigs and poultry.

7 ENVIRONMENT

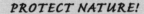

PROTECT NATURE!

Many us are not just worried about the effects of the food we eat on our health. We also care about the environmental impact of the way our foods are grown, processed and distributed. Our political leaders should help us to put our money where our mouth is.

- GM crops need to be tested for their longer-term ecological impacts. Governments should work both nationally and internationally – and again with all concerned – to find acceptable, credible and above all safe ways forward.

- International pressure should be brought to bear on those countries where GM crops are being developed and grown with little or no effective testing, to ensure that they take health and ecological issues properly into account.

- To date, government subsidies for organic and low impact farming have been minuscule compared to the vast sums poured into developing GM technology. This must change – in the organic sector's favour.

- All companies should be looking to reduce 'food miles' and source as much as possible locally.

- Fruit, vegetables and meat, among other things, should be labelled with their varieties. Companies must offer more varieties and promote biodiversity. Food manufacturers and retailers will need to do more to sustain and promote real biodiversity.

8 ETHICS

BE FAIR!

The business world is beginning to recognise the need to adopt 'future-friendly' policies. Campaigns for animal welfare, human rights and child labour, among others, have already had major impacts on the supermarket world. Fair trade products are beginning to appear on supermarket shelves and are likely to spread rapidly.

- Companies should implement fair trade principles wherever they operate in the food chain.

- Animal welfare standards should be more actively promoted, all the way through our food chains. And these standards should apply equally to imported produce.

9 COST

DON'T CUT CORNERS!

One reason why the BSE crisis hit the UK so hard was that the food industry here had been among the most aggressive in keeping food prices low. But the recent dioxin scare in Belgium has shown that this is not just a UK problem. Cheap food means cheap farming and cheap ingredients, but does not automatically guarantee low overall costs – particularly when health, social, animal welfare and environmental costs are brought into consideration.

- As consumers, we must be prepared to pay the 'real' cost of the food we eat.

- As citizens, we should vote for and support politicians, parties and governments that pledge to move us all in this direction.

- The food industry should learn to accept the costs of taking proper account of safety, health, environmental and ethical issues.

- Food manufacturers and retailers should invest in research to test the health effects of functional foods before they are widely introduced.

- Such initiatives need to be backed up with effective education, and

other information programmes designed to build real public understanding and support.

10 INNOVATION

DON'T HOG THE BENEFITS!

The introduction of GM food was handled badly in part because the
industry concentrated on products that would make big profits for
themselves and for farmers. Consumers have been exposed to the
'risks' without getting any of the benefits.

- Whether foods are organic, functional, GM, or some combination
  of all three, producers and retailers will need to think about how to
  pass a significant share of the benefits on to the consumers.

- Finally, but most importantly, The food industry and food companies should support 'future-friendly' initiatives throughout their
  activities – so that today's benefits are not achieved at the expense
  of tomorrow's world.

The time has come for a global debate on the future of food. As
Rockefeller Foundation president Gordon Conway put it in a recent
speech to Monsanto executives, we need to adopt 'a pace moderate
enough to measure unforeseen effects – and measure carefully
enough to detect those effects before they do harm'. He also stressed
that the dialogue should 'involve everyone on an equal footing – the
seed companies, consumer groups, environmental groups, independent scientists, and representatives of governments, particularly
from developing nations.'[191]

★ A DOZEN NEW FOODS STARS ★

So what does all this mean in practice? Below, we spotlight a dozen food initiatives that we see as 'New Food Stars'. The thirteen – our 'baker's dozen' – organisations involved show some of the ways in which new foods can be, and will need to be developed and introduced if they are to succeed.

In each case we have selected companies or products on the basis of some particular thing they have done well, rather than on their overall performance. So, while these New Food Stars may not be doing everything well, each sets a spectacularly good example in at least one aspect of the methods that all food companies will soon have to adopt if they want to be successful.

★ BABY ORGANIX ★

There are growing concerns about the potential impact of some foods and additives on the immune systems of babies and children (page 170). The *Baby Organix* brand made by Organix Brands plc, is a leader in the field of organic products for the very young. When it comes to healthy food, it makes sense to get started early.

★ BEN & JERRY'S ★

This company helped make corporate social responsibility cool. They help fund rainforest conservation, although they aren't organic and they don't use free-range eggs. These people are serious about maintaining the integrity of their food chain. Our main reason for making this award: **Ben & Jerry's** campaign for the right to label their products as free of GM dairy hormones (page 156).

★ *COLUMBUS EGG* ★

In developing the *Columbus Egg* (page 160), **Dean's Farm** aimed to produce chicken feed similar to the original diet of the jungle fowl. The result: eggs that are lower in unhealthy fats and higher in healthy fats, such as Omega-3. And, if you are sensitive to these things, all without a trace of GM. **Dean's Farm** have recently introduced free-range versions, and organic eggs are also on the way.

★ CO-OP WHOLESALE SOCIETY ★

With its 'Campaign for Honest Labelling', the **Co-op** has been unusually open. They were the first supermarket to label vegetarian cheeses made with GM enzymes (page 153) as 'Made using genetic modification and so free from animal rennet'.

★ GREEN & BLACK'S ★

A long way in style from traditional organic fare, **Green & Black's** were an early venture into organic luxury – but, more importantly, they were also the first company simultaneously to embrace 'fair trade' practices and organic principles throughout their food chain.

★ RACHEL'S DAIRY ★

These folk are early 'New Organic' mainstreamers. You find **Rachel's Dairy** products on the shelves of many supermarkets, but scaling up production meant that the founders had to re-mortgage their farm twice. The third time around, they sold out to an American organic dairy products firm, but the founders are still involved, and are determined to keep putting their principles into practice.

★ SAFEWAY & SAINSBURY ★

Before the anti-GM wave hit, both **Safeway** and **Sainsbury** showed how GM foods and other new foods *should* be introduced. They labelled their GM tomato purées voluntarily, provided clear consumer information and passed on some of the savings in lower product prices. There are a number of lessons here for anyone planning to introduce new foods. Both companies now have 'GM-free' policies and are very strong on their organic offerings.

★ SEEDS OF CHANGE ★

Originating in the USA, **Seeds of Change** was established to help preserve biodiversity and it is still working in that area. In support of the **Henry Doubleday Research Association** (HDRA) in the UK, it uses ingredients that help re-establish endangered vegetable varieties. Owned by **Mars, Seeds of Change** now offers a wide range of organic pasta sauces and soups, plus tomato ketchup, available at many major supermarkets.

★ THE VILLAGE BAKERY ★

Beginning with a basket of home-baked organic bread sold around the corridors of the BBC's HQ in London, the **Village Bakery** was founded in 1976 in Cumbria. It uses traditional wood-fired ovens to produce a large range of organic bakery products sold in supermarkets and other stores nationwide.

★ WAITROSE ★

Waitrose, part of the John Lewis Partnership, has emerged as a strong supporter of organic food production through the **Waitrose** Organic Assurance Scheme. This actively encourages producers to switch to organic methods, helping farmers make what can be a difficult transition. **Waitrose** now offers over 500 organic products, most of them available in all their stores. **Waitrose** recently won the 'Organic Supermarket of the Year' award.

★ WEETABIX ★

One of the most impressive answers to our GM Food Survey came from **Weetabix Limited** of the UK. They explained the work they had carried out on 'traceability' and on the 'identity preservation' of raw materials and ingredients. They were particularly open, honest, comprehensive – and convincing.

★ YAKULT ★

Yakult Honsha stresses that *Yakult* is a food, not a medicine. We were struck by the company's commitment and openness: they welcome anyone wishing to look round their factories – the nearest to the UK is outside Amsterdam. Another potential model for the new foods sector.

Contacts List

Action & Information on Sugars, Tel: 01276 605 451

Advisory Committee on Novel Foods and Processes (ACNFP), Secretariat, Ergon House, c/o Nobel House, 17 Smith Street, London SW1P 3JR Tel: (MAFF below)

Advisory Committee on Releases to the Environment (ACRE), The Department of the Environment, Transport and the Regions, Floor 3/G9, Ashdown House, 123 Victoria Street, London SW1E 6DE Tel: 0171 890 5275 Fax: 0171 890 5259 www.environment.detr.gov.uk/acre

Baby Organix - see **Organix Brands**

Banana Link, 38 Exchange Street, Norwich NR2 1AX Tel: 01603 765 670 www.laslett.com/bananas

Ben & Jerry's Ice-cream, 3A The Deans, Bridge Road, Bagshot, Surrey, GU19 5AT Tel: 01276 473 366 Fax: 01276 473 132 www.benjerry.co.uk

British Allergy Foundation, Deepdene House, 30 Bellegrove Road, Welling, Kent GA16 3BY Tel: 0181 303 8583

British Dietetic Association, 5th Floor, Elizabeth House, 22 Suffolk Street, Queens Way, Birmingham B1 1LS Tel: 0121 616 4900 www.bda.uk.com

British Nutrition Foundation, High Holborn House, 52–54 High Holborn, London WC1V 6RQ Tel: 0171 404 6504 www.nutrition.org.uk

Coeliac Society, PO Box 220,1B Octagon Court High Wycombe, Bucks HP11 2HY Tel: 01494 437278 www.coeliac.co.uk

Columbus Eggs, Dean's Farm, Bridgeway House, Upper Icknield Way, Tring, Hertfordshire HP23 4JX Tel: 01442 891811

Compassion in World Farming, 5a Charles Street, Petersfield, Hampshire GU32 3EH Tel: 01730 264 208 www.ciwf.net

Consumers' Association, 2 Marylebone Road, London NW1 4DF Tel: 0171 830 6000 www.which.net

Co-operative Supermarket, CWS Retail Ltd, New Century House, PO Box 53, New Century House, Manchester M60 4ES Tel: 0161 834 1212 www.co-op.co.uk

Elm Farm Research Centre, Hamstead Marshall, Nr Newbury, Berkshire RG20 0HR Tel: 01488 658298

English Nature, Northminster House, Peterborough PE1 1UA Tel: 01733 455000 Fax: 01733 568834 www.english-nature.org.uk

Five Year Freeze – see Genetic Engineering Alliance

Food & Chemical Allergy Association, 27 Ferringham Lane, Ferring, West Sussex BN12 5NB Tel: 01903 241178

Food & Drink Federation, 6 Catherine Street, London WC2B 5JJ Tel: 0171 836 2460

Food Commission, 94 White Lion Street, London N1 9PF Tel: 0171 837 2250 www.foodcomm.org.uk

Food Ethics Council, Minster Chambers, Church Street, Southwell, Notts NG25 0HD Tel: 01636 812 622 www.users globalnet.co.uk/~foodeth

Freedom Foods, Royal Society for the Prevention of Cruelty to Animals (RSPCA), The Causeway, Horsham RH12 1HG Tel: 01403 264181 www.rspca.org

Friends of the Earth, 26–28 Underwood Street, London N1 7JQ Tel: 0171 490 1555 www.foe.co.uk

Genetic Engineering Alliance, 94 White Lion Street, London N1 9PF Tel: 0171 837 0642

Genetic Engineering Network (GEN), PO Box 9656, London N4 4JY Tel: 0181 374 9516 www.dmac.co.uk/gen.html

Genetics Forum, 94 White Lion Street, London N1 9PF Tel: 0171 837 9229 www.geneticsforum.org.uk

Genetix Food Alert, c/o 23 Fleming Street, Glasgow, Scotland G31 1PQ Tel: 0141 554 6099 Fax: 0141 556 5589 www.essential-trading.co.uk/genetix.htm

GenetiX Snowball, One World Centre, 6 Mount Street Manchester M2 5NS Tel: 0161 834 0295 Fax: 0161 834 8187 www.gn.apc.org/pmhp/gs

Genewatch, The Courtyard, Whitecross Road, Tidewell, Buxton, Derbyshire SK17 8NY Tel: 01298 871 898 www.genewatch.org

GMO Campaign, 41 Harboard Road, Oxford OX2 8HL Tel: 01865 513 224 www.millennium-debate.org

Greenpeace, Canonbury Villas, London N1 2PN Tel: 0171 865 8100 www.greenpeace.org/uk

HDRA Organic Wine Club – see Vinceremos

Henry Doubleday Research Association (HDRA), Ryton-on-Dunsmore, Coventry CV8 3LG Tel: 01203 303517 www.hdra.org.uk

Joint Health Claims Initiative – *see* Food & Drink Federation, LACOTS or Sustain.

LACOTS – Local Authority Coordinating Body on Food and Trading Standards, PO Box 6, Token House, 1a Robert Street, Croydon CR9 1LG Tel: 0181 688 1996

MAFF Helpline, Ministry of Agriculture, Fisheries and Food (MAFF), Whitehall Place, London SW1A 2HH Tel: 0645 335577

Marine Stewardship Council – *see* World Wide Fund for Nature

Monsanto plc – Nutrition & Consumer Food Sector, PO Box 53, Lane End Road, High Wycombe, Bucks HP12 4HL Tel: 01494 511 411 www.monsanto.com

New Nutrition Business, Editorial Office, Suite 1, Prospect House, 67 Boston Manor Road, Brentford, Middx TW8 9JQ Tel: 0181 758 9414 Subscriptions: 01865 767575

Novartis Nutrition, Station Road, Kings Langley, Herts WC4 8LJ Tel: 01923 266122

Nuffield Council on Bioethics, 28 Bedford Square, London, WC1B 3EG Tel: 0171 631 0566 www.nuffieldfoundation.org

The Oil Merchant, 47 Ashchurch Grove, London W12 9BU Tel: 0181 740 1335

Organic Farmers & Growers Ltd, 50 High Street, Soham, Ely, Cambridgeshire CB7 5HF Tel: 01353 722 398 www.organicnetworks. com/ofg/index.htm

Organic Food Federation, The Tithe House, Peaseland Green, Elsing, East Dereham NR20 3DY Tel: 01362 637314 www.organicfood.co.uk/off

Organix Brands plc (Baby Organix), Organix House, 4 Fairfield Close, Christchurch, Dorset BH23 1QZ Tel: 01202 479701 www.baby organix.com

Out of this World, 106 High Street, Gosforth, Newcastle upon Tyne N3 1HB Tel: 0191 213 5377 www.ootw.co.uk

Pesticide Trust, Eurolink Centre, 49 Effra Rd, London SW2 1BZ Tel: 0171 274 8895 www.gn.apc.org/pesticidestrust

Rachel's Dairy, Unit 63, Glanyrafon Industrial Estate, Aberystwyth SY23 3JG Tel: 01970 625805

Safeway Stores plc, Head Office, 6 Millington Road, Hayes, Middlesex UB3 4AY Tel: 0181 848 8744 www.safeway.co.uk

Sainsbury, Stamford House, Stamford Street, London SE1 9LL Tel: 0171 695 6000 www.sainsbury.co.uk

Seeds of Change, Freeby Lane, Waltham on the Wolds, Leicestershire LE14 4RS Tel: 01664 415200 www.seedsofchange.com/uk

Soil Association, Bristol House, 40–56 Victoria Street, Bristol BS1 6BY Tel: 0117 929 0661 www.soilassociation.org

Sustain (formerly **SAFE Alliance**), 94 White Lion Street, London N1 9PF Tel: 0171 837 1228 www.gn.apc.org/safe/

UK Register of Organic Food Standards (**UKROFS**), Nobel House, 17 Smith Square, London SW1P 3JR Tel: 0171 238 5915

Vegan Society, Donald Watson House, 7 Battle Road, St Leonards on Sea, East Sussex TN37 7AA Tel: 01424 427393 www.vegansociety.com

Vegetarian Society, Parkdale, Dunham Road, Altrincham, Cheshire WA14 4QG Tel: 0161 928 0793 www.vegsoc.org

Village Bakery, Melmerby, Penrith, Cumbria CA10 1HE Tel: 01768 881515 www.village-bakery.com

Vinceremos Wines and Spirits Ltd, 261 Upper Town Street, Leeds LS13 3JT Tel: 0113 257 7545 www.vinceremos.co.uk

Waitrose Ltd, Southern Industrial Area, Bracknell, Berks RG12 8YA Tel: 01344 424 680 www.waitrose.co.uk

Weetabix Ltd, Weetabix Mills, Station Road, Burton Latimer, Kettering, Northants NN15 5JR Tel: 01536 722181

Whole Earth Foods, 269 Portobello Road, London W11 1LR Tel: 0171 229 7545 www.earthfoods.co.uk

Women's Environmental Network, 87 Worship Street, London EC2A 2BE Tel: 0171 247 9924
www.gn.apc.org/wen

World Wide Fund for Nature (**WWF**), Panda House, Weyside Park, Godalming, Surrey GU7 1XR Tel: 01483 426 444 www.wwfuk.org

Yakult, 12–16 Telford Way, Westway Estate, Acton, London W3 7XS Tel: 0181 740 4111

Notes

1 Judith Wills, *The Food Bible*, Quadrille Publishing, 1998
2 Jean Anderson and Barbara Deskins, *The Nutrition Bible*, Quill/William Morrow, 1995
3 Patrick Holford, *The Optimum Nutrition Bible*, Piatkus, 1997
4 Lynda Brown, *The Shopper's Guide to Organic Food*, Fourth Estate, 1995
5 We are indebted for many of the facts in this section to *The Food Chronology: A Food Lover's Compendium of Events and Anecdotes, from Prehistory to the Present*, by James Trager, Aurum Press, 1995
6 Shirley English, Smart spud asks for drink of water, *The Times*, 26 June 1999
7 Seeds of Change, *Consumer Reports*, September 1999
8 David Derbyshire, Now it's the Franken-Fish, *Daily Mail*, 29 July 1999
9 Steve Connor, Not to be sneezed at – the pollen-free flower, *Independent*, 24 July 1999
10 GM company facts, *The Food Magazine*, April/June 1999
11 *Gene Protection Technologies: A Monsanto background statement*, Monsanto, April 1999
12 Charles Arthur, Modified crops 'do not yield any more', *Independent*, 8 July 1999
13 Rhoda H. Karpatikin, Who Controls the Food Supply?, *Consumer Reports*, September 1999
14 Jane Bradbury, Tim Lobstein and Vivien Lund, *Functional Foods Examined*, The Food Commission, 1996.
15 'Enhanced food' is latest trend, *Buffalo News*, 9 May 1999
16 ibid
17 ibid
18 Bradbury, Lobstein and Lund, op.cit.
19 *Consumer Groups Call for Greater Regulation of 'Functional Foods'*, International Association of Consumer Food Organizations press release, 26 March 1999.
20 *Functional Foods: Public Health Boon or 21st Century Quackery?*, CSPI
21 Tim Lobstein, Organic standards: where do we draw the line?, *Food Magazine 44*, January–March 1999
22 Rachel Carson, *Silent Spring*, Penguin, 1999.
23 Theo Colborn et al, *Our Stolen Future*, Dutton Books, 1996.
24 Deborah Cadbury, *The Feminization of Nature*, Hamish Hamilton, 1997.
25 David Derbyshire, Downfall of a farmer who gambled with rogue pesticide, *Daily Mail*, 5 June 1999.
26 Andrew Smith, Planet Organic, *Observer*, 27 June 1999.
27 Lynda Brown, op.cit.
28 2092/91
29 Andrew Smith, op.cit.
30 Charles Arthur, Cinnamon kills 99% of E. coli bacteria, *Independent*, 7 August 1999
31 Hilary Schrafft, Ideas pour out in convenient wrappers, *Financial Times*, 11 May 1999
32 When being seen to be green could backfire on you, *Inside Food & Drink*, February 1999
33 Martyn Halle, Could this eliminate salmonella in eggs?, *Daily Mail*, 28 July 1999
34 Food Irradiation: Solution or Threat?, *International Organisation of Consumers Unions briefing paper 3*, London, September 1994.
35 *Effective? DHA-fortified foods*, Hokkaido Shimbum, April 28, 1995
36 Clover Healthcare
37 Anderson and Deskins, op.cit.
38 Judith Wills, op.cit.
39 ASA Monthly Report
40 Celia Hall, Scientists study sweetener after cancer fears, *Daily Telegraph*, 4 August 1999
41 Edited by Michèle J. Sadler and Michael Saltmarsh, The Royal Society of Chemistry, 1998
42 Jerome Burn, Unsung friends of your body, *Financial Times*
43 *Diet and Health 2*, Unilever Research Laboratorium, 1996
44 Lester Packer, *The Antioxidant Miracle*, John Wiley & Sons, 1999.
45 Anderson and Deskins, op.cit.

46 Lynda Brown, op.cit.

47 Jean Anderson and Barbara Deskins, op.cit. Vitamin entries are largely drawn from this source.

48 Researchers hunting scores of new functional food compounds in plants, *Food Labelling & Nutrition News*, 25 March 1998

49 ConAgra's gut feeling, *New Nutrition Business*, October 1998

50 Dean Madden, *Food Biotechnology: An Introduction*, International Life Sciences Europe, Brussels, 1995

51 A. E. Bender, Functional foods: Cautionary notes, in *Functional Foods*, edited by Michèle Sadler and Michael Saltmarsh, Royal Society of Chemistry, UK, 1998.

52 Mick Whitworth, Live like a Viking: eat bark, *Inside Food & Drink*, December 1998/January 1999

53 See, for example, Richard Rance, *The Miracle of Super Blue-Green Algae*, Colorado Springs, 1994; or Gillian McKeith, *Miracle Superfood: Wild Blue-Green Algae*, Keats Publishing, 1997.

54 Tim Lobstein, Organic standards: where do we draw the line?, *Food Magazine 44*, January-March 1999

55 The main source of information for this section is *The Nutrition Bible*, Quill / William Morrow, 1995

56 Ian Murray, Tea and chocolate, *The Times*, 6 August 1999

57 According to the American Heart Association's Council on Epidemiology and Prevention.

58 New cancer hope in a soya snack, *Daily Mail*, 25 May 1999

59 *Food Magazine*, July/September 1999, and M.A. Lappe, E.B. Bailey, C. Childress, and KDR Setchell, Alternations in clinically important phytoestrogens in genetically modified herbicide-tolerant soybeans, *Journal of Medicinal Food*, 1:4, 1999

60 Noimasa Hosoya, Health claims in Japan: Foods for specified health use and functional foods, paper presented at Codex meeting, September 1998

61 National Wildlife Federation Bio-technology Policy Center, Fact Sheet, Washington DC, 1992. Quoted in *Spilling the Genes*, The Genetics Forum, London, October 1996.

62 The GM 'new wave': nutritional enhancement, *New Nutrition Business*, June 1999

63 Blueberries championed as antioxidant in the US, *New Nutrition Business*, February 1999

64 Robin McKie, Forget the pills ... find your thrill on Blueberry Hill, *Observer*, 19 September 1999

65 Wilson da Silva, Killer genes that make the pips squeak, *New Scientist*, 29 March 1997

66 Lynda Brown, op.cit.

67 Raisins rank among the top antioxidant foods, *New Nutrition Business*, June 1999

68 Charles Arthur, Strawberries get a sweet gene, *Independent*, 10 July 1998

69 Andy Coghlan, Exquisite taste, *New Scientist*, 3 April 1999

70 Kate Murphy, Eat your superveggies, *Business Week*, 10 November 1997

71 Beans benefit bowels, *New Nutrition Business*, May 1999

72 Reseach adds to cancer link for garlic, *New Nutrition Business*, May 1999

73 Andy Coghlan, Tubby tubers, *New Scientist*, 2 August 1997

74 Evelyn Wright, Beat Hep B, go eat a potato, *Business Week*, 9 August 1999

75 Lynda Brown, op.cit.

76 US Environmental Protection Agency, as reported in *Pesticide News 35*, March 1997

77 *World In Action*, 13 October 1997

78 Nick Nuttall, Limp lettuces face crunch in GM trials, *The Times*, 14 June 1999

79 *Observer*, 27 June 1999.

80 Lynda Brown, op.cit.

81 Processed tomatoes more 'functional' than fresh, *New Nutrition Business*, February 1999

82 *Buffalo News*, 9 May 1999

83 More studies look at benefits of nuts, *New Nutrition Business*, June 1999

84 Eat peanuts for weight loss, *New Nutrition Business*, May 1999

85 Japanese researchers working on cholesterol-lowering GM rice, *New Nutrition Business*, March 1999

86 Hartmut Meyer, On China's miraculous GE-world, GENET, 2 August 1999

87 Nick Nuttall, Scientists give rice a vitamin supplement, *The Times*, 5 August 1999

88 Sathnam Sanghera, Milking the world wide web for the best-quality product, *Financial Times*, 27 March 1999

89 Michael Brower and Warren Leon, *The Consumer's Guide to Effective Environmental Choices*, Three Rivers Press, New York, 1999.

90 *Growing Organically 156*, HDRA, Summer 1999.

91 Mix your beef with cherries to lower carcinogens, *New Nutrition Business*, February 1999

92 *Observer Life*, 27 April 1999

93 Scandal of the farmers pumping up their cattle with smuggled hormones, *Daily Mail*, 14 June 1999

94 Genet News: Extracted from Yahoo News of June 24: [http://dailynews.yahoo.com/headlines/sc/story.html?s=v/nm/19990624/sc/canada_pigs_1.html]

95 Dr Tim O'Brien, *Farm Animal Genetic Engineering*, a report for the Compassion in World Farming Trust, revised December 1998.

96 ibid.

97 Sausages: a new method to lower cholesterol?, *New Nutrition Business*, March 1999

98 Deborah Mackenzie, Can we make the supersalmon safe?, *New Scientist*, 27 January 1996

99 Michael L. Weber, So You Say You Want a Blue Revolution?, *The Amicus Journal*, Autumn 1996

100 Lyndon Davies

101 Dr. Tim O'Brien, *Farm Animal Genetic Engineering*, a report for the Compassion in World Farming Trust, revised December, 1998.

102 Sources include: Centre for Veterinary Medicinal Products, *Veterinary medicinal products containing Bovine Somatotropin: final scientific reports*, European Commission, Brussels, 1993. Quoted in *Spilling the Genes*, The Genetics Forum, London, October 1996.

103 BST campaign latest, *The Food Magazine 45*, April / June 1999

104 Joanna Blythman, Milk and money, *Guardian Weekend*, 14 November 1998

105 James Erlichman, Milking her brand, *Guardian*, 17 July 1999

106 H.M. Customs & Excise, Data prepared by Statistics Branch C, ESG, MAFF

107 Sue Dibb & Tim Lobstein, *GM-Free*, Virgin Books, 1999

108 H.M. Customs & Excise, Data prepared by Statistics Branch C, ESG, MAFF

109 Yoghurt benefits highlighted, *New Nutrition Business*, May 1999

110 Bio Yoghurts, *Which? Online*, June 1997

111 The case for coconut oil, *New Nutrition Business*, April 1999

112 *Inside Food & Drink*, June 1999, page 19

113 Third trial provides more evidence for Olibra, *New Nutrition Business*, April 1999

114 Anderson and Deskins, op.cit.

115 Baby Organix, Fact Sheet on GMOs and Baby Food, 1999

116 Nick Nuttall, Baby food giant cuts out GM products, *The Times*, 31 July 1999

117 Safe Alliance, Food facts: soya

118 Whole grains reduce overall death rate, *New Nutrition Business*, March 1999

119 Lynda Brown, op.cit.

120 Our medical correspondent, Lost US wheat 'best for cancer', *The Times*, 28 July 1999

121 K-sentials for kids: essentials for Kellogg, *New Nutrition Business*, March 1999

122 Lynda Brown, op.cit.

123 Sue Dibb and Dr Tim Lobstein, op.cit.

124 Anderson and Deskins, op. cit.

125 Omega Protein in sauce deal, *New Nutrition Business*, March 1999

126 Anderson and Deskins, op.cit.

127 *Buffalo News*, 9 May 1999

128 Roger Dobson, *Sunday Times Style*, 1999.

129 Chocolate may help you live longer, *New Nutrition Business*, February 1999

130 Merck Pharmaceutical backs Fruit & Fibre Bar, *New Nutrition Business*, March 1999

131 Anderson and Deskins, op. cit.

132 Lynda Brown, op.cit.

133 Tea time, *The Times*, 3 July 1999

134 Sue Dibb and Dr Tim Lobstein, op.cit.

135 Swedish researchers believe they have found key to green tea's anti-cancer properties, *New Nutrition Business*, April 1999

135 Argentina begins export drive for the "green tea of South America", *New Nutrition Business*, February 1999

137 Soft drinks undermining Americans' health?, *New Nutrition Business*, February 1999

138 Michael F. Jacobson, Liquid candy: How soft drinks are harming Americans' health, Center for Science in the Public Interest, www.cspinet.org

139 New study adds to data on grape juice antioxidants, *New Nutrition Business*, March 1999

140 Tropicana adds calcium, *New Nutrition Business*, March 1999

141 Ben & Jerry: Smoothie operators, *New*

Nutrition Business, April 1999

142 Microalgae under the microscope, *New Nutrition Business*, April 1999

143 Richard Ehrlich, A bit of a smoothie, *Independent on Sunday*, 30 May 1999

144 Pepsi dumps Josta, *New Nutrition Business*, April 1999

145 Consumers' Association, Energy Drinks, *WhichOnline*, October 1996.

146 Sunny Delight is the soft drink star, *New Nutrition Business*, June 1999

147 Take a deep breath, *New Nutrition Business*, April 1999

148 Beer and apples good for health, *New Nutrition Business*, May 1999

149 *Observer Life*, 27 June 1999.

150 Whisky Galore!, *New Nutrition Business*, February 1999

151 Joanna Simon, Lab côtes, *Observer Life*, April 1999

152 Tim Atkin, Fortified winks, *Observer Life*, 22 November, 1998

153 Patrick Holford, op.cit.

154 International Food Information Council (IFIC), Internet, October 1998

155 Patrick Holford, op.cit.

156 Steve Connor, Not to be sneezed at – the pollen-free flower, *Independent*, 24 July 1999

157 Vaccine made of dirt boosts asthma fight, *Guardian*, 18 September 1999

158 Nick Nuttall, Scientists raise hope of new drug crops, *The Times*, 5 July 1999

159 *Daily Mail*, 13 May, 1999

160 Patrick Holford, op.cit.

161 Dr Bob Arnot, *The Breast Cancer Prevention Diet*, Newleaf, 1999

162 *Daily Mail*, 25 June 1999

163 British Nutrition Foundation fact sheet

164 Patrick Holford, op.cit.

165 Judith Wills, op.cit.

166 Patrick Holford, op.cit.

167 Neal Barnard, *Foods That Fight Pain*, Bantam, 1998

168 The Imperial Cancer Research Fund

169 Patrick Holford, op.cit.

170 Michael D Lemonick, Beyond depression, *Time*, 17 May 1999

171 Neal Barnard, op.cit.

172 Judith Wills, op.cit.

173 Neal Barnard, op.cit.

174 Can vegetarians lose their appetite for love?, *Daily Mail*, 26 May 1999

175 Patrick Holford, op.cit.

176 David Pillig, Hungry to beat the obesity blues, *Financial Times*, 17 July 1999

177 *Which Health?* December 1998

178 *Which Health?*, December 1998

179 *Food Magazine 40*, February 1998

180 *Financial Times*, 5 March 1999

181 Helen Rumbelow, Gym-shy women seek muscles in a bottle, *Daily Telegraph*, 22 May 1999

182 Judith Wills, op.cit.

183 *Guidelines for a healthy vegetarian diet*, British Nutrition Foundation, 1997

184 *Anthony Barnett and Patrick Wintour*, Revealed: science blunder that gave us BSE, *Observer*, 8 August 1999

185 New Foods: the future of positive health, *Dragon International*, May 1999.

186 *John Vidal*, McLibel: Burger culture on trial, Macmillan 1997

187 *Evolving dangerous tastes*, Healthy Eating, May 1999

188 We willingly declare an interest here. We have worked with Denmark's Novo Nordisk, the world's largest enzymes company, for over 10 years. We have done so because we believe they are a good company and their technology is as future-friendly as they can make it. SustainAbility, the company we co-founded in 1987, also worked for a period for Monsanto, but unilaterally resigned the contract on 1 January 1999. The background can be found at www.sustainability.co.uk

189 Jasper Becker, Safety fears as scientists play god, *South China Morning Post*, 10 July 1999

190 David Castle, How Iceland led the way, *Inside Food & Drink*, June 1999

191 Rhoda H.Karpatkin, op.cit.

Index